Ms Pati
7 McCold Dr.
Zelienople PA.
16063

MW01717510

The Scotts From A Hill

In Pittsburgh, Pennsylvania

Copyright © 2017 by Patricia Scott

All rights reserved. No part of this book/manuscript may be reproduced in any form or by any electronic or mechanical means, including information or storage and retrieval systems, without permission in writing from the author.

Printed in the United States of America.

ISBN: 978-1-63385-225-9

Library of Congress Control Number: 2017913758

Published by

Word Association Publishers
205 Fifth Avenue
Tarentum, Pennsylvania 15084

www.wordassociation.com
1.800.827.7903

There
never
was
a
coward
where
the
shamrock
grows.

1850

The story begins with our paternal ancestors, John Scott and Ellen Wills, who were born c. 1850 in the Southern District of Connaught in the Irish Republic. There, they married in 1875 and soon departed the Motherland forever, taking with them all they possessed—their personal honor and pride, and the deepest yearnings of their hearts, that they and their children would soon enjoy a better life. They went away paupers, and where they went turned into a worse hardship for them.

England was in the grip of the Industrial Revolution. Streams of destitute Irish found work in its mines and mills, dangerous work that resulted in countless lost lives due to mine cave-ins and blast furnace explosions that occurred regularly and without warning. John worked in the seaport town of Barrow-in-Furness, enduring brutal manual labor appropriated in demeaning ways and carried out in deplorable conditions. Bitter cold air blasted in at will and heat escaped through wide gaps in unstable corrugated tin walls and roofs of the foundry buildings. Incessant rains turned working and living quarters into a bog year in and year out. Neither the air above nor the earth below ever cleared of smoke or dried out. The British Parliament was only beginning to address vital health issues in this congested slum of tenements and row shacks, without public water or sewers, and where hunger, disease, epidemics and death were rampant.

The hearts of John and Ellen Scott turned continually toward their beloved Ireland in wonder: *Had they made a terrible mistake*? In the Barrows, the Scotts' first child, George, was born, next Samuel (our grandfather Sam Scott), and then Mary. The little family crouped continually. Smog hemmed them in, reducing visibility to night in broad daylight. With slightly more than a few miserable coins to spare and nothing to lose, they boarded ship at Lancashire and left England for America in 1879. A story survives of the crossing that when the ship reached American shores, three-year-old Samuel ran up and down the deck, flailing his arms and singing at the top of his lungs: *America, America*! In his wee British accent, the tune came out: *A Miracle, A Miracle*!

In Boston, John was hired as a tool maker for a dollar a day on the thirteen-hour shift. After work, he joined cronies at the Hibernian Club to imbibe on double shots of barrel whiskey at two cents a glass to drown out the sorrows, loosen the tongue, and exercise natural sociability. He then headed home to his dear wife and children with the wind at his back, as well as a bad cough from which the damp and dirty air refused to deliver him. While in Boston, two more sons were born to the Scotts, James and William.

In 1892, mid-west agents for the railroad industry arrived in Boston scouting laborers. With free rail passage guaranteed, John signed on with Union Pacific in St. Louis, Missouri, where he and his family moved into a flat in walking distance of the railroad yards. The Scotts believed that the hardships they had endured were now behind them. However, their great expectations for a better life did not come to pass. John died in 1897 of a heart attack on the job; Ellen died in 1898 in a cholera epidemic. Both were buried in a potter's field on the outskirts of St. Louis. As for their surviving children—George, Samuel, Mary, James, and William—they would fend for themselves.

Our paternal ancestors, Patrick O'Donnell and Brigid Feeney, were born c. 1850 in the Northern District of Connaught in the Irish Republic. Patrick belonged to a family of story tellers and Brigid to a family of songsters. They grew up together in the same Parish and were sweethearts. Both families had made the Atlantic crossing in 1878 from the seaport at Sligo, having had sufficient means for their passage. The Feeneys were first to sail; the O'Donnells crossed upon receiving the good news that jobs were plentiful in New England. In Boston, Patrick found work in a textile mill, where he discovered Brigid bent over a cloth-weaving machine. With the industrial machinery grinding, no one seemed to notice Patrick sweeping Brigid up into his arms. Their joyous reunion resulted in marriage and relocation to join relatives in Pittsburgh, Pennsylvania.

In Pittsburgh, they settled in an industrial district known as *Shantytown* in the shadows of an iron ore foundry and boiler works near the confluence where met the Allegheny, Monongahela, and Ohio rivers—*The Point.* There, for five dollars a month, they moved into a row house. Brigid despaired of the smog and pollution but Patrick saw an opportunity and joined a ditch-digging crew laying the city's first sewer lines.

With a baby on the way, they joined the nearby St. Mary of Mercy Parish, known as Father Jimmy Sheedy's Church of Poor Irish. The Sisters of Mercy of Ireland maintained the church sacristy and a schoolhouse where they prepared immigrants for citizenship and taught skills to place women in upper-class domestic positions. Brigid joined the local ranks, taking in laundry for downtown hotels and boarding houses.

Shantytown had full use of a public facility called the *Water Shed*, where water flowed into huge concrete vats that were cracked and leaking. Water for home use had to be boiled on outdoor fire pits in iron cauldrons shared in common. A story survives of an Irish washerwoman who in 1845 started a fire in a woodshed, causing a conflagration that burned down half the town. Fires burned down huge sections of Pittsburgh from time to time and were the worst threat to the city's survival next to the problem of its contaminated drinking water.

In 1881, Brigid gave birth to the O'Donnell's first child, John, and returned to the scrub board, there to stay until Bart was born in 1883, both delivered by a Shantytown midwife. Their third child, Mary Catherine (our grandmother), was born during a flash flood on July 21, 1885, a catastrophe that left the population of Shantytown sheltered for many days at the Court House on Grant Street. Patrick soon found a safe place for his family to live on higher ground in the neighborhood of Lawrenceville.

There, the O'Donnells settled in the Tenth Ward on a bluff in the 6000 block of Butler Street in a pitch-roofed frame house with fiber plaster walls and plank-wood floors. The home had no electricity or indoor plumbing, and was situated adjacent to a trolley turnaround called *the Loop*. Out back flowed a freshwater spring on a slope leading up to the Quill's Hill limestone quarry, which supplied stone foundations for homes under construction in the area. Just down the block from their house stood Pittsburgh Public School No. 18 where they enrolled their children. The redbrick schoolhouse served grades one through four. Upper grades transferred seven blocks away to McCandless Public School on Butler Street.

Catholics in public schools were obligated to attend Sunday school for religious training. With St. Kieran's Church on 53rd Street under construction, the O'Donnells attended Sunday Mass at St. Mary's on 46th Street. Patrick earned formidable respect in the Parish, considering his generosity when the collection basket passed by him during the homily.

On the job, he asserted his leadership skills when two of his friends died in a sewer excavation cave-in, and he lobbied to make safety improvements that no doubt saved lives. For his trouble, he earned a few extra and much needed dollars in wages. Counting his blessings, he considered himself rich. Although never more than a ditch digger, our great grandfather managed to provide a modest standard of living for his family, which by his reckoning made his work noble. Had he known that during the worst part of the Great Depression his yet to be born grandson, Vincent Paul Scott, would become a ditch digger, he would have been proud. The purpose of providing for family was the same, and by Patrick's lights nothing was more important than family. Little is known about his siblings except that they all worked in the mills, imbibed heartily, and carried their religion on their sleeves.

In Northern Ireland, Province of Ulster, County Down, resided our maternal ancestors, the Quinns and Dorans of Mourne Barony, and the Grants and McManuses of Drumboniff. John Grant and his wife Rose McManus lived on the outskirts of Belfast where they eked out a living in the linen mills, although it has been reported that John did well in gaming enterprises and Rose shored up profits far from tax collector purviews. They brought ten children into the world between 1851 and 1869—all baptized at St. John's Church in Clonduff Parish, Hilltown.

It is believed that their frame house burned down due to a mishap that exploded the fireplace and that their Parish quickly rebuilt the structure to spare a hefty fine from the Crown. Catholic doctrine mandated the hasty baptism of newborns as fear existed among Ulster's Catholics that, unless their children were brought up in the faith, their minds might fog up under the influence of *Black Irish Traitors*, as Irish Protestants were called. No good Catholic would send a child to the national school; instead, they relied on Parish priests to teach religion and impart hedge schooling in open fields and in drafty barns. As for John's and Rose's children, decades of political unrest and hunger ignited the desire for change—stay and fight or leave. Mary, Michael, and Elizabeth stayed; Roseann, Ellen, Catherine, Margaret, Arthur, and Celina Grant made the crossing in 1888, John in 1906.

James Quinn and his wife Mary Doran brought six children into the world between 1850 and 1860. They lived in a stone house and farmed bottom land where corn grew and cows grazed, property owned by an aristocrat who lived in a Glasdrommond mansion in Mourne Barony, County Down, which faces the Irish Sea eastward and westward adjoins County Armagh, site of St. Patrick's first cathedral. As for the Quinns' daughters, Bridget and Catharine, and their sons, Richard, John, Patrick, and James, they left the beloved motherland in fear of the unknown.

In 1871, the boys made their way to Liverpool, England and signed on board *Ship America, Ship Master Joseph J. Lawrence*, so recorded. The vessel, burdened with fifteen hundred tons and a thousand passengers, made stops in Irish seaports to top off the load—destination New York harbor. It is known that the Long Island Railroad facilitated the transport of immigrant passengers to points of exit from New York City for other destinations. The Quinns traveled by rail to Pittsburgh, with whistle stops across

Pennsylvania's rugged landscape. At the Allegheny Railroad Depot in Lawrenceville, they were met by their sisters, Bridget and Catharine, who had crossed ahead of their brothers and welcomed them to their residence, a boarding house at the corner of 49th and Hatfield Street in Pittsburgh's Ninth Ward.

The demand for laborers made it easy for the brothers to quickly find work. The Quinns were easy to track in U.S. census reports and in City of Pittsburgh and Fire Insurance Directories, predecessors to the telephone book. Patrick Quinn and his brothers, Richard and James, returned to Ireland in 1889 with good reason. At Barony Parish in County Down, Patrick witnessed the marriage of Richard to Ellen Donnovan, and James to a Margaret Quin (one n) of no relation. Unfortunately, neither woman survived the crossing.

It is unknown how our grandmother Margaret Grant and our grandfather Patrick Quinn met. In my research, documents obtained from the Pittsburgh Diocese archives show that they were married on May 5, 1892 at Sacred Heart Church in East Liberty, along with Patrick's brother Richard and Margaret's sister Roseann—a double wedding—both couples married in the same place on the same day. Patrick, said to be easygoing, and Margaret, no nonsense, dressed stylishly for their big day—he in a white linen shirt, wool vest, waist coat, and a bowler hat with a grain ribbon; she, in long tresses piled high, wore a full-length linen dress beneath a shag wool coat and high-buttoned shoes. With nothing between them but a well-traveled wooden trunk stamped *Made in Belfast*, they caught a streetcar to Lawrenceville and exited at the Penn Avenue junction with 34th and Butler Street,the *Fork of the Road*. There, the industrial hovel of Lawrenceville came into view. The area teemed with smoke and soot, but they breathed in a feeling of hope at the joyous gathering of relatives. The newlyweds were taken in by

Margaret's brother, Arthur Grant, in a row house at 5400 Carnegie Avenue in the Tenth Ward, two streets up from the main drag. Patrick's brother, Richard, lived one street down on Dresden Alleyway. At the corner of 55th and Butler stood a four-story brick and mortar building, the *Dublin Pub and Boarding House*, where resident laundry was daily aired outdoors from pole to pole for all to see. The Pub itself was a long narrow room with

an ornate tin ceiling and a hand-carved mahogany bar stocked with Irish liquor and barrel beer. A side entrance to a private lounge allowed women the comfort of classy seating, good drink and food. Dublin's was the area's most popular laboring-class hangout. Pittsburgh's class society was well in place.

The rich attended balls, the opera, and private theater, and they hosted plays and musicals that drew small crowds. The Art Society drew large exhibits. The Symphony Society sponsored concerts in public parks. Pittsburghers took advantage of the utilitarian culture, such as writers' circles and the science, astronomy, and history clubs. Singing societies, such as the Orpheus Club in

Lawrenceville, flourished in ethnic neighborhoods; the patriotic clubs served veterans of the wars.

Our Quinn grandparents had no time for all that. Margaret being ruddy and robust, set up housekeeping; Patrick being quick-thinking and agile, worked a six day, twelve-hour shift and walked many blocks to the Crucible Works in the Sixth Ward. In the worst part of winter, he paid a nickel to ride the horse drawn hack that ran on a single track along Butler Street. On the job, he shoveled coal into a furnace with a rhythm that maintained the precise temperature to turn iron into steel. Good humor in challenging circumstances earned him even more—longer hours and an increase in wages from twelve to sixteen dollars a week.

In 1893, the Quinns moved to a house on the 54th Street hillside accessible by cobblestone walkways and wooden stairways. There, James (Jimmy), Richard (Dick), and Joseph (no nickname) were born. With three handsome boys to do them proud, the Quinns settled into the good life, unaware that their joy would turn to sorrow when, in 1897, whooping cough would strike down their son James.

Under a cloud of gloom, four-year-old Jimmy was buried from St. Kieran's and interred at St. Mary's Cemetery 46th Street—Section 56, Grave 44. Grief-stricken Margaret stopped singing, and Patrick worried that she might never stop sobbing.

In that household, there seemed no beginning or end of each hour of the day or day of the week, but only the unspoken sorrow in a world that seemed to go on without end.

In 1899, our Uncle Frank was born, named for St. Francis of Assisi, and everybody cheered up. In 1901, our mother, Rose Helen Quinn, would be born, and in 1903, her sister, Mary Margaret Quinn, would be born. The family was moving on.

1900

Turn-of-the-Century Pittsburgh drew throngs into downtown to celebrate. They came on foot and by horse and wagon, on trolleys and steamboats. The Monongahela River wharf accommodated parking for people driving the new motor cars. Hundreds lined the waterfront, the bridges, and the Mount Washington cliffs overlooking downtown, to view the city's spectacular fireworks. Everywhere, people were hearing about Pittsburgh's prosperity and were flocking here in droves.

Our boat-building and glass-manufacturing industries flourished. Westinghouse Airbrake Company brought in the unskilled and turned them into machinists. The Pittsburgh Reduction Company manufactured aluminum products and hired immigrants off the street to operate their assembly lines. It would become the Aluminum Company of America, the largest producer of aluminum in the world. The Pittsburgh Paint and Glass Company employed chemist graduates of our universities and developed innovative ways to produce products that last. Vital industries maintained their headquarters in downtown office buildings, where only the best and brightest were hired.

In 1901, shortly after John and Ellen Scott were buried in a potter's field on the outskirts of St. Louis, our grandfather, Sam Scott, and his brother Jim headed for Pittsburgh, Pennsylvania. They were neither fugitives of the law nor reprobates on the run. They came by steamboat in search of their fortunes, stopping in mill towns along the Mississippi and Ohio rivers, peddling wares such as box matches and horse liniment, acquired through pilfering to pay their passage, and they bartered for food that kept them alive. I can just see these two excited young men, in thread-bare shirts, pants, worn out shoes, and desperately in need of a bath, walking down the gangplank the minute the boat docked at the bustling river wharf with freight stacked sky-high, and I can just hear them shouting: *Wow, look at all them hills*!

At the ages of eighteen and fourteen, they felt that they had done enough hard living to qualify as grown men. They wanted steady work for fair wages; however, the sight of another dirty mill town made them wish they had never left St. Louis, haunted as they were by their father's admonition to avoid foundry life after what he had lived through at Barrow-in-Furness. He had hammered away on the perils of mill work, but his job on the St. Louis Railroad had turned out no better; all of it enough to compel Sam and Jim to steer clear of the Pennsylvania Railroad Company, where *Now Hiring* signs were posted all over the Strip District, the central warehouse and merchandise distribution hub bordering downtown.

The spirited brothers were determined to stay out of the mills but felt qualified to work at the loading docks on Smallman Street. Sam soon developed a resentment for what he felt to be a mean-spirited work ethic, meaning a measly dollar-a-day to cover a dingy boarding-house room and a pot-luck supper. He heard about a dairy farming co-op that was hiring and took a walk over to Penn Avenue to check it out. A position posted for a driver to deliver milk to private customers on its Butler Street horse and wagon route captured his attention, so he applied.

The boss, a bear of a man with an eye patch, a dense beard and a European accent, instructed him to back the horse and wagon out of the stall and lead it back in. He had never driven a wagon before and knew nothing about horses, but he didn't let that stop him. He did what he was told to do and got the job. He became adept at guiding the horse around hard turns on narrow streets without tilting the wagon. Not easy to do considering that it shared the road with ice wagons, meat wagons, grocery wagons, and police and fire wagons—plus motor vehicles that spooked the horses.

Sam was beginning to feel the good life when his wages increased. Sun up to sun down, he worked the route and became popularly known as Sam Scott the Milkman. At day's end, he stalled the horse at the 34th Street stables, ate a twenty-five cent supper at a corner saloon, and lodged in an upstairs room that he shared with his brother for twenty-five cents more. The Butler Street Bath House nearby made a convenient spot to wash and groom; he wanted to look good when he made his rounds.

His favorite stop was at 5500 Butler Street, the Protestant Home for the Aged and Incurable, where he was greeted by beautiful nurses and housekeepers. The thirty-two-room mansion, situated in amongst a forest of oak trees, was the former summer home of Jane Holmes, daughter of a prominent Pittsburgh banker; she had donated the property to be used as a nursing home.

With all due respect to delays, by the time Sam reached the 62nd Street trolley loop, he and his helper, a boy pulled out of grade school, were famished. They sat on a bench in the tin shelter used for waiting commuters and devoured the contents of their metal lunch buckets. There came an occasion when Sam looked up and noticed a girl in a gingham dress walking out of a frame house on the bluff across the way. She had a smile on her face and was swinging a milk bucket; she headed for a cow tied to the porch railing and sat down to milk it. Sam, not one to let an opportunity slip by, strode up the bluff whistling *Dixie*, tipped his straw hat, and said, *how do you do*? She just kept right on milking the cow. He spoke up louder, asking how much she wanted for the cow, and she said it wasn't for sale.

Bet you fifty cents the cow's name is Betsy, says he.

Bet you fifty cents the cow's name is Cherry, says she.

And what, may I ask, is your name? says he.

My name is Mary Catherine O'Donnell. What's yours?

People call me Sam Scott the Milkman. You can call me Sam.

Hmmmm, she replied with a shrug.

Well, Mary, do you see that horse and wagon down there? They belong to me.

Hmmmm, she repeated.

It was Sam's nature to assume that her tone meant he was welcome to stop and say hello to her at every opportunity. The mere sight of him and his haughty tone highly annoyed her parents, Brigid and Patrick O'Donnell. After all, their daughter was only fifteen; but their cold-shoulder treatment towards Sam made him all the more determined to win Mary's affection. He got as far as sitting on her porch making small talk. The only place that they could be together privately was to take a walk up to the new Sharpsburg bridge at 62nd Street. The old plank wood bridge spanning the Allegheny had been replaced with a steel and wood truss bridge, which first opened as a toll bridge until its three-hundred-thousand-dollar debt was paid off.

Sam's wages improved when he won a canteen service contract at the nearby Union Steel Casting Plant. There, he routinely jumped off the milk wagon to coax Mary's cow off the main drag and back up the bluff. She had no command over the family pet. The cow knew it, too, and roamed as it pleased, even as far as the mill yard, where workers would burst into laughter at the scene of the impatient man and the obstinate cow. Sam did not appreciate their teasing in a foreign language. On the other hand, they couldn't understand his British twang, although they made out enough of it to realize he was cursing the cow and not them.

Word was that between Sam and Mary, a fleeting romance begun in the fall ended in a marital union the following springtime with apparently no witnesses to the historic event. The O'Donnells vehemently opposed the arrangement, which broke Mary's heart. She dearly loved and desperately wanted the approval of her mother and father and her four brothers; it was not to be. The estrangement brought hard times on the whole family with both Patrick and Brigid in slowly failing health.

In that era, it was common for girls to avoid scandal by marrying early and starting a family. The great fear was to have a baby out of wedlock, and the great dread was to bear an illegitimate child that would be forever shunned by society and denied the rights of so-called *respectable* citizens. Literature abounds of passionate stories of the shame, disgrace and desperation of young women who fell in love and had a baby while their lovers either deserted them, died in the wars, or refused to get married and hung around waiting for the victim to figure out what to do. Protecting the illegitimate child was of the essence. In hardship cases, mothers would sometimes flee the hospital after giving birth and leave their babies behind, or abandon them on doorsteps, hoping they would be taken in and adopted.

So goes a story that our grandmother, Mary O'Donnell, had a baby who died, leaving her in a state of deep sorrow. The story goes on that in her grief she answered a newspaper ad for a baby to be adopted, an infant born in the spring of 1902 and baptized Vincent Paul after Saint Vincent DePaul. Moreover, his parents, a supposedly acclaimed Irish song-and-dance team with a successful show on the road, gave their baby away because they couldn't cope. The gaping hole in this story is why anyone would let a sixteen year old girl adopt a baby in the first place.

Sam and Mary moved into an attic apartment cattycorner to a steel alloy mill in Lawrenceville's Ninth Ward. Heppenstall's used metallurgical technology to produce an advanced heat treating process for tempering steel. The mill expanded with die block, black smith, and hammer press divisions. Mary asked Sam to apply there, knowing full well that the pay was far better than a milkman's wages; he told her to mind her own business. Apparently she tried. A year later, Lillian was born, and before they knew it, along came Samuel, then John, forcing the family to move to a three-room house on Kent Alleyway at its intersection with 54th Street, ironically in the shadows of the Quinn family's residence.

Sam's milk delivery route continued to expand and he started taking Vince along on Saturdays. It bothered Sam that on Sundays, Mary left the little ones with him and took Vince to church. To get even, Sam started chiding Vince that only *sissies* go to church and *real men* go to work. Well, Sam won that argument; *his boy* couldn't wait for Sundays to roll around so that he could work the milk route with his dad. Mary, mortified, stopped going to church altogether, bearing the anguish of what people might think if she showed up without *her boy*. He was keenly aware of his mother's moods and melancholy and shared a likeness to her, a little in her features and more in her ways. She was already depending on him in ways that an eldest child is so often held bound.

In 1908, Vince turned six and his mother enrolled him at St. Kieran's School. Sam found out, pulled his son out of class, and marched him down to McCandless Public School on Butler Street. From that day forward, Sam went out of his way to play down the importance of education to let Vince skip a day of school here and there to work the milk route. He managed to keep up his grades and advanced in his schooling, never expecting what was in store for him down the road.

In 1913, his father pulled him out of school permanently at the end of sixth grade, declaring that he was old enough to work the milk route full-time like other boys his age. Mary's grand dreams for his high-school and college graduations were shattered. She turned to the church, asking Father James Doyle, the pastor of St. Kieran's, to intercede. He dropped by one day in hopes of persuading Sam to reconsider his rash decision to take Vince out of school; Sam escorted the priest out the door.

Mary braved one more battle with Sam to allow her to have their children baptized when their daughter Anne and son

Bartholomew came into the world a year apart. Sam said, *Go to hell.* He wanted nothing to do with the church and simply did not care what people thought of him. He had even gone as far as refusing to attend the funerals of Mary's mother and father who died one year apart from each other. It's a mystery how his reputation as the most popular milkman in Lawrenceville remained intact.

Sam easily steered his horse and wagon clear of motor vehicles that now clogged the main streets. On roughly graded side streets, the pitch of the road was often so steep that the wagon would drift backwards downhill; getting the horse to pull the wagon uphill in the snow required strong urgings.Vince loved that horse and refused to see it whipped. He borrowed sugar cubes from his mother's pantry to carry in his pockets. In precarious situations, he would jump off the wagon, treat the horse to sugar cubes, pet its mane and talk to it in comforting words. In no time, the wagon was moving again.

Pennsylvania winters tested the metal of men—winters no less brutal on the boy. No son could possibly have felt more torn between pleasing the two people he loved most. He adored his mother and idolized his father, but once on that milk wagon guiding the horse, he quickly forgot about their endless squabbling. He learned the routine, created a more efficient way to manage it, and soon had his father catching up with customers on payday before the men reached the saloons and squandered their wages. Here was a twelve-year-old boy determined to work the milk route from dawn to mid-day and sell newspapers until dusk for the sake of family.

In 1914, the assassination of heir to the Austrian throne ignited World War One, the Great War. Our steel mills triumphed, producing the equipment needed by our European allies. A permanent pall of smoke hovered over Pittsburgh, eradicating the noonday sun and painting the midnight sky with the orange glow of its blast furnaces. The nation had not yet become militarily engaged in the war, but it was deeply involved, providing the ammunition.

Vince, too young for the draft, saw no future in delivering dairy products. The day he was guiding the wagon around a sharp corner and was attacked by a big black dog, incurring fifty stitches to close the wounds, he started thinking about alternatives. With time on his hands to recuperate, he started poring over newspaper want ads. One published in the *Pittsburgh Leader* piqued his interest:

"POSTAL TELEGRAPH & CABLE CO. SEEKS MESSENGER BOYS FOURTEEN YEARS AND OLDER INTERESTED IN A CAREER IN THE HEART OF THE GOLDEN TRIANGLE WITH OPPORTUNITIES FOR ADVANCEMENT."

Vince dressed in his best and caught a streetcar into town. He knew his way around and located the Keenan Building on Liberty Avenue. He walked many flights up to the manager's office in the eighteen-story brick edifice erected in 1907 for Col. Thomas J. Keenan, chief owner of the *Penny Press*, precursor to the *Pittsburgh Press*. He was interviewed and hired on the spot, but with his wages not enough to buy round-trip streetcar tokens, he rode to work and walked home after long days on the beat.

War-time contracts flowed over Postal's cable lines at a fast and furious pace. The swift-footed new kid on the block understood the importance of putting classified messages into the hands of railroad and steel executives at their corporate offices in town. He was making an impression that sometimes stirred the more experienced messengers to give him fake addresses and send him on wild goose chases. He ended that mischief by memorizing the names and addresses of Postal's downtown clients. He taught himself how to decode messages and type them with two fingers on a cast-iron typewriter. The manager did not exactly train him, but gave him the latitude to show what he could do and in no time promoted him to apprentice clerk.

Two years into Vince's career with PT, several homes on Kent Alleyway went up in flames. The Scotts took shelter in a nearby house where their seventh child, Rosemarie, arrived unexpectedly; she was fine. However, the house had no indoor plumbing or electricity and the family quickly moved to a remodeled house on Holmes Street. Vince never came home from work empty-handed, even if all he could afford were a few chocolate drops for his mother. His father seemed to grow more critical with every advancement he made. One day, he mustered up the nerve to tell Sam that he wanted to go forward, not backwards. The encounter did not go well, not well at all. His hot-headed father demanded him to quit his job and get back to a real man's work on the milk wagon.

A new city ordinance banned horse-drawn vehicles on city streets. Sam was forced to switch to a motorized milk wagon and learn how to drive it. He set out with an instructor and had trouble working the clutch and shifting out of neutral into low gear, along with the multi-tasking effort of steering away from a demon of a barking dog that was chasing after the truck. It began to drift backwards downhill and ran over the dog. The truck jumped a curb and crashed into a wooden fence, tearing off its gate. Sam jumped off the truck, profaning the Lord on high, blamed the instructor for causing the accident, and quit his job. Hours late for supper, he arrived home drunk and bragging; he had finally mustered up the guts to tell his boss where to shove a lousy milkman's job.

Mary confronted him with the consequences of his rash decision; he walked out, slamming the door behind him. Days later, he returned gloating over his new job selling merchandise—everything from hand tools and household gadgets to homeowners' and life insurance. He canvassed affluent neighborhoods, charmed people into opening doors, and sold pots, pans, and vacuum cleaners right out of catalogues, but little of Sam's wages passed into Mary's hands. Their bickering made family life downright unpleasant, and then they had a terrible row. He threatened to leave, so she called his bluff, saying he'd never pull a dirty trick like that on their family. She never expected him to take her up on it.

Then came the terror of how she'd survive without a husband, and, on her knees, she prayed to God that he'd come home; a month later he did. Theirs was a tense relationship—he making like he wanted to go along with whatever she wished and she seeing right through his pretentiousness. Nevertheless, on the fourth day of July 1918, the last of their brood, Lawrence, was born, and on the eleventh day of November 1918, the Armistice was signed, ending World War One.

All that long while, our grandmother and grandfather, Margaret and Patrick Quinn, had been saving in a shoe box to buy a house on level ground. They had grown weary of trudging up and down steep 54th Street to get to work, the stores, the schools, and the church. Their son Richard had finished trade school and worked at the Union Steel casting mill. Joseph had dropped out of high school to join ranks with his father at the Crucible mill.

Unlike his feisty father, Joseph was shy and soft-spoken. He had inherited his mother's upper respiratory weakness and coughed all the time. No one could have predicted that he would suddenly die of tuberculosis and be laid to rest at St. Mary's Cemetery in the same grave with his brother James. Margaret went there day after day, grieving hopelessly. Patrick swore on their sons' graves that he would improve the quality of their family life.

In 1919, the Quinns bought their dream home at 5621 Butler Street. The twenty-year old redbrick house abutted a vacant lot on one side and an alleyway on the other. Out back, redbrick row houses lined Berlin Alleyway, where railroad tracks provided access to the loading docks of the Hanlon & Gregory Galvanizing Company, a block-long mill facing Butler Street. This vital throughway carried heavy traffic, including the streetcars that shook everything in the Quinn household as they rumbled by. Half a block away at 57th Street stood the sprawling Atlantic Oil Refinery, which occupied several acres and a number of oil storage tanks between Butler Street and the Allegheny River. The refinery's towering exhaust stack spewed perpetual smoke and flames. In the polluted and noisy environment, Margaret suffered anxiety and respiratory misery, a troublesome worry for the family until daughter Mary surrendered a career in nursing to help out at home, with the amiable assistance of daughter Rose.

Our mother, Rose Helen Quinn, graduated from St. Raphael's High School for Girls in Morningside. Upon completing her studies at Duff's Iron City College, she was placed in a secretarial position in a corporate office downtown. She walked tall and dressed appropriately for the job in a gray suit, a tailored white blouse, and white gloves—a thoroughly modern young lady looking forward to the passage of the 19th Amendment to the Constitution giving women the right to vote. The bill had passed the House and was guaranteed to pass in the Senate. All this, and her fascination regarding a certain fellow she had recently run into on a streetcar, were ideas to ponder as a new decade, soon to be called the *Prosperous Years*, began.

1920

Prohibition—the newest law of the land—was considered a nuisance in Pittsburgh. The melting pot had more secret watering holes than any city of its size: a bar on every corner and a saloon in the middle of every block. Local newspapers published editorial and cartoon protests against the law, and politicians promised to have prohibition abolished. The Dublin Pub was closed, but like every tavern in the district, its backdoor business boomed. Our saloons filled our steel workers' great need for strong drink to flush down the mill grime.

Doc Young, a Tenth Ward pharmacist, understood that just about everyone had symptoms of respiratory disease due to the widespread pollution. He prescribed two shots of whiskey a day for a bad cold and two shots of brandy for a bad cough. If your condition did not improve in a couple of days, he sent you across the street to Doc Donaldson, with an admonition that if you didn't take medical advice, Byrne's Funeral parlor right next door might get your business. Thirsty laborers appreciated sound advice from professionals willing to bend rules and dispense liquor—for medicinal purposes, of course.

A frosty Guinness adequately satisfied Patrick Quinn's thirst. However, when his dear wife came down with a bad cough and cold, he had no choice but to drop in at Young's dispensary seeking advice. The Doc suggested diluting strong tea with honey and brandy. Maggie refused it, so Patrick summoned Kate Grant, who stood over her sister until she sipped the brew all the way down. It helped, but over the holidays, she took a turn with complications that could not be treated.

Our grandmother, Margaret Grant Quinn of County Down, Ireland, died in Pittsburgh, Pennsylvania, on a bitter cold January day 1921; she was fifty-eight years old. Her death certificate, signed J. Donaldson, states cause of death as pneumonia with possible tuberculosis. Her family believed it was mill smoke that killed her. Her wish was to be buried near her sons, James and Joseph, in St. Mary's Irish Cemetery on 46th Street. The century-old cemetery had no more space; hence, she was buried at Calvary Cemetery in Hazelwood, a difficult journey up and down city hills in cold funeral cars for a loving family bearing wounds of loss and grief. Everyone was in shock. Our grandfather appealed to the Diocese to have his sons' remains moved to Calvary for burial beside their mother in Section M, Lot and Row 610. Three headstones in the form of Celtic Crosses were later placed at the site, one for James and Joseph, one for Margaret, and one reserved, all bought and paid for by Patrick Quinn himself.

Perhaps the tragic loss of his dear Maggie distracted him. He'd be walking down Butler Street on the way to the mill and get halfway to town before realizing where he was. The congenial fellow who had always been so cautious and precise with his timing had lost his concentration. One morning shortly after our grandmother's death, our grandfather was coming up out of a furnace pit and struck his head on an overhead beam, a blow that knocked him unconscious. When he woke up his sight was gone.

His eldest son Richard, uncle Dick, then twenty-seven, stepped in as head of the house, a gentle soul with a sharp wit and mischievous but harmless disposition. He had been pitching in from his factory wages all along to help keep his little brother in school. Francis, uncle Frank, was twenty-two

years old in his second year at Duquesne University studying for the priesthood. Like his mother, he was soft spoken and pious. With the family's income diminished, Frank quietly dropped out of school and found employment at the Nuttall Foundry on McCandless Avenue below Butler Street. He attended the five-thirty morning Mass at St. Kieran's before punching in at work on the ten-hour shift. He also carried a rosary in his pocket and was always prepared with an uplifting word whenever the need arose. Unfortunately, our grandfather refused to be cheered.

His cronies, bewildered and frustrated by Patrick's gloom over the loss of his wife, and the loss of his sight and no income, took his case to the union, sued Crucible, and won him a settlement of seven dollars and fifty cents a week. At the time of the accident, he earned twenty-seven dollars a week. Medical bills piled up as specialists attempted to restore his vision. The Pittsburgh Association for the Blind provided him training to use a long cane, sweeping the sidewalk and feeling the curb if he went for a walk, but he stayed home. Cooped up and despondent, he was urged to join his friends at Dublin's Pub, where he had socialized ever since his crossing from Ireland.

It wasn't easy, but once re-established in his old routine, our grandfather's disposition improved. Troubling for Mr. Quinn was a rumor he picked up at the Pub that his daughter Rose was interested in a certain fellow who he was not exactly thrilled about. It wasn't so much the young man that bothered him, but his father, Sam Scott, whose reputation was well-known in town.

Vince Scott had a reputation for getting to work on time, but his pocket watch tended to run a little slow. To enhance his timely obsession, he invested in a Bulova watch on easy credit at S. H. Deroy's in town. Radios being a hot item, he invested in a Kent table radio with a high fidelity tuner for five dollars down and five dollars a month. He had wanted to own one ever since he heard the first radio broadcast announcing results of the Harding-Cox election over a crystal set at the telegraph office.

KDKA had made its historic 100 watt broadcast from the Westinghouse plant in East Pittsburgh. Its station on Wood Street downtown reported news at the top of the hour and half hour, played records to fill time slots and featured local entertainers live on the air. Most commercials lasted ten seconds. *Drink Maxwell House coffee, good to the last drop,* lasted five seconds. Vince appreciated the value of a radio in the house, sensing it helped keep his anxious mother distracted from worries of the night with news of the day.

The commuting public protested overcrowded streetcars and demanded City Council to pass an ordinance banning streetcar strikes, a move that provoked conductors to call surprise strikes that forced people to walk. Those who could afford to were buying cars and driving, creating downtown traffic chaos and no place to park. Service stations opened, new roads were planned, and new buildings and bridges were going up—a boon to the gas, oil and steel industries. Steel company stocks soared, but the labor force owned none of it; they began walking out in strike after strike. Vince saw the process as self-defeating because his friends who worked in industry lost work and wages sometimes for three and four months a year and longer while he held down a steady job.

His supervisor, Harry Grimes, called him in one day to ask how he felt about moving to the front office position of assistant solicitor for new accounts. Elated by the promotion, he consulted the tailor at Gordon's Clothing Store on Butler Street, opened an account, and invested fifty bucks in a dark-blue herringbone suit, a white shirt and tie. He couldn't wait to show off his smart new look to his mother and when he walked in the door, she said, *Son, you look like a million bucks*. He next bought a gray wool overcoat for fifteen dollars, a red wool scarf for two dollars, a gray Stetson hat for five dollars, wing-tipped black leather shoes for twelve dollars, and galoshes for three dollars, purchases to prepare him for the approaching winter. For all his efforts to do the right thing, he was unprepared for what was about to happen.

After long hours at work, and especially on cold nights, he looked forward to the hot supper plate his mother had waiting. On that night reserved by fate, he came in out of a freezing rain, shivering, and went straight to the kitchen, where he found her sitting at the table with her hands folded in her lap and a blank stare on her face. He asked, *What's wrong, mom?*

In a flat tone, she said: *Your father's gone, he's deserted the family.* She reached into her house dress pocket, handed him a scrap of paper and said, *Read it.*

It said: *Mary, I can't go on this way. I am forty years old with nothing to show for. I'm clearing out and heading back to St. Louis where I came from. The railroad hired me. I'll send some money home when I get paid. Sorry for the inconvenience. Sam.*

Soon after, in a fit of revenge, she marched all of their eight children down to St. Kieran's, rebellious as they were to be put through a baptism ritual at that point. Living as she was in the shadows of the Parish and in fear of gossip, she avoided church, listed Vince as head of household, took her desertion grievance to a lawyer on Butler Street, filed for child support, and had Sam subpoenaed back to Pittsburgh for a hearing in the Family Division of the Court of Common Pleas of Allegheny County.

On a frigid February day 1923, Sam breezed down the judicial corridor looking like he owned the place and strolled up to Mary who was standing just outside the courtroom. One look and she knew he had recovered all of the bold conceit he had possessed the day he jumped off a milk wagon, strutted up the bluff and flirted with her while she was milking the family cow so long ago.

Vince shortly arrived, and his mother immediately noticed that he was wearing glasses—a pair of round wire glasses exactly like hers. They were both near-sighted and the resemblance between the two was striking. He had anticipated an embrace or affirmation of some kind from his father, but Sam simply gave him a slap on the back and circled Mary. She, after all, looked stunning in a black velvet hat with a prominent feather and a tailored black wool coat with a black velvet collar. She had bought the whole outfit at the Goodwill just for the occasion. She could barely stand the sight of him. He sensed it and began to whine about how hard it was trying to earn a decent wage in a cramped cage selling train tickets to cranky passengers. She simply could not muster up the poise to say hello.

Jim Scott presently arrived, also looking prosperous as the owner of a grocery store in Etna, a city borough on the other side of the Allegheny River. He had come to the hearing hoping that a reconciliation might take place between his brother and sister-in-law for the sake of their children. Mary had never taken to Jim, nor he to her, but the desertion had softened his heart toward her. He offered Sam a hand shake, said hello to Mary and asked how she was getting along. Sam suddenly leaned in, kissed Mary's cheek, and told Jim she'd be just fine. Sam's cavalier attempt at a conversation made her blood run cold, especially when he handed out the line about what harm a little kiss could do and how she looked so lovely he couldn't resist.

On her lawyer's advice, she had brought along her sons to strengthen her child support case, but she was beginning to wonder if it would do any good. The boys' attention was focused entirely on Sam and Jim, who paced up and down the corridor smoking cigarettes. During the wait for the hearing to get underway, nerves frayed and a terrible argument erupted between Sam and Mary.

To everyone's surprise, Vince started sticking up for his father. Jim could stand it no longer and turned on his nephew, asking when he was going to wise up. Vince more or less told his uncle to mind his own business. It wasn't the sort of talk Jim expected, and in the heat of the moment, he said, *Listen here Vince, I don't know why you're sticking up for your old man. That bum's not your real father anyhow, you're adopted.*

Dazed and confused, he stormed out of the courthouse and stopped for a drink in every back room from town to Lawrenceville. Hours later he arrived home to find his mother in a desperate mood. She cried out that she had been worried sick all day over him and went on to tell him that she was sorry about what his uncle had said. He asked if it was true. Her answer was neither yes nor no. She told him she loved him as her very own, considered him her son, and asked that he always think of her as his real mother. He never again raised the subject with her, but the thought of being an adopted child would haunt him all his days.

Early in the century, the Commonwealth did not mandate immediate reporting of births or adoptions. Many such records are inaccurate and far more do not exist. Opinions handed down indicate that more than one version of Vince's adoption story survived. In some quarters it was believed that Sam had fathered a child to a woman who either ran off or died, and that Mary took the baby in. There might be a nugget of truth in this story, but the story of the song and dance team had the strongest legs.

Some days after the hearing, Mary got busy making dinner and whipped up a lemon meringue pie, her children's favorite desert. She placed it in the broiler and pulled up a chair to keep watch as it browned. There came a rap at the door and Sam burst in, making her so angry that she slammed the broiler door shut, causing the pie to splatter all over the place. She ordered him out and never saw him again.

What was he doing there in the first place? He already knew that her appeal for child support had been denied because the courts frowned on common law arrangements, and Mary could not prove that she and Sam had ever married. Ironically, during the phase of my research to prove that our Scott grandparents had indeed been legally married, I found no records anywhere. (Interesting enough is that when I worked with Aunt Rose Scott on this story, she told me that she too had gone through the court house archives searching for proof that her mother and father had married and had no luck either. What I hadn't revealed to her was that I also searched the records for proof that Aunt Rose had been married and no luck there either. But she did share with me the story of how in 1934, she married a bum and threw him out of her mother's house six months before giving birth to her one and only child. Thanks to our grandmother who raised Sheila, our aunt was able to return to work and hold down a demanding but good paying job.)

Years of frustration spurned Mary Scott's outrage, but there was no sense crying now; she had cried over Sam for twenty miserable years—*a big waste of time,* as she put it. She lamented that people would feel sorry for her and dreaded that she'd be the talk of the town. In that shamed-based society, his brothers turned on Vince for sticking up for their father. He packed up to leave and changed his mind, knowing that his mother needed him more than ever. The wall between him and his brothers would take years to fall away. Vince himself was not one to let go of a grudge once he decided to hold one. At home, he kept to himself and stuck it out; such was the nature of his nobility, his loyalty and his love.

To spare herself the social embarrassment of not having a husband, she listed herself in the city directory first as a widow and then as divorced, although one never took place. Despair overwhelmed her. What would become of the children without a father? What would become of her without a husband? She became more reclusive than ever.

Sam Jr. had what is called *charisma*, a trait that easily likened him to his father's public style, except for the fact that our uncle loved his family. He went to his uncle Jim's grocery store in Etna and asked for a job. There, he learned to drive a pickup truck and huckster produce. His mother was leery of the pocket money he flashed, more than peddling vegetables paid, but with help from next in line John, both did well. John soon felt confident enough to quit high school and deliver dairy products to private customers for the Meadow Gold Dairy Company.

With the mid-twenties booming, Bart resigned from eighth grade on the objection that school was getting him nowhere. He joined a construction crew, vowing to work his way up in the home-building industry, and he bragged about retiring by age fifty as a millionaire. His brothers smirked and his sisters giggled, but in due time, he started his own construction company, building homes all over Stanton Heights, less than half a mile from his mother's house on Holmes Street. That was our uncle Bart Scott, and he would have the last laugh.

Vince worked to mend fences and looked out for young Lawrence, who he encouraged to do well in his studies, hoping his baby brother would go on to high school and graduate. Lawrence preferred tagging along with Sam on the huckstering route rather than attending school. Their mother secretly dreaded a day might come when she'd find their names in the newspaper crime list. Vince figured this out and stopped bringing home the newspaper. Instead, he left it on the streetcar for the next person to read.

On Butler Street, streetcars rocked along a double track guided by a central headlight; their braking systems could be heard for some distance before they screeched to a jolting stop. The crowded Number 1 Butler Street operated from town to the 62nd Street Loop and turned around. Service improved when the Number 1A was added and continued over the bridge to Sharpsburg and beyond to Aspinwall, where it turned around at a new car barn. Streetcar rides to the outskirts were an inexpensive form of family entertainment on Sunday afternoons and on weekday evenings.

One day after work, Rose Quinn waited for her streetcar at the stop in front of Rosenbaum's on 6th Street in town. The streetcar turned off Penn Avenue and jumped the track. People started walking when service on the route was brought to a halt. Well over an hour passed before engineers were able to bring in a crane to hoist the streetcar back onto the track and get it moving. When the conductor finally opened the door, anxious commuters piled on, and Rose was pressed aside by the rush of the crowd. Somehow, she managed to squeeze in and hold onto an over-head leather strap just as the door closed.

At the next stop, Vince Scott hopped on. The minute he spotted the lovely girl he had met on a streetcar what seemed ages ago, his heart skipped a beat, and so did hers. It felt like forever for the streetcar to get to the fork of the road at Butler Street and Penn Avenue, where a number of people got off. He quickly guarded a seat and asked Rose if she'd like to sit down. She nodded and sat down. He asked how she was doing. She said fine and started reading her newspaper, after all, she barely knew him.

In that era, a respectable woman could acknowledge a man's interest in her without becoming too friendly. It was up to the respectable man to figure out how to pursue her, so Vince had to figure out how to get Rose's attention off that newspaper before the streetcar reached his stop, which was several blocks ahead of hers. She seemed not to notice him getting off, absorbed as she was with the news from Ireland and how long it would be until they all started shooting at each other again.

To Vince's good fortune she was on the next evening's streetcar; he asked her right off if she'd like to go see a movie Saturday night. She said yes and his heart skipped two beats. He agreed to call on her at eight o'clock, although he was not exactly quiet when he rapped on the door at 5621 Butler Street. Moreover, Patrick Quinn was not exactly quiet either. Being in no mood to entertain an unwelcomed pursuer, let alone the son of Sam Scott, he hollered, *Who's pounding on that door?* Rose simply invited Vince in. Blind or not, her father stomped upstairs when Vince started tinkering on the piano and singing in a rapid cadence the one tune he knew:

Eighteen long years I have lived in a flat,
and all that I got is a dog and a cat.

Oh, the lady next door, she is chuck full of joy,
the stork came and brought her a new baby boy!

Rose seemed to enjoy his bit of showing off, until her father bellowed, *Hey you black sheep down there, stop that racket.* Smartly, she invited Vince out for a walk through the neighborhood. Sensitive though he was, he tried to overlook the fact that Mr. Quinn didn't like him and remained undaunted in his pursuit of the girl he loved. He seldom told his mother where he was going and was thankful that she didn't ask. He was not quite ready to speak to her about the joy of his heart.

Soon, they were seeing each other steadily. He set his pocket watch ahead so as not to be late for an important date. Strutting along the main drag smoking a cigarette in his cavalier way, he stopped here and there to glance at his reflection in the store windows. He wanted to make a good impression, not just on Rose, but on a formidable rival, Mr. Quinn.

But then came the day when himself answered the door and told Vince to go away. His impulse was to do just that but, on the other hand, he'd not want to risk a reaction that might hurt Rose's feelings, even though she understood that he did not want to be where he wasn't wanted. She explained how her father had been blinded in a mill accident and had never been the same. Vince sympathized and it saved everything for her. Her sister Mary and brothers Dick and Frank more easily stood up to their father, which made it easier for Rose to stick up for Vince. All courage vanished for both of them the day Mr. Quinn answered the door and asked Vince directly, *What no good are you up to now?*

The lovebirds had been meeting each other anyplace but her house as it was less stressful. They often double-dated with Rose's best friend Nettie Brunich and Vince's best friend Billy Garrigan. The coziest place to meet was at the show, especially with the season changing and the evenings growing cold. Then winter set in and Rose was forced to bring Vince inside, at which point Mr. Quinn started up again. There was tension in that house alright. Vince felt it, and to bolster his morale, he began to stop at Dublin's Pub on his way to call on Rose.

One evening, he arrived on time in a happy state and went straight to the piano, hit the keys with two fingers, and started bellowing his tune for all its worth. Mr. Quinn failed to see the humor in a song about a dog and a cat, a stork and a baby boy. He had had about enough of it and told Vince to keep away from Rose; he was no longer welcome in that house. In that case, the courtship went underground.

The downtown theaters featured new releases, but they had to watch their timing to avoid missing the last streetcar home or they would have to hail a taxi, an expensive ride with the meter running while the taxi stood in snarled traffic. What better place to go out of the weather than the swanky Arsenal Theatre in the heart of Lawrenceville to see first-rate films and eat popcorn? A comfortable setting, but their predicament dragged on through the winter.

The *New York Times* headlined a story January 1924 of an explosion and fire at the Pittsburgh Steel and Spring Company in Lawrenceville that killed twelve men. Residents on Stanton Heights saw plumes of black smoke and fire billowing into the air and said it looked like the end of the world. A few weeks later, the *Pittsburgh Gazette Times* headlined a story of a disaster at the Atlantic Oil Refinery on Butler Street just up a ways from the Quinns' house. An explosion had ripped open a steel pipe through which hot oil was being forced under high pressure from a benzene still. The force of the explosion rocked the district and a 10,000 barrel oil tank burst into flames. More tanks were threatened, resulting in an all-city fire alarm.

The *Pittsburgh Press* reported that a tank of crude oil collapsed and the ladder of a burning tank broke, hurling three officers and four hosemen into the inferno. Four fifty-foot diameter gasoline storage tanks and seven oil storage tanks were destroyed; damages totaled over $100,000. Fifteen thousand barrels of oil flooded Atlantic's tank yards. Another hundred thousand gallons of oil spilled into the Allegheny River, killing its catfish, a vital resource for thousands of families. Flames leaped from the refinery smoke stack, and dense smoke made fighting the fire more difficult. Eighty people were injured in the disaster, among them, fifty children, many who had ignored orders to get off the roofs of the forty garages, a row of remodeled horse stables adjacent to the refinery.

Even though the Quinns' house was miraculously untouched, they were forced to take shelter with Grant relatives in the Ninth Ward as a ten-block area had to be evacuated due to dense smoke and burning buildings. Below zero temperatures caused gas shortages, and frozen water pipes added to the discomfort. Traffic barriers were erected from 51st to 62nd Street. Streetcars were forced to leave passengers off at the 47th and Plummer Street turnaround, an inconvenience finally lifted in time for the Saint Patrick's Day Parade in town.

In May 1924, Vince turned twenty-two and decided it was high time he made his intentions known. He proposed to Rose and she accepted. Now all that he had to do was *face the music*, as he put it, meaning an encounter with Mr. Quinn. A scotch and soda along the way provided the spunk to brace himself when the other himself opened the door—the perfect time to get to the point: *Mr. Quinn, I came here to ask for your daughter's hand and I intend to marry Rose with or without your permission.*

Mr. Quinn looked like he had just been shot, but shook his head mightily, and point blank retorted: *How dare yee suggest to me Mr. Scott that you intend to marry me daughter Rose.* Then, in an uncharacteristically vulnerable moment, he softened his tone and asked Vince to please come in and sit down. It was a lot for the older gent to take in and ponder before he had a word or two to say to an upstart, but if marrying Vince was his daughter's will, he would give her a good send off.

Vince headed home rehearsing in his mind how to break the news to his mother. She was tidying up and offered him a cup of tea. She filled him in on family news and he fumbled with words leading up to what he wanted to say, beating around the bush, until he nervously blurted, *Mom, I met a real nice girl a while back and we're going to get married.* His mother upped and left the room.

Downcast, he kept his appointment with Father Doyle at St. Kieran's. In forty years of service to the community, the priest now struggled with poor health and relied on two assistants to help with an overwhelming Parish workload, but he had remained a close friend of the Quinns and would look out for Rose. To put it mildly, Vince sweated out the interview. The priest knew of his turbulent family background and had never forgotten the day Sam Scott showed him the door so long ago. He now prayed for peace in both families and it worked.

In September, Vincent Paul and Rose Quinn Scott professed their vows before family, friends, relatives, and the curious. She made a lovely bride in satin, he a dashing groom in gabardine. He admitted to feeling uncomfortable in church but went along with the program—and *begorra,* what a match! He had worried that his mother's hard feelings would become a roadblock, but she had come to the wedding after all. The newlyweds moved into an apartment on the corner of Keystone and 53rd Street, half a block up from the church. Rose attended Mass regularly and Vince occasionally—he being a sort of unconverted Irish pagan—banging the kneeler down to genuflect and jamming his fingers to his forehead and a blow to his chest to make the sign of the cross with a loud prayer, as if to say: *Look at me, I'm here*!

In October, Mr. Quinn received a visit from a man identified as Harry Wilson, president of American Spiral & Spring Manufacturing Co (the Spring Works). He showed up without an appointment and bluntly stated that the company had purchased the vacant lot next door to the Quinns and a mill would be built on the site. Heavy machinery would create an annoyance but would cause no harm to Mr. Quinn's property, but the company was willing to take it off his hands for $6,000 and would give him time to think it over.

Days later, Mr. Wilson returned with a new offer—the company didn't need the house but was willing to buy the ground for $3,300 and Mr. Quinn could take his house wherever he wanted to. Our grandfather promptly showed that man to the door, saying that he had no place to go or take his house with him and, furthermore, he had worked in mills all his life and loved factory noise.

The Quinn household went into an uproar when freight trucks pulled into the vacant lot and deposited huge steel beams and corrugated tin sheeting inches from their house. Construction began and industrial equipment was installed, including five heat-treating furnaces; water, oil and paint tanks; metal grinders and flatteners; iron shears; drill presses; and banding machines. Then two six-hundred-pound drop hammer presses started pounding away. Mr. Quinn complained to the company that the

plaster in his house was cracking. He was ignored and started thinking the hammer presses had been deliberately placed on the wall abutting his house to drive him out for not selling his ground and taking his house elsewhere. Then the mortar and bricks started crumbling. His only recourse was to sue. He talked to a lawyer in town and was advised that in our sluggish judicial system, it could take years for the case to be heard. Our Quinn uncles, Dick and Frank, had no recourse but to try to keep the house from falling down. Daily, Aunt Mary wiped plaster dust off the furniture and windowsills and swept and scrubbed dirt and debris off the floors and everything else in the house.

Our father and mother joined Keystone Street's annual bucket brigade to clean up their neighborhood. The exterior of those houses required harsh chemicals to remove a heavy coating of soot and grime, but Dad's and Mom's apartment, furnished with Quinn family donations, was well kept thanks to their mutual appreciation for a higher standard of living. Mom wore a housedress when she cleaned, and at some point, it dawned on Dad that she appeared to be needing a larger size. He loved to shop and picked out two of the finest at a local dress shop, one to wash and one to wear, as he put it, and nice enough to wear on their evening strolls.

One evening while working around the apartment, she let out a quiet shriek. He suggested that she sit down before she fell down. She finished what she was doing, sat down in her mother's rocking chair, and began to stitch with a needle and thread—hand stitching infant sleeping gowns of white linen. He seemed at ease in his comfortable chair by the window, smoking a cigarette and working the crossword puzzle in the *Sun Telegraph.* Then he spread the newspaper out on his lap, dealt himself a game of Solitaire, and turned on the radio, there to relax until bedtime.

In the middle of that warm June night, she let him know that her time had come to deliver. For a moment, his mind went blank and then he became frantic. He got dressed and, not owning a car, ran all the way to the Quinns' house a few blocks away and pounded on the door. Unassuming, our uncle Frank felt for the rosary in his pocket and got his sister and brother-in-law to nearby St. Francis Hospital in no time at all.

1925

In the dawn of a new day, Vincent Paul Scott, Jr. was born and post-haste baptized by Father Doyle of St. Kieran's in keeping with Irish Catholic traditions. Dad wanted to protect his little family and purchased a Metropolitan Life Insurance policy for five hundred dollars at a quarterly premium of fifty cents, with twenty-five cents to be added to the premium for each newborn, a spirit that would prevail until his means to pay disappeared. He ruled out incurring the expense of owning a car but considered having a telephone installed for the sake of convenience. Mom said what she would appreciate more was a washing machine.

He had good credit and purchased a sixty dollar top-of-the-line wringer-washer that went by the improbable name *Gain-a-Day,* a drudgery saver manufactured on the third floor of the Pittsburgh Gage & Supply Company on Liberty Avenue in the Strip District. Anybody could buy one and take it home for twenty-five dollars down and five dollars a month. Dad forked over the cash and paid a driver to haul it home and set it up.

Mom could not wait to get it going. She was already carrying their second child and was entirely grateful to be the owner of a modern invention that not only washed clothes but wrung them out. She appreciated full well that most of her neighbors still did laundry on a scrub board and wrung everything out by hand. Dad did not want that for Mom, bearing in mind the hardships that his mother had endured.

Mary Catherine O'Donnell Scott was still living on Holmes Street with Lillian, Ann, Rose, and Lawrence. Sam, John and Bart had moved out on their own and were gainfully employed. Our grandmother rarely socialized in the neighborhood but treasured visits from her sons, especially Dad when he brought her first grandchild along. She was, from the first time she laid eyes on Vinny, extremely proud of him.

Aunt Mary never turned down an invitation to babysit. It amused her how Vinny could stay awake for hours on end, waiting for his mother and father to return from their adventures at the local grocery stores or an early movie at the show. One night, Dad stayed up late with Vinny so Mom could lay down. All of a sudden, their yearling picked himself up off the floor and made his way around the room holding onto the furniture, sort of like he had been planning the event all his life. Dad woke Mom up to see Vinny on his feet for the first time. She didn't mind it at all; she was not sleeping well as her time to deliver was near.

In August 1926, Sis was born and named Rosemary after Mom and Aunt Mary. Second in line of the twelve Scott kids, Sis came into the world bearing all the marks of beauty and genius perfect for our parents' boasting. Uncle Frank, of course, was on hand to drive Mom straight to St. Francis Hospital, a good deed that would become a family tradition.

Sunday was family day with the Quinns, the one day a week when Mom didn't have to cook supper, but impossible to visit properly in that disruptive atmosphere. The blow of the hammers next door caused a terrible vibration that shook the dining table and the floor beneath it. Talk at the dinner table always alluded to the possibility of *suing the bastards.* Our grandfather could not stay home for any length of time because the hammers dropped at a rate of nine or ten blows a minute, a racket that blew out his hearing. Frank and Dick couldn't sleep during the day when working night shift. They appealed to the superintendent of the mill for relief and were ignored.

The plant whistle blew incessantly, the industrial equipment roared, and our poor blind grandfather feared the roof of his house would cave in on him. He was eating breakfast one morning when a jolt shook the house, the lantern above the table burst into pieces and a shard of glass put a gash in his head. The hammers started up, the coal stove pipe crashed to the floor and black smoke filled the house. Then came the last straw—the kitchen ceiling caved in and he thought he was going out of his mind—the perfect opportunity to get on with his case.

The lawsuit was filed by Attorney Thomas L. Kane *in re: Patrick Quinn vs. American Spiral & Spring Manufacturing Company in the Court of Common Pleas of Allegheny County at Docket No. 2748 January Term 1927.* The complaint was heard by a Court *en banc* (three judges) who issued a decree *nisi* (case dismissed). It found our grandfather guilty of laches (undue delay in asserting his legal rights) and set the amount in controversy at less than $2,500 (meaning action should have been brought before a magistrate not the court). The decision would have to be appealed to a higher court and would take months and a small fortune to prepare.

Dad came into good fortune when his boss at Postal Telegraph promoted him to office manager. His wages were sufficient to pay the rent and utilities, monthly installments on insurance and hospital bills, household supplies, with a little extra *pin money*, as he called spending money for cigarettes and beer. The landlord got wind of his prosperity, raised the rent, and Dad started looking.

He found an apartment on Holmes Street, two streets up and in the same block as Grandmother Scott. It had two large rooms at street level and a kitchen and bathroom in the lower level facing a back alleyway. The place had been cleaned and painted, and the rent was affordable. Mom said it would do, so they moved in—a big mistake. The plumbing malfunctioned and water leaked inside the wall between the bathroom and kitchen. A storm hit, the stairway wall light exploded, and the power went out. The landlord, who lived on the upper floors of the house, replaced the fuse, looked at the burnt out light socket, and said he'd fix it when the wall dried out. Mom was afraid to light the gas heater that Dad installed to help dry out the place for fear it might set the house on fire.

The epidemic of house fires had everybody on edge. The *Sun Telegraph* covered news of an Equitable Gas Company explosion on the Northside that blew out windows on Mt. Washington, shook downtown buildings, and caused homes at the site of the blast to burn down. But where would people go without the risk of jumping out of the frying pan and landing in the furnace? Dad planned to take his time looking for the next place to live to avoid another big mistake.

In September 1927, Joe was born and named for Mom's brother, Joseph, whose photograph hung on her bedroom wall. Every chance she got, she held baby Joe up to it and told him that he was named for his Uncle Joseph, which would become a

source of pride for Joe all his days. Dad started setting his clock to get up a little earlier so that he had time to make the family breakfast before going to work, a selfless act that became an ideal to strive for all his years.

The holiday season approached, and he clipped newspaper coupons for culinary specials on sale at Donahoe's in town. The quality of its food enhanced the nutritious meals that Mom served on a finely set table, but she was always relieved when the holidays were over. *Too much work*, she said.

A move was in the works for the Quinns, pending the outcome of the appeal to the Supreme Court of Pennsylvania, Docket No. 86 March Term 1928 in dissent to the decision of the Court of Common Pleas. Exhibits filed included the lower court's official transcript and photographs of the front, side, and back of our grandfather's crumbling house. Among the eleven witnesses appearing on his behalf were his sons Richard and Frank and daughter Mary and, of all people, his son-in-law Vincent P. Scott, Sr., who testified, or rather, gave the court a piece of his mind, *For God's sake, Your Honor, you can't sit down in peace and eat a decent meal in that house and enjoy a half-decent conversation with all that racket going on.*

In that emotionally charged atmosphere, the court transcript brilliantly captured not only our grandfather's story of pain and suffering but his wonderful brogue. At one point in his testimony, when asked how the noise of the Spring Works affected him, he passionately explained:

Ah, the noise, it affects me all right...and the house. It shakes the floor up and down and 'tis on my nerves. I want to go to bed and I can't lie down for the bed goes the same as the hammers and the rolls, crushing in the wall and... I tell you it's fierce. Those hammers are fierce. Everything going and the place shaking...I'm not able to stay in the house. I've got to get out. The noise...I can't do it. There is no comfort in me house. One day the lantern came down when the hammer started and caught me on the head. Six dollars ninety cents that cost me. It knocks the stove pipe down when the hammer is working. Then I am in a fix. I went to the corner to get a policeman but I couldn't get none, I couldn't see so I could get protection as good as anybody else. You want me to tell how we come to buy the place? There was nothing only the brick house … not a thing. The lots were all empty. He [Harry Wilson] pays me a visit and offers to buy me property. He only wants the ground, says the house is worthless to him and I can take it wherever I want. That would be no good. I have no place to move. He says the machinery will make a nuisance but no harm to me. The machinery…it puts you crazy. It has me crazy anyhow. Nervous…I don't know what to do. Am wishing to put bricks through the windows, I am. That's what I have a notion to do…men like that doing a thing like that on a poor blind man…God help us…a poor blind man and his family have no pleasure in the house.

The move to a better house that Dad and Mom had planned was postponed; she was expecting her fourth child in four years. He encouraged her to get off her feet in the evening while he did the supper dishes and washed diapers. He knew that even with the convenience of an electric washer, feeding wet wash through the wringer and hanging it out to dry put a strain on her, especially in the dense humidity and heat once summer arrived and Dolores was born.

While Mom was in the hospital, Dad took time off work to take care of Vinny, Sis, and Joe, ages three, two, and one. The reality was that the flat on Holmes Street, though kept in order—a place for everything and everything in its place—was too small and the big bed overcrowded. Mom had to get up nights with infant DeeDee, which made for Dad a hard time getting back to sleep. He felt an urgency to look for a bigger house and saw a *For-Rent* sign in the window of a flat one street down on Lotus Way. The place seemed roomy enough until they moved in, but there, Dad would be listed in the next city directory as head-of-household, Manager-P.T. & Cable Co.

The Atlantic's tropical storms that season produced three hurricanes, coastal flooding, and heavy rains inland. Pittsburgh got slammed. Dad came in out of a cold hard rain one night, hung his coat and hat on the door nail, set up the ironing board, and dried out his soaked newspaper. The November 7, 1928 front-page headline read: *Franklin Delano Roosevelt Wins Race for Governor of New York.* A sub-headline read: *Anyone who governs New York has a good chance to be President with any luck.* Dad couldn't wait for FDR to run and straighten out the mess the country was in. The noble cause for the common man was to make America greater. Pittsburgh's manufacturing and building industries boomed. Gulf Oil erected an eleven million dollar headquarters on Grant Street. The expansion of our factories and railroads indicated that nothing could stop our economic growth.

People were still in awe of radio when stories began to appear of television systems being tested. Dad's curiosity piqued when he read a story about color television sets on sale to the public. The story did not say where one of these sets could be purchased or what to do with it once you bought one. Television networks did not yet exist but inventors were creating technology faster than it could be introduced to the market.

Meantime, the Supreme Court of Pennsylvania was about to hand down its decision in Plaintiff Patrick Quinn's appeal. At the last-minute, Defendant American Spiral & Spring proposed settling the case. The Company did not want a story to get into the newspapers of its noisy factory driving a poor blind man out of his house and home. He accepted their offer to buy his house and the ground for $6,500 and pay court costs totaling $3,500. With sufficient funds in hand to pay for a move, Dick and Frank, suggested that they all get as far from Butler Street as possible and pleaded with their father to move to Aspinwall. He refused.

As if by divine intervention, our mother and father paid our grandfather a visit and made an effort to reason with him. They defined the advantages of a wealthy blind man living in a modern house on a quiet tree-lined street with access to a candy store down the block, a bank around the corner and a Hibernian Club next door. It took time for him to get used to the idea of living somewhere else, but alas he consented, saying, *What choice does a poor old blind man have when he doesn't have a say*? Ever-so-slowly, he adjusted to his new neighborhood but desperately missed his cronies, the Butler Street racket, and the Dublin Pub. He stayed in his fancy Aspinwall room sulking with his radio blasting. It would take some time for the new character on the block to get used to things.

In September 1929, Mom and Dad celebrated their fifth wedding anniversary. Our hopelessly romantic father gave our hopelessly practical mother a gift of candy and flowers—all for the love of his life, *his girl*. He began to measure progress by the lack of a salary increase and the addition of longer hours to his office work load. Mom needed more help than ever, and at times exhaustion forced her off her feet. She struggled to keep up with chores that increased with every child she bore. She saw that the children were growing and starting to need *things*. One day she mentioned this to Dad and, to her astonishment, he said he'd buy all those *things* when his ship came in. She crossed her fingers hoping that his ship wouldn't sink.

October 29, 1929, *Black Tuesday*, the Wall Street Exchange collapsed, wiping out over thirty million dollars in stocks that decisively ended a decade of prosperity. Congress initiated emergency regulations to mitigate losses, and across the country, twenty million Americans suddenly went on the dole. Dad blamed former president, Herbert Hoover, and expressed distrust for politicians who promised everything during their campaigns and did nothing after they were elected. Dad's opinion was this: *All that ever happens when you go to the polls and vote is—out with the old bums and in with the new bums—nothing ever changes because the system has been entrenched in corruption from its very founding.*

Allegheny County was a Republican stronghold, but with the new voting machines installed in almost every precinct, people went to the polls in droves to vote Democrat—a vote for a better country, a better world, a better universe, and a return to prosperity. Postal Telegraph hired more messengers in a surge of business transactions as companies started going under and others tried to stay afloat. Dad, with his wages frozen at thirty dollars a week, worked overtime at the main office without overtime wages and managed the satellite office in the Strip District on Saturdays for a pittance.

Job stress started his hair thinning and his eyes bothering him. His optician prescribed new lenses for his old round wire glasses. He thought they made him look smart, and he wanted to look smart on the job—after all, he was particular about how he presented himself. His boss, Mr. Grimes, took note and offered him a job at PT's headquarters in Gary, Indiana, suggesting that Dad fly out there at company expense to look the town over.

He had reservations about flying on what he conceived to be a parchment, toothpicks, and glue aircraft, but his decision to check out the job generated huge excitement on Lotus Way. The entire neighborhood gathered to watch PT's private plane fly over Scott's house with Dad on board. The kids waved and cheered: *Aero-plane, aero-plane, our Dad's on an aero-plane!*

Well, he looked the job and town over with a heavy heart. A substantial salary offer tempted him, but he would have to tell his boss that his wife didn't want to move and he would never go against her wishes. For the present, PT spared him the humiliation of joining the millions of Americans unemployed.

In 1930s Pittsburgh, the average worker lived payday to payday, and families were still putting food on their tables, even with food prices sky-high. All this time, Prohibition remained in effect and hard liquor flowed in alluring back rooms. Dad sometimes imbibed at watering holes on the way home from work. Mom knew, but her style was to create molehills out of mountains, not the other way around. She understood that he bore the frustration of nothing left over on payday to save for the day they moved to better themselves. His name was on every house-rental list in Lawrenceville.

Nevertheless, the wonder of it all was that no matter which house the Scotts lived in, there was always a baby in the bassinet and a toddler in the highchair handed down the line from Vinny. Skip, the fifth wonder of Scott World, named Francis after his sponsor, was hastily baptized at St. Kieran's and slept right through the drenching, so said Uncle Frank.

Drenching rains never stopped Dad either; he escorted Vinny to kindergarten at his *alma mater,* McCandless Public School. His hope was that all of *his* children would attend public school where the education was free. Mom feared that in public school *her* children might come under the influence of bible-believing Protestants but accepted the risk to prevent Vinny from falling behind when it came time for his transfer to St. Kieran's School. The student body was required to attend morning Mass and march in formation from the church to the school as required in all Parishes. The school was staffed by an order of the Daughters of Charity of Baltimore and burgeoned with students. Extra classrooms had to be set up in the parish

convent to accommodate the overflow, which often spilled out onto the sidewalk on warm afternoons—bright students with hands raised to answer questions: *Yes Sister. No Sister.* A sweet scene familiar to our ancestors of Ireland being schooled in drafty barns and open fields.

Vinny was enrolled at St. Kieran's in time for first grade without an argument from Dad. He took number one son in tow and taught him how to part and comb his hair with every strand in place, polish his brown oxfords to a high shine, and tie them neatly. She taught him to dress smartly in a short-sleeved shirt, short pants and knee socks. Who could have been more proud of their first born than Mr. and Mrs. Scott? She gathered up the little ones and escorted Vinny to school, a tradition she would cherish as one by one her children came of age. At home, he was called *Sonny*, but in school he was called *Vince*. Sister gave him a desk to share with two boys at the back of the room. He had no trouble seeing the blackboard and could feel the adulation of his teacher.

Vinny wanted to make friends, but a few of his classmates turned that into a bullying nightmare because he wore short pants and could read Book One from beginning to end, flawlessly; Mom and Dad had given him a home-schooling head start. Nevertheless, he loved first grade and took pride in his work. He had reached an age when Mom and Dad began to depend on him in the way the eldest is often depended on—a cultural tradition. When Sis started kindergarten at McCandless

PS, Vinny met her after school and walked her home. A first child can be a bit of a mystery to a younger sibling who sometimes wonders why a big brother or sister takes life so seriously—a cultural phenomenon.

One winter day, Mom kept both of them home and Vinny couldn't stand it. What would Sister think of him if he didn't show up? Mom tried to explain that the snow was too deep, there was ice under the snow and, besides, it would be freezing in school. He cried so hard that she let him go, bundled up and bearing the brunt of icy wind and blowing snow. He knew, of course, that school never closed because the Sisters of Charity would be waiting to welcome brave students who showed up for class. During those early years, he gladly traveled to school in a blizzard or two.

During the December 1931 blizzard, Anne was born. The hospitals had instituted an accounting system that required a contract to pay bills on monthly installments. Hard-pressed for funds as he was, Dad fell into a state of shock at the realization that he belonged to the invisible class of hard-working poor. The A & P on 54th Street only accepted cash, so he opened a credit account at Shall's Grocers on Butler Street. They charged more but delivered free. He dropped off an order one morning on his way to work and—to Mom's surprise—the groceries arrived while she was bathing Anna in the kitchen sink.

Joe never forgot that day. Imagine a little boy walking right out the front door of his house and wandering into a grocery van to explore. Well, the rear door suddenly slammed shut behind Joe and the van drove off, taking him on a bumpy ride. It stopped curbside at Shall's, the rear door banged opened, and the little stowaway was discovered, bearing a look of sheer wonder on his tear-drenched face. It seemed he may have started down a path of running away. Mom sobbed for joy to have her boy back safe and sound, even though she never had time to realize that he had gone missing. With six children underfoot and no yard or indoor space to play, she prayed for a big house and an even bigger yard. Dad, by sheer luck, found one on 57th Street and she wanted to see it.

The white frame house stood on a bluff, a walk up a steep brick-paved walkway between two other frame houses to get there. It had an up and downstairs, new wallpaper and paint, and linoleum flooring. The view from the front porch was quite like a scene from an old-country village nestled between two big hills with tar pitch and slate roofs and swirling chimney smoke.

Mom said, *No child of ours shall ever be left inside.*

And Dad said, *Not bad for fifteen dollars a month.*

1932

The first of May in Pittsburgh was Moving Day, the fourth move in eight years for the Scotts. Uncle Frank drove the moving truck, and everybody else walked from the old neighborhood to our new home on the wooded slope at the foot of the Quill's Hill limestone quarry. First thing Joe explored was the backyard where he found a rusty tricycle in the weeds. He got it going on a dare-devil ride down the brick path—a crash landing—but joyous to have left behind the crowded flat on Lotus Way with garbage and broken glass and rats as big as or bigger than cats.

Dad said we had moved *to better ourselves*, a pronouncement that had become one of his best propagandizing expressions to keep us motivated. Now, the big project of putting our new home in order was at hand. Ahead of time, he had gone to the main Goodwill store in the Strip District to buy a twenty-dollar 1901 Kalamazoo cooking range made in Michigan to be delivered to our new address. The wood and coal burning cast iron monstrosity with an overhead oven took three men to haul in sections up our brick walkway and to reassemble at no charge.

As night shadows fell, the family felt a sense of security and peace—then off to bed with lights lowered and windows opened to let in the breeze. The pleasant thing about morning was the ceaseless piping of sparrows and the six o'clock tolling of the *Angeles* bells. With a church right up the street, Dad cursed its bells with every gong—a racket to him that he fought off in his sleep.

St. Mary's Slovenian Parish was established at the turn of the century. Just up-a-ways, 57th Street ended abruptly at its intersection with Christopher Street and continued on an incline of over three hundred public steps up the side of the house-and-tree-lined slope to Sunnyside Public School on upper McCandless Avenue. At that elevation, a panoramic sea of factory buildings, tar-pitched roofs, two-way streets, and the one-way alleys of Lawrenceville came into view.

Pittsburgh neighborhoods were in hard times. Poorhouses were filled and people scrounged to live. The fifty thousand people first listed as starving swelled to a hundred-fifty thousand. Churches and synagogues opened their doors to feed the hungry. The Pittsburgh Association for the Poor conducted clothing and food drives. Catholic Charities offered emergency funds to keep families from being forced out of their homes and into the streets. The Good Fellows and the Odd Fellows gave food and clothing handouts. St. Augustine's Parish, run by the Capuchin Order on 36th Street, operated a soup kitchen, but the disheartened resorted to stealing bread from stores and bottled milk off door stoops. Shootings, lootings, robberies, and burglaries occurred; thieves were difficult to track down, and hard-ups who received stolen goods were hardly willing to turn in criminals.

All of it left our citizenry with no choice but to approve a five million dollar emergency relief bond and establish a welfare fund to support families on the dole. Father Jimmy Cox of St. Patrick's Parish in the Strip District held a rally at the University of Pittsburgh's stadium in Oakland to announce the formation of the Jobless Party and his run for office on an economic reconstruction platform. Thousands of hunger marchers followed him to Washington, D.C. to urge Congress to pass an unemployment insurance bill; the marchers were fed by the Helping Hand Society of Pittsburgh.

Dad cursed the day he'd have to go begging. He knew there were people with more money than they knew what to do with and people worse off who could have used their help. To cope, people planted backyard and potted vegetable gardens. No gardens were more splendid than those of our 57th Street neighbors who grew everything from lettuce, onions, green beans, peas, carrots, celery, parsley, garlic, and tomatoes to beets, parsnips, zucchini, cabbage, kohlrabi, and potatoes.

You could buy local produce in season at Sullivan's Candy Store right down the block from our house. Their shelves brimmed with not just fruits and vegetables, but homemade breads, cakes and pies—in a candy store! Its candy case brimmed with a colorful array of every sweet treat imaginable; apothecary jars atop the display case were stashed with stick candy, pretzel sticks, jaw breakers, bubble gum, licorice sticks, Tootsie Pops, and Sugar Daddies.

Almost every day, Mom sent Vinny and Sis to Sullivan's with a store list and a penny each for candy. The store bell jingled when they opened the door, signaling the proprietor, Paddi Sullivan, to tip his brown derby, wipe his hands clean on his white apron, and step over to the candy counter prepared to give his little speech for the children's amusement. *Well now then, what can I do for yee kids? Yee say yee want to buy candy? And how mooch money do yee have to spend*? The kids had no trouble understanding his brogue, but he sometimes had difficulty communicating with older customers.

One of his loyal customers, a snazzy dresser and skilled machinist, spoke such poor English that even his fellow-Slovenians couldn't understand him. Jake's and Paddi's banter often sounded like they were arguing. After all, ethnic strife existed in that era, but it wasn't like that on 57th Street. When Mrs. Sullivan died an untimely death, the Slovenians were first to extend their condolences with nourishing food plates and pastries.

Mom had unknowingly sent Vinny and Sis to the store that very morning. Mr. Sullivan was locking up and, with tears flowing, had to explain why. Shivering with the awful truth of a death in the neighborhood, the kids raced home with instructions to deliver his sad news: *Go home, dear children and tell yeer dear mother that me dear wife died in her sleep last night. She's gone to heaven; she's gone to her eternal reward. Go now and tell yeer whole family to pray for poor Mrs. Sullivan's departed soul.*

The outpouring of sorry songs and sherry that late night were too much for Dad; come morning, he slept in. Mr. Grimes came to the house, apologized for the intrusion, waited for Dad to get dressed, and drove him to work, knowing that if Dad missed work he didn't get paid. It wasn't the first time. Aunt Mary worked in the same office and saw the handwriting on the wall. Dad had hired her part-time to take up the paperwork slack. Sometimes, he found himself in a bind ahead of payday and asked her to lend him a few bucks out of the office cash box. At first, he paid it right back, and if he didn't, she got scared and put the money back herself. Mom realized that Dad would eventually face a comeuppance, but she believed in second and third chances because he often gave away his last coins to a comrade in need of drink.

Uncle Frank, who rarely lost his temper, one day right in front of the kids told Dad to wise up. The incident put a strain on relations, strained further when Aunt Mary butted in. She got so mad that she told Mom to leave Dad. No one was more shocked than Aunt Mary when, a few days later, she came home from work and found her sister and all six Scott kids there.

In that household, there were no spare rooms, so the living room was transformed into an overnight accommodation with pillows and blankets strewn everywhere. The kids thought they were on vacation, too excited to fall asleep, but by morning were sleeping soundly when Aunt Mary headed out. Oh, but when she got home that evening, they were still there, and the house had been turned upside down. She didn't have the heart to scold the kids but bawled out her sister for not keeping a closer watch.

Mom was distracted with worry and angry at the letters Dad wrote; they all sounded the same: *Oh how much I love you and miss you. Oh how sorry I am, my dear Rose, my girl. Please come home. I cleaned the house spotless for you. I haven't touched a drop since you left. I'll give it up and take the pledge.* He telephoned from work to say how much he loved and missed her. He missed the kids, too, and begged her to bring them home; she said not until he sobered up for good. She knew he'd never take the pledge and relied on a belief that he had more than a weakness; he had a disease that needed treatment. Uncle Frank said Dad's drinking was nothing but a bad habit and she was too soft on him, but in spite of it all, Uncle Frank drove her and the kids home to the same old thing. She had no choice; it was time for Vinny and Sis to start school in the new Parish.

At St. Mary's on 57th Street, the Irish were welcome. Mass was celebrated in Latin, the sermon delivered in Slovenian and English. The elementary school, staffed by the Sisters of Notre Dame, had two grades per classroom, fifteen students per grade, five desks per row, no uniforms, and a strict dress code—girls buttoned up to the chin, hems below the knees, hair cut short or long in braids; boys in button-down shirts and long pants, and hair cropped close. Sister Mary Cletus, the local order's senior advisor, taught first and second grade. She gently enforced class rules—*be on time, be seated quietly, no raising of hands out of turn, no speaking in class unless called upon, no bathroom breaks except at recess, no special privileges.* Sister required a great deal—self-control, manners, responsibility, abiding by the rules; discipline was the order of the day.

Mom gathered up her brood and escorted Vinny and Sis to school. Everything was going well that first day, until the principal rapped at the classroom door and asked Sister Cletus if she could identify a little boy who had wandered into the school. Sister showed the wonder-struck child into the classroom and asked if anyone recognized him. Vinny and Sis jumped up out of their seats exclaiming that he was their little brother. Joe had bawled his eyes out that morning because he wanted to go to school with them. He never settled down until, a few days later, Mom walked him to kindergarten at McCandless Public School. Joe never forgot how overjoyed he felt to discover so many modern toys to play with and to be served a half-pint bottle of milk at recess, thanks to a federal program providing free milk.

In Pittsburgh, there was concern over the numbers of boys hanging out on the railroad tracks, stealing food from boxcars, and being exposed to the habits of hobos who camped out drinking themselves to death. Mom saw the sorry look of children hopping trains in the newspaper photographs. She knew her kids would never do such an awful thing, not to her—it would have killed her.

It just about killed Dad when he was informed that an employee at PT with more seniority would replace him as manager. He had no choice but to accept a clerk's position at lower wages and found himself back almost where he had started sixteen years ago. The demotion devastated him, but he looked for a second job to make up the difference. He heard that Hubbard's tool and die shop up near the Sharpsburg bridge was hiring part-time on a pick and shovel assembly line, work that lasted him but a few months. It embarrassed him to think of how he'd ever pay the book bills and tuition at St. Mary's. He started harping on a stale theme that the kids belonged in public school because God was everywhere and the education was free. Mom reminded him of their promise to holy mother church to raise the kids in the faith.

She was carrying their seventh child when Winston Churchill came to town. The Prime Minister praised the city as the industrial capital of the world. FDR campaigned at Forbes Field on his New Deal program and the City Brass played his theme song, "Happy Days are Here Again!" Here was an American hero—a crippled man in a wheelchair with brilliant leadership skills, who addressed compelling problems of the common man and carried the Electoral College in a grand sweep.

In January 1933, Roosevelt assumed the presidency, and every bank in the country closed. He went on the radio to explain why in a way people understood. The banks had to close to go off the gold standard and replace gold with paper dollars backed by the Federal Reserve so the banks could reopen restored. He believed in the power of radio and delivered fireside chats right after the dinner hour when families tuned in. He always started with, *My Friends*. It made people feel as if he knew them. His quips and warm laughter reflected the buoyant confidence of a tough-minded leader with a quick grasp of what had to be done.

In his first hundred days, Congress passed dozens of emergency relief acts, the most costly being the Work Progress Administration. The WPA developed a massive road rebuilding program throughout the country. The labor force on relief either signed onto road crews or lost their relief money. Dad thought his family would never have to go on the dole and proclaimed that, if it did, it would be over his *dead body*. Fear existed that the Depression and gangland crime and violence might never end; and it persisted until it dawned on Congress to end Prohibition. To celebrate the repeal of the 18th Amendment, the Pittsburgh Brewery on Liberty Avenue offered men and women alike their first glass of legal beer—FREE. Imagine Dad going off the wagon to imbibe with that festive crowd. People started saying things were looking up, and they were right.

In April, Eugene was born. Huey was just another Scott genius with an easy disposition, the first to be born at West Penn Hospital in Bloomfield because St. Francis Hospital in Lawrenceville had upgraded its guidelines. Families unable to pay their debts were referred to surrounding hospitals to redistribute the financial burden.

The Scotts were registered at West Penn's free wellness clinic for routine exams and medical treatment. It took two streetcar rides to get there, but its staff ran an efficient clinic and children received good care. Mom took Sis along to lend a hand. This conscientious seven-year old girl adored the new baby and carried him all over the place so he wouldn't be stuck in a crib all day long. He reached for her when he wanted held and cried every time she left the room. Otherwise, he hardly ever cried. He didn't even cry when baptized, and *the priest went wild with holy water,* Sis said.

In June, out of nowhere it seemed to us, Grandfather Quinn died. His death was the result of complications after a fall down the stairs in the middle of the night when he made a wrong turn on his way to the bathroom. At first, his kids thought he broke his neck, but in the emergency room he was diagnosed with a broken collar bone. In recovery, he became so disoriented that he could not be released and was transferred to Woodville State Hospital for Men way out in the boondocks. Our poor grandfather rebelled and was put in isolation.

Uncle Frank had driven the family out there to see him as often as possible. They had expected him to get well, but he refused to eat and demanded to be taken home; at age sixty-eight, he died in his sleep. His death was attributed to arteriosclerosis and senile psychosis—old-age disease. Perhaps the fall of a blind man down a flight of stairs caused a brain injury. It would explain why a feisty character of such independent nature went down so hard. Honored by age-old friends and devoted family, Patrick Quinn was buried from St. Kieran's and laid to rest in Calvary Cemetery alongside his beloved Margaret and their sons, James and Joseph—a fine wake and funeral and a burial in a family grave marked with three Celtic Crosses in honor of their beloved Ireland.

Aunt Kate Grant remained a stabilizing family force throughout the years and would be the last to go of the Grant-Quinn generation. She lived in a grand house in West View that she had inherited from a widow she worked for as a domestic and had cared for in old age. She found it trying to keep up with the place, so it was listed and she moved in with the Quinns at their Aspinwall residence. Her property sold for half its worth; however, the proceeds were a boon to the family at large with Dick and Frank unemployed, both courting the possibility of marriage, and Aunt Mary holding down the fort.

Hard times for Mom and Dad meant one hardship after another trying to keep a roof overhead and food on the table with bill collectors on the prowl. The grim news at PT was that Dad's job was eliminated with more layoffs to follow. On his last work day, he picked up his wages, went straight home, and handed over his pay envelope. Mom asked him not to take it so hard, but he sat slumped in his chair looking every bit like one in mourning. Suddenly he picked up and left the house cowering in defeat; he had made mistakes that he knew he could never live down and, over his *living body,* went downtown to the welfare office and surrendered to the dole.

After the holidays, a relief agency rep came to the house to assess our situation. Dad asked her to leave, fearing that people might find out we were destitute. In those days, children believed everybody belonged to the same class. You could only be sure you were poor if you stood in a food line. Dad heard there were jobs at a steel mill up river and walked there only to learn it was a lousy joke. Vinny knew all about it because he walked there with Dad, seven miles out and seven miles back. By the time they got home, the soles of their shoes were gone, their socks were shredded, and their blisters were bleeding. They washed up and changed and headed right back out—the boy to sell raffle tickets and the man to the saloon—a blessing in a way because he was a happy drunk.

In frustrating times, the Holy Name Society of St. Mary's appealed to the Parish men to enjoy a social bottle of beer or two on Sunday afternoons, but Dad steered clear to avoid prying questions about how things were going at home. Mom prayed in earnest, and alas, he received a letter from his father. Dad was the only person on that side of the family who had kept in touch with Sam, Sr.

As a sales agent for the St. Louis Railroad, he worked on commission and sometimes earned free train tickets. Enclosed with his letter was a roundtrip ticket to Chicago and an invitation to the World's Fair. Dad hadn't seen his father in ten years, but he just didn't feel like traveling. Mom encouraged him to make the trip, saying it would be a whole lot better than hanging around with nothing to do but complain. He said he'd feel guilty, and she said, *Just go*! Dad packed his bag and hopped that train.

He was pleasantly surprised to be greeted at the station. His father, still of youthful appearance, showed Dad around. He marveled at the skyscrapers and the World's Fair exhibits, which drew forty million people in the depths of the Depression. Three days in Chicago gave him time to renew the bond between them, and the long train ride back to Pittsburgh gave him time to come to terms with the harsh reality that he had lost his job at PT because of his drinking.

In the aftermath, he put on a mask of acceptance and fell victim to the great curse—alcoholism. Mom held out hope that he would go before Father Doyle and take the pledge. The Irish believed a pledge only worked if sworn before a cleric to curse a disease that ran in some families like cancer ran in others. Dad had never trusted those mysterious men in long black robes, and some of the pressure lifted when Father Doyle died. The whole town came out to mourn the loss of a man who had served Ireland and the Pittsburgh Diocese for fifty-five years.

With Mom's trusted friend gone and Dad jobless and drifting deeper into despair, she seemed to lose her mooring. She watched as the family slipped into destitution, a hardship far more devastating than being just plain poor like everyone else. To release anxiety, she sang her stress song in a low tone: *Yelp us! Oh yelp us! We need thy very help! Oh, the Lord he does know. He does know it all! Yelp us! Oh yelp us! We need thy very help! Oh, the Lord he does know. He does know it all!*

She sang her song when the washer broke down in the middle of a cycle, and she sang it when supper burned on the stove, and when her husband came home smelling like a beer barrel, and when she questioned how he had the heart to waste money on booze and cigarettes with seven kids to feed. Almost as if he had heard his sister's cry, Uncle Frank showed up with a crate full of groceries.

He never came empty handed or stayed long at our house, and he never failed to hand out nickels for the kids to spend at the candy store. He lifted Mom's spirit with news that he had been called back to his job as a crane operator at the new Westinghouse plant (the old Nuttall Foundry) on Butler Street. The date for his marriage to Grace Rosewell of Lawrenceville was set for early summer; they would be moving in with her family on Keystone Street. Word also was that Uncle Dick's marriage to Olivia Young of Aspinwall was set and they would move in with her family on Western Avenue, right around the corner from Aunt Mary and Great Aunt Kate. It would be delicious pickings for the Scott kids that summer with all the parties and picnics the relatives could dream up.

Dad received word to report to the WPA or lose his eighteen dollar weekly welfare subsidy. He was assigned to a crew on an Atlantic Refinery project, a trot down the street to its oil transfer station on the bank of the Allegheny River, where oil pumped from river barges fed into pipelines that ran three-hundred miles to a refinery in Philadelphia. He accepted ditch digging as necessary employment, never forgetting that his grandfather, Patrick O'Donnell, had worked on the first crew to sewer the Point.

What got to Dad was being powerless. He felt that his boss ordered him around as if he was nothing more than the dirt underfoot and he couldn't take that. Then a foreman spotted a flask sticking out of Dad's hip pocket and sent him home for a day without pay. His trumped-up excuse to Mom was that he got thirsty on the job. She told him to stop bringing home bad news to darken their doorstep. Here was a man in filthy work clothes who had once worn a herringbone suit and linen tie on the job.

In the spring of 1934, Sis, dressed in white linen, received her first holy communion. Like Vinny had a year earlier, she memorized the questions and answers in the catechism and learned the hymns and prayers of the Church. No child bore more joy than she felt to see a gold star next to her name on the classroom bulletin board for selling enough chance cards to pay for her prayer book and rosary.

A Blessed Mother service and procession of the holy communicants was scheduled for the following Sunday afternoon. Sis, all in white, arrived way ahead of time and no one was around. She went looking for her friends who played in the alley way by the candy store. Finding no one there, either, she crossed Butler Street and went to the *Scrappy,* a junk yard by the railroad tracks, to look for treasures, a pastime of the curious at large.

The *Scrappy,* a military scrap yard in World War One, rose in a huge rusty heap of metal scrap brought there by junk dealers. Sis was moseying along the tracks when she suddenly tripped over a railroad spike and fell flat on her face, causing her nose to bleed all over her Holy Communion dress. In a panic, she ran all the way to Keystone Street, pounded on the Rosewells' door, and fell into Aunt Grace's arms. With her tears quickly wiped away, her dress washed and ironed, and food in her belly, she skipped all the way to church just in time to march in procession in honor of the Blessed Mother, thanks to the abundant blessings of her beloved aunt.

In September, the new school year began. Vinny, Sis, and Joe returned to St. Mary's bringing along DeeDee who started first grade. She felt pretty good skipping off to school, as Mom had styled her abundant blonde hair, but all there was to hold it back from her eyes was a safety pin. Sister Mary Cletus assigned her to a desk upfront because she had poor eyesight, even with glasses. In the orderly classroom, Sister began the day with an Our Father and Hail Mary, then picked up her pointer and accidentally knocked the safety pin out of DeeDee's hair, which fell down in her face, blocking her vision. She stormed out of the classroom and all the way home without stopping. The next day, she had to promise Sister that she would not leave school before the bell rang and she never did. Dad had talked to her about that, even though neighborhood safety was not a big problem back then.

The Aspinwall relatives threw a party to celebrate Dad's and Mom's tenth anniversary. With another baby on the way, she needed his help more than ever, but he had his lost focus. Sometimes a rotten feeling would come over him that turned him to drink. He wanted her to be happy and knew he fell short; she knew it too. When she murmured, his eyes bulged like a man on death row—his guilty look—and her *Yelp Us* song became a dirge.

The Season of Advent arrived, and Mom decided to take in the early Mass; to her surprise, the new pastor was at the altar. Father Matthew Francis Kebe, a Slovenian immigrant with full U.S. citizenship, was fifty-two years old, clean-cut, and shaven; his gold wire glasses enhanced his austere manner and reserve. He subscribed to the National Geographic and belonged to the Audubon Society, but his main focus was Parish business. He neither flaunted intelligence nor boasted of knowledge, and nowhere existed such impeccable records as those written in his distinct hand. Presently, he prepared for the busy holidays and asked for volunteers to clean and decorate the church. He also ordered an additional supply of coal to keep the church warm during the extended hours he would be spending in the confessional to accommodate longer penitent lines.

Dad did his penance hauling coal from the Junction Coal Company supply barn down by the river. When our coal ran out, free coal was available through the emergency fuel relief act, but only enough to last a few days. Hence, Dad had to scout for more along the railroad tracks. Vinny and Joe followed behind him, picking up lumps of coal that had fallen off the gondola cars, tossing them into a wheelbarrow and hauling it home. Fallen trees on the hillside behind the house provided another source of fuel. The man and his boys dragged dead tree trunks and limbs into the yard and split them into logs to fuel our coal stoves. Keeping the home fires burning in northeastern winters challenged everyone, especially during the holidays.

Christmas Eve was upon us, and Dad went shopping for a holiday tree. While he was out, a neighbor was summoned to place an emergency call to Uncle Frank. Dad arrived home and found Aunt Grace there. She explained that Frank had taken Mom to the hospital. The kids asked Dad why she had to go to the hospital again. Compelled to explain, he told them that she had to get her sprained ankle fixed. Sis objected to this stale tale and asked Dad why every time Mom came home from the hospital she brought a new baby with her. He said it was the right thing to do. Aunt Grace chuckled with amusement, but Sis saw a big question mark hovering over Dad's brain and didn't buy his story. It became a waiting game until, shortly before midnight, Lawrence was born. A few days later, Mom brought the baby home. Sis had hoped for a baby doll from Santa Claus and didn't get one. She took one look at Larry and sighed sweetly; by her lights, she had received a real baby doll from heaven.

On the Feast of Epiphany, Father Kebe said Mass, ate a healthy breakfast prepared by the housekeeper, Miss Mary, and got ready for his rounds. The tradition of blessing homes represented the journey of three wise men from the Far East to Bethlehem bearing gifts of gold, frankincense, and myrrh for the Christ Child. The gifts symbolized prosperity, good health, and harmony for another year. He pulled on his galoshes, draped his black overcoat over his black cassock, tucked in his wool scarf, put on his tossle cap and gloves, and headed out into the weather bearing a prayer card, a holy water asperser, and some chalk. He was well prepared to escalade Lawrenceville's steep streets and city steps, which he called *stairways to heaven*. The Scotts were his last call of the day.

He arrived at supper time, perhaps by design to catch Dad home and possibly convert him. The kids were already seated at the table, with Huey propped in the highchair and Larry in Mom's arms. Once warmed by the fire of the coal stove, the priest placed the sign of the cross on each of their heads. He sprinkled the air with holy water to protect us from evil, recited scripture in Latin, and wrote in chalk above the front door: *19 C + M + B + 35.* The symbols represented one thousand nine hundred thirty-five years since the journey of the Magi. He offered his blessing with the Sign of the Cross: *In nomine Patris et Filii et spiritus sancti.* Upon leaving, he paused to offer a few encouraging words for Dad.

The Epiphany blessing seemed to inspire Dad with more awareness of Mom's needs. She did not always feel well and had gained weight with each child she bore. She hadn't been to a beauty salon in ages and made do with a comb, a pair of scissors, and a mirror. With less time for Mom to take care of herself, Dad hired a woman from Dresden Alleyway to lend a hand for fifty cents a week.

Ethel Fox, robust and talkative, stood four and a half feet tall. People said she was not all there, but, in all fairness, she had never gone to school. She had a knack for keeping little Scott kids happy with sweet treats. She appreciated nature and loved the outdoors. One day she discovered a wounded sparrow; it died in her hands. Her sobbing made the atmosphere feel heavy. She brought a kitten to the house and Mom said take it away. Ethel built it a home in the narrow space between the house and retaining wall out back, and it stayed there.

Little Huey chased that kitten everywhere. He loved it so much that at potty time he refused to go inside; he peed right where he was. Sis saw this and asked what the heck he was doing. He had a slight slur in his speech, but she knew what he meant when he cried: *Me leaky in da lane in da blue.* His way with words tickled her enough to ask the same question over and over just to get him talking.

Vinny, Sis, and Joe talked up a storm that summer selling tickets for St. Mary's carnival fair on a rented lot at 51st and Butler Streets. Parish volunteers ran the concession stands, roulette wheels, and bingo tables and sold raffle tickets to huge crowds—three tickets for a quarter; half the take was the big prize. Carnival personnel operated the mechanical rides at a nickel a ride. Another nickel bought an ice cream sandwich or a cone of popcorn. Hot humid weather guaranteed a thunderstorm before the night ended, with people running for cover under tents or huddled together at food booths, dodging hail and lightning strikes.

Joe walked to the fair with Mom one day. It had been raining and a rainbow appeared in the sky. She didn't speak a word, but he could feel something deep moving in her soul. He had the idea that she singled him out for special attention, and found out later that she treated all of her children with the same tender love. What Mom and Dad spent at the carnival fair had to be left out of our church envelopes, but the carnival experience profited the Parish after overhead deductions and miscellaneous costs to maintain the school building. Inflation forced tuition and book bills up from two to three dollars a year—a pittance when you think about it, but multiplied by the five Scott kids presently in the system, it added up and made a difference in ability to pay.

Government economists said the Depression in Pittsburgh was behind us and the hard-working poor saw no relief in sight. Steelworkers earned four hundred dollars annually and coal miners around six hundred. Electrical workers earned around a thousand dollars annually, firemen twelve hundred and police officers thirteen hundred, jobs few and far between and only available through local politicians. U.S. Congressmen fared well at eight thousand a year; the waitresses who served them made around four hundred a year, including tips earned on twelve-hour shifts.

Dad wondered how anybody expected him to get ahead on a ditch-digger's wages, and he did not hide his consternation, like *shit and goddam* with every sling of a pick or shovel, or *the hell with it, I'm going out and tie one on*. The Pub had been renovated and re-named: Neid's Hotel and Tavern. The owner, Paul Neid, allowed labor force customers to run up a small bill payday to payday. He cut Dad some slack because of our big family and knew when to cut him off.

Mom ran up a modest bill at the slaughter house and butcher shop on 57th Street. The proprietor, a burly Slav with a shock of white hair and a gregarious style, knew his customers by name and offered a boisterous greeting when the doorbell jingled and they walked in. The floor was covered with saw dust, the walls with smoked sausages and bulk garlic hanging from iron hooks. The meat case brimmed with plump chickens and choice parts, pork roasts and chops, prime beef roasts, spare ribs, beef stew and steaks and freshly ground beef.

A big sign in bold letters above the meat case posted *Soup Meat—Forty Cents a Pound, Soup Bones—Two for Twenty-five Cents, and Soup Bones Free with a Five Dollar Order.* The butcher always put free bones and extra meat in with Mom's order, knowing she hardly ever had five whole dollars in her purse at one time. Moreover, he cheered her with encouragement in his earthy accent, *No worry Mrs. Scott, next year be a better year for sure*!

1936 started with heavy snowfalls and drifting snow, followed by an early March thaw. Ice gorges breaking up on the Allegheny upstream blocked networks of creeks and streams feeding into the river downstream. In downtown Pittsburgh, the river spilled over its bank and continued to rise through the night. The St.

Patrick's Day Parade was cancelled. Next day, the three rivers at the Point crested higher than they had ever risen to forty-six-and-a-half feet. Emergency boat crews motored through deep

waters, plucking flood victims out of windows and off roof tops. Sixty people drowned. A hundred thousand were rescued before the flood waters added more to the death toll. Four hundred people were seriously injured, and not all in harm's way could be located or helped. The National Guard was called in to protect businesses, and relief workers provided food and shelter, blankets and medicine.

Dr. George T. Noden, newlywed, had just opened his medical practice on Butler Street and found himself putting in eighteen to twenty-hour days attending to the urgent needs of flood victims. Anyone without the means to pay was treated, regardless. Many people became sick because the water was contaminated. Water trucks were set up in neighborhoods, and every kind of vessel imaginable was filled to haul safe water home.

The curious walked along the river banks looking for useful items that drifted ashore—pots and pans, anything that could be cleaned up, including furniture that could be restored.The river's rush pushed boats, barges, trees, and debris downstream. Every now and then a house would float by with a screeching cat or cackling chicken on its roof. Amid the terrifying devastation, people could not help but to laugh, only to be filled with dread when the Waverly oil tanks near the Allegheny River exploded. The scorched and smoky air drove residents indoors while the fire raged out of control. People living on the hillsides gazed in awe of that fiercely magnificent destruction.

When it happened, Sis heard a huge blast and called everybody outside to watch the fire and smoke billowing up from the river. Mom scooted everyone back inside and pushed the door shut. Sis put on her boots and said she was going for a walk. Mom said, *oh no you don't,* so she went upstairs to look out the window and watch the oil tanks exploding. It was days before the firefighters could get near that wild blaze so bright that we walked through our house without turning on the lights at night.

In the dreary weather, Mom came down with a bad chest cold. She boiled water, added a few drops of camphorated oil, and breathed in the vapors, a sound like she was breathing her last. Alas, the visiting nurse arrived and made arrangements for Joe, DeeDee, Skip, and Anna to be taken in at St. Raphael's Orphanage on Penn Avenue until Mom got well. The nuns provided good care, and the kids soon made friends. A favorite activity was the daily walk for exercise, an adventure in being careful not to trip over the streetcar tracks crossing the street to spend their pennies at a candy store.

Vinny earned candy money as a newsboy. His newspaper drop-off point was at Union Steel; pick-up time was six-thirty a.m. He tightly folded each newspaper to assure it wouldn't fly apart when tossed, loaded his paper sack, and climbed steep inclines of city steps to deliver the paper to customers who lived at the top. Newspapers sold for three cents each, he earned a penny a paper and was already looking for a second job, but he was too young to work for the Works Progress Administration.

The WPA hired laborers *en masse* on a Lawrenceville road building and repair project. On 57th Street, neighbors watched in awe as the cobblestones were dug up, the road was re-graded, and the cobblestones were re-laid. Heavy equipment moving up and down the road represented true progress. Communities rallied with unemployment easing, and this aided a revival of patriotic spirit.

Dad had enormous civic pride and proudly paraded his *shoe-leather express*, as he called his brood, to the Butler Street parades. Tenth Ward parades started at the Allegheny Cemetery and passed through its formidable iron gates onto Butler Street. Children, fearing the gate house guard, steered clear of mischief

on hallowed ground where thousands of soldiers were buried dating back to the Revolutionary War, along with Pittsburgh's banking families and its acclaimed composer, Stephen Foster. The Decoration Day parade, later renamed Memorial Day, formed at the cemetery where community leaders stepped up to the podium and delivered patriotic homilies. Dad thought the politicians talked too long and heckled them to get things moving. But, he never got tired of hearing the band play FDR's theme song, "Happy Days are Here Again." Uniformed men raised flags and rifles and marched in cadence to the blare of trumpets, trombones, tubas, and the fief and drum corps.

That year's Fourth of July scene on Butler Street was a panorama of patriotic banners, red, white, and blue crepe paper streamers, balloons, bicycles, and honking horns. Marching bands exploded in a fanfare of "Yankee Doodle Dandy," the real-life story of a dandy born on the Fourth of July. Once passed the fire house, the illustrious uniformed began to discreetly step off to the side and into the beer gardens.

Dad walked the kids as far as 55th Street, where he pointed in the direction home and slipped into Neid's Tavern on a promise to bring home a big surprise. He arrived home not too late or drunk carrying a big bag of fireworks. When the sun settled behind the western hills, he established his position on the hillside and set off a fantastic display of everything from firecrackers to Roman candles. A night never forgotten with neighbors cheering Dad as a true patriot, if only for a few hours. Mom was suspicious about where he got all those fireworks because they were illegal. It had to be somewhere between the cemetery and Neid's Tavern.

Talk at Neid's was that gas lines in the Strip District had exploded, blowing out windows in St. Stanislaus Church on Smallman Street and damaging one of its bell towers. Faith believers said St. Stan came through with a miracle—no one was killed. The inferno destroyed the old Postal Telegraph office, damaged the Pittsburgh Banana Company, and sent hundreds of injured to local hospitals.

On July 17, 1936, Mom was rushed to West Penn Hospital where Eileen was born. A visiting nurse came to the house to check up on the baby because she was born with a heart problem thought to have been caused by too much oxygen administered during delivery. Mom herself was not well—nine births in eleven years and poor nutrition compromised her health, and her legs were horribly swollen with varicose veins. At her West Penn wellness clinic follow-up, the attending physician advised Mom to get out and walk more to improve her circulation. She informed him that she did enough walking the floors with Eileen in the middle of the night. No one at our house seemed to question why we always had a new baby, until Sis poked a huge hole in Dad's broken ankle theory when she rushed home one day with an unbelievable story that she had heard on the street: *The stork brings the baby and it comes out of Mom's stomach.*

It was impossible to believe that our Great Aunt Kate was suddenly dead at age seventy-five of liver cancer, according to the coroner's report. She had never bothered with doctors; instead, she had declared her intention to die a natural death. Everybody wore their finest to her funeral at St. Kieran's. Aunt Mary, named executrix of the estate, inherited $3000. Aunt Kate also left five hundred dollars each to her nephews, Richard and Frank Quinn, and to her niece, Rose Quinn Scott. Mom told Sis not to tell Dad, because he went right through her last inheritance when Grandfather Quinn died. This time, Mom hid the money in a shoe box in the back of the closet buried under a pile of things. She wanted it saved for a rainy day. Sis wondered what Mom was waiting for with Dad's job gone.

News spread that Hubbard's had restarted and was hiring. The plant expanded operations in a series of corrugated tin buildings just beyond the Sharpsburg Bridge and produced electrical materials, cable lines, hand tools, and pole line hardware. Dad mulled around the house with no inkling of a job to be had. Mom knew that he was trying to avoid the inevitable—*working in a lousy mill.* Then out of the clear blue, he said he was taking a walk up Butler Street to Hubbard's office to re-apply. He shaved, put on a clean sport shirt and trousers, splashed on some *Old Spice*, walked to the shop to fill out an application, and was hired on the spot.

In muslin work clothes and steel-tipped work shoes, he charged up Butler Street postured as if to lead General Sherman's March from Atlanta to Savannah, Georgia, trying to end the Civil War. He reported to work on the daylight assembly line, a job that would take some getting used to, so much for solving the war on poverty. Dad hit it off with the foreman, a grace that humbled him enough to admit that he didn't really mind working in a mill. His starting wage was five dollars a day, overtime included. The company was an open shop and had no union.

Labor unions had thrived since the 1880s, albeit through violence. Our national skilled labor force began to organize and founded the American Federation of Labor (AFL). The unskilled organized a union of their own, the Congress of Industrial Organizations (CIO). Employees of forty-two Pittsburgh steel plants pledged support to form all nationwide steelworkers into one trade union. At mills where the CIO succeeded, the labor force won a guaranteed wage.

The work force at Hubbard's was divided on joining the CIO under threat of being fired. Dad voted with the majority and went off to work with a will or ego, whatever it was. Mom couldn't put a finger on it. Friday came, payday. He gave her his pay envelope and stood over her, telling her to count out the thirty bucks he earned that week and to make sure it was all there before he took a few dollars out of it for pin money. She could hardly imagine what had come over him.

Working on the eight-to-four daylight shift, Dad got home around four thirty feeling more energy than ever. He washed up and shaved, changed into clean clothes, ate supper and took the little kids for a walk up the street to check out the WPA's new water and gas line diggings. At evening, he settled into his chair to relax and read the paper, listen to the radio, and re-establish his old comfortable routine. Home sweet home felt good.

In the protracted years of the Depression, government economists said the worst was over, but financial relief came in dribbles. Every penny Dad paid to keep the lights on and the house warm greatly relieved family stress. Neighbors gave us their kids' outgrown clothing and shared from their abundant backyard harvests. Our huckster uncle, Sam Scott, Jr., gave us left-over produce that earned him our gratitude. For all Grandmother Scott's worry while he was growing up, he had turned out good. He partnered with Jim Scott at his grocery store in Etna, a prosperous enterprise. Us kids thought that side of the family was rich, even though we barely knew them or socialized with each other. *Who cared*?

Our landlady appreciated how well we took care of her property and was sorry to inform us that we had to move. Her eldest son was getting married and needed our house. Being upset hardly describes our disappointment. Vinny felt so bad about it that he wrote on the side of the house in big letters with white chalk: *This House is a Dump*!

Dad naturally had the last words, *Listen up yins kids. I have an announcement. We are going to move. We're moving to better ourselves*!

1937

It was time for Mom to tell Dad about the inheritance. She had been thinking of a possible down payment on a house. He looked about ready to drop dead when she brought her shoe box out of the closet and started mumbling something about money missing. He nearly fainted when confronted but confessed a tragic story of woe and regret. He had been searching for his dress shoes, discovered the shoe box, and couldn't understand why all that money was there. He left it alone, but it wouldn't leave him alone. She asked what he did with it and he raved, guilty culprit that he was, before admitting he had paid a few bills and used some of the money on booze.

Her stress song echoed deep into the hills. His doomsday searches until he found a house on an even higher hill held her spellbound. Skeptical as she was, she agreed to take a look. They had thirty days to move. Mom never went anywhere important unless she wore her Sunday best, but climbing the 57th Street steps taxed her stamina because her Cuban-heeled shoes were too tight. They reached the WPA retaining wall at the bend of the road at Duncan Street and 56th and ½ Street, as our Pittsburgh hill streets were juxtaposed, later to be identified by the U.S. Post Office as the Duncan Street Wall.

Mom sat down to catch her breath for a while. She had never been diagnosed with asthma and wondered if she had heart trouble, as even the one flight of stairs at home challenged her. Dad, even more breathless on two packs of Camel's a day, sat down beside her and lit up. They could see the house from there, and he said, *Well hon, what do you think*? 5614 Duncan Street, first in the row of eight turn-of-century frame houses, was desperately in need of a paint job. A sign in the window read: *Landlord across the Street.* Cattycorner to 5614 in a brown shingle shanty lived the proprietors of a storefront where they sold stale bread, outdated staples, and penny candy.

Tiny, a small woman in a housedress, bright lipstick and high heels, was on duty when Dad walked in and said he wanted to see the house. She hollered out back to her husband, the Major, a large man, bald and sun-browned. He had apparently earned the title for his endless braggadocio about serving in the Great War. Truth was, he never served a day; he had flunked the conscript exam. He explained to Dad his authority to show the property, lease and maintain it, and collect the rent for an absentee landlord.

The front of the house was swept clean, but roof slates and chimney bricks lay in crumbled piles on the side of the house. The small back yard was piled high with junk and the retaining wall had collapsed. The slat board fence surrounding the yard lay in ruins. Dad noticed Mom's deep frown and shoved a fist into his side, boasting, *Don't worry Rose, I'll nail that thing back together in no time.*

They stepped inside the house and she looked glum. He went on and on about how he could fix the whole place up with little effort. She shook her head, no! The house needed too much work and was too small for ten kids. She had said *ten* kids because another baby was due. However, even with six small rooms, three pot-bellied coal stoves, and a dirt cellar, it had an upstairs bathroom and a side lot where the kids could play. Eighteen dollars a month rent made for a good deal.

Moving day was an exciting time with many trips lugging anything and everything anybody could carry in a peripatetic procession of happy Scott kids up and down that big hill. Uncle Frank loaded his car with household furnishings; Uncle Sam hauled heavy items in his truck—iron beds, springs and mattresses, a wooden ice box. It was a miracle that the kitchen floor didn't cave in when the *Kalamazoo* was re-assembled and its stove pipe attached to the chimney. A four-legged gas range with a side oven left behind by the previous occupants was vented to a second chimney wall. An enamel-coated cast-iron wall sink took up a chunk of corner space, leaving barely room for the table, a table bench, and some chairs by the window, and the washing machine by the cellar way door; but it was Mom's kitchen and, by the time she got through with it, it would be immaculate.

Our nextdoor neighbors, the Besals, were first to welcome us to the neighborhood. The best news was that they owned a telephone and the Scotts were welcome to use it in an emergency. Emergency repairs on the house were made thanks to an account Dad opened at a hardware store on Butler Street, where he bought everything a handyman could use. Joe Monroe, two doors down, lent Dad a ladder, and together they patched the leaking roof. Dad put screens in the windows, repaired the screen doors, and hung fly paper from a light socket to catch bugs that flew in every time someone went in or out.

One Saturday, the Major stopped by to collect the rent. It wasn't the rent but the condescending manner in which he approached Dad that got him so mad he was ready to take a swing. The Major took flight and reported to the property owner that Mr. Scott was a dangerous man. Subsequently, he was notified that the rent went up a dollar, hereafter to be paid at Schramm's Real Estate on Butler Street.

Then Dad lost three days' work when a foreman at Hubbard's discovered a hammer and chisel missing from the inventory. Dad had more or less borrowed the tools to work on the house, and as he put it, *a scab at the shop had stool-pigeoned.* After explaining to the foreman why he needed the tools, he got to keep them, along with a little less in his next pay envelope. Mom called Dad a *thief* and he said, *Please don't cry, hon. I was going to pay for the tools when my ship came in.* She said, *How do you know your ship didn't sink*?

Dad dove into an ocean of challenges to fix up the house, his way of trying to turn a rut into a groove. Mom used the last drop of her inheritance to turn our house into a home. It took a ton of patching plaster to repair large sections of plaster missing from the lath board walls before the painting began, and it took hours of sanding and refinishing to spruce up the mahogany mantle and sliding doors between the living and dining rooms. The kitchen walls and wainscoting were painted, the linoleum replaced, and wallpapering the whole house was underway. Vinny had a big hand in helping Dad with that job because Grandmother Scott had hired him that spring to help re-wallpaper her kitchen on Holmes Street and she had taught him the ropes.

In all the excitement, Sis was sent next door on an emergency mission to call Uncle Frank, who got Mom to West Penn just in time to deliver *me*, the tenth Scott kid in twelve years, named Patricia for Grandfather Patrick Quinn. The Metropolitan insurance man showed up and found Mom washing clothes in the kitchen. He curiously observed Huey and Larry playing on a pile of dirty laundry on the floor, Eileen propped in the family highchair, and me sleeping in a laundry basket on the table. He added me to the premium—ten children times whatever, but Mom had no cash on hand to pay him; he'd be back to collect at another time. We had no health insurance, and Dad said not to worry, the important things were covered, and he had confidence in his position on the assembly line at Hubbard's.

One day he was on his way upstairs to clean up and change. Mom was cooking supper and heard him muttering: *These work clothes are so filthy they could stand up and walk all by themselves.* He came downstairs a new man, wearing his short-sleeved plaid shirt and tan khakis, smelling of *Old Spice* and bearing razor nicks that he called *battle wounds*. After supper, he relaxed in his chair by the window to read the paper, listen to the radio, and smoke cigarettes; he looked every bit the part he played—king of the house.

1937 turned out to be a great year with Dad earning full wages. Hubbard's labor force belonged to a CIO sub-union called the Amalgamated Association of Iron, Steel, and Tin Workers, which threatened a walkout for higher wages. The company issued a warning that if it happened, they'd all be fired. They walked out anyhow and won a guaranteed seven-dollar-a-day wage, overtime pay, paid holidays, a forty-hour work week, and grievance procedures. Dad had taken a lead in those efforts. Like every other U.S. industry under pressure to fill contracts for defense buildup in England and France in anticipation of invasions by Germany and Italy, the company had given in to union demands.

On the Feast of Epiphany in January 1938, Father Kebe made a special call at our house. Warmed by the fire of the coal stove, he blessed us with holy water, recited a prayer from his breviary and wrote in chalk above the kitchen door: *19 C + M + B + 38.* One thousand nine hundred thirty-eight years since the journey of the Magi, three years since Father had blessed our house, and it elevated our family spirit.

At St. Mary's, Vinny was feeling the demands of attending Washington Trade School on 40th Street every Monday to learn manual skills, like building book cases and work tables, as required by the Catholic School District, and keeping up with his after-school job delivering newspapers. He had been saving up and bought a red bike to make the route more efficient. Word got around that he could deliver papers on time in any weather. He started with twenty-seven customers, but the route swelled and became more difficult when it snowed and he had to walk. He recruited Joe, suggesting that he might like to earn a little cash. Joe said *heck no* at the prospect of hauling heavy newspaper sacks up and down city steps. Then he thought about the prospect of candy money and took the job. Vinny showed him the ropes and together they made headway until the first serious snowfall.

Nowhere but in Pittsburgh were four seasons defined so precisely and turned so suddenly harsh. The boys bundled up and headed through snow drifts delivering the daily news. They arrived home with their faces windburned and their hands and feet frozen. The house was toasty, but they went straight to the cellar and refilled the coal bushels before Dad got home. With three coal stoves in the house, he had to get up in the middle of the night to stoke the embers and rebuild the fires. Hard coal sold for four dollars a ton; three fifty a ton for five tons and over. The coal truck often lost power at the junction of Christopher and Duncan Street; hence, the driver dumped the coal in the middle of the road and people on the hill had to haul it home in wheel barrows, wagons, bushel baskets, and buckets.

Running out of coal sometimes caught Dad by surprise. He put on his overcoat and tossle cap and scanned the perimeter. Once assured that no one was watching, he went into Besal's back yard and stole a few lumps of coal from their abundance. No doubt they knew and understood, and he most likely returned the coal. Until more coal could be delivered, he sent the boys scouting. They were used to it and rigged up a sled to haul scraps of wood and coal home. Dad built such big fires in the living room stove that the stove pipe would turn hot orange and had to be monitored in the event of a chimney fire.

It was a good day when the coal truck roared onto Duncan Street. Dad rushed inside to warn everybody to *hold your ears* while the coal was dumped, shaking our house to its very foundation. It took all day to shovel a two-ton load through the chute into the cellar—two days for a four-ton load. The cellar door was kept closed to prevent coal dust from rising up through the house, but something about our restocked coal supply gave us a sense of security in the depths of winter. Nowhere was the onset of a new year, a new spring, and pleasant weather more appreciated than by we Scotts on our new hill overlooking the old homestead on a bluff at 57th Street Rear, and the Atlantic Oil Refinery complex on the bank of the Allegheny River.

At St. Mary's, Anna started first grade. Mom helped her dress and styled her abundant black hair. Anna did not like the way Mom combed it, pulling it roughly, but she enjoyed the compliments of girlfriends who said she had beautiful hair. In school, she joined Skip who was in second grade. He cautioned her that he had made a few mistakes—like holding a pencil in the wrong hand, for which he suffered a slap on his left hand with Sister's ruler. Anna was a timid and fearful child, scared of her own shadow, and not knowing why. Mom wisely prepared her with suggestions about observing classroom rules to avoid negative attention. Unwisely, Sister Cletus put her in the last seat in the last row. Anna saw neither the blackboard nor the text on the page and could not pass tests. She brought home her first report card and fell into Mom's arms, sobbing.

A few days later, Mom took her for a walk to Shall's grocery store— her big day out with Mom. They took the shortcut from Duncan Street through the Homey Hill to Butler Street, a rugged tract of land owned by the Protestant Home for Incurables. They made it to Shall's but returned with empty shopping bags. The account had been closed. Anna cried all the way home, but Mom created a delicious miracle for supper—like Jesus turning water into wine, Anna said.

That evening, Mom took Anna on her lap at an upstairs front window. They leaned out and counted headlights of cars rolling over the Sharpsburg bridge, a form of meditation for Mom. She often sat at that window during the day watching what the kids were doing down on the street. One day, she and Anna were looking out, saw DeeDee in a brawl with one of the Chirico girls, and rooted for DeeDee all the way. Special times like that for Anna gave her the courage to bear up against unpleasant encounters in school. Sadly, she would be held back one year on the pretext that she was retarded. Joyfully, she would be joined by Huey in first grade when the time came.

A heated rumor was circulating that the Irish were being kicked out at the end of the school year. Mom made an appointment with the pastor and learned that he was under orders from the bishop to comply with the mandate—students must attend school in the Parish where they were baptized, meaning for us going to the Irish Parish, St. Kieran's. The Sisters of Notre Dame wanted to keep the Scotts, but they had no voice, and feuding among ethnic rivals persisted.

Dad heard about the latest rumpus at supper time. Someone had hurled a rock through a window at St. Mary's and the Scott kids were blamed. He railed to the point of blasphemy that his kids should put up their dukes if they were accused of crimes they didn't commit. Mom said she didn't want her kids implicated in a holy war; there was enough of that trouble in Ireland. The *Pittsburgh Catholic* newspaper published a story indicating that an effort was being made at the school superintendent's office to preserve the status quo. Turned out that Divine Providence had no voice; the Bishop had the final say—the dreaded mandate would stand.

The September 1939 school year began, the road rose to meet Vinny, and he entered Central Catholic High School for Boys. He had expected to attend a public vocational school to prepare for a career in industry. By chance, he had taken an aptitude test arranged by Catholic Charities that qualified him to attend Central, a bus and streetcar ride from Stanton Avenue in Lawrenceville to Fifth Avenue in Oakland.

As for Sis, Joe, DeeDee, Skip, Anna, and Huey, the shortcut to St. Kieran's on Carnegie Street was through the Homey. In fear and trembling, they arrived at school, handed over their fateful transfer slips, and took seats in their respective classrooms. The sadness of changing schools made every disappointing new encounter feel worse.

Sis in eighth grade dwelled on all the work she faced when she got home. One day she said to Mom, *What did **you** do all day?* Sis felt the rebuff but knew she was her mother's most dependable assistant. In school, she suffered from boredom and was glad when Sister asked for help handing out text books. Sis took her geography workbook home and showed it to Vinny. He opened it and saw an ink-stamped legend: *This Book Belongs to St. Kieran's.* Beneath it he wrote in indelible ink: *Saint Kieran's Stinks.*

When the indelible protest was discovered, Sis was sent to the principal's office. Sister Mary Elda looked at the inscription, slammed the work book down, and said, *Who wrote this*? Sis started shaking and said she didn't know. Sister called her a liar: *Rosemary Scott, you tell me the truth or I'll force it out of you. Tell me who wrote in your geography book or I'll give you a lie detector test. I'll hook wires up to your heart and brain. You tell me the truth or else*! Sis came across with whatever the principal wanted to hear, and from that day forward, secretly called her *Sister Mary Evil.* Eighth grade turned out for Sis a worse nightmare than the nightmare Vinny lived through there as a lad in first grade. St. Kieran's was a good school and the Sisters of Charity enjoyed an excellent reputation as educators. However, its elderly principal, impassioned to keep students under control, was convinced that the styles the Scotts wore were influenced by Marxist ideologies. She brought it to the class's attention that girls in short dresses and flowered babushkas were *communists* and boys in knickers and knee socks were *fascists*. School bullies started calling the Scotts DP's, *Displaced Persons*. Mom wondered why a Catholic principal did not use common sense. We Scotts wore whatever we had.

Joe rebelled when the principal ordered him to go home and come back in normal clothes. In the stress of it all, he was rushed to the hospital with a ruptured appendix. On returning to school, the principal accused him of feigning illness to shirk responsibility. Sis told the principal that she never saw Joe so sick in his whole life, not even when he had scarlet fever, missed a month of school at St. Mary's, and had to repeat fourth grade because he had eaten green apples.

Sis was issued a one-day suspension for insolence and broke down in sobs when she told Mom the humiliating story. Mom believed every word of it. She was not one to express emotions—more like her silence and body language told you what was on her mind. But in this case, in no uncertain terms she reminded Sis of how well the nuns at St. Mary's treated the Scott kids, especially in times like the day Anna had been taken to the convent and served a sausage and pancake breakfast after she fainted from hunger in class.

Skip and DeeDee smartly steered clear of trouble in their new school environment, and if it wasn't for feisty DeeDee watching her back, Anna would never have survived St. Kieran's, she said. She was scared to death of a run-in with the principal and still couldn't see the blackboard or read text on a page. Her teacher, however, sized Anna up as a bright student at a disadvantage and arranged for her eye exam at the free eye ware clinic, where she was fitted with glasses.

Things were just starting to settle down at St. Kieran's when Huey took a seizure in class and Joe and Sis brought him home. She was sent to the pharmacy for a remedy—a spoonful of tonic—and he was back in school the next day. The principal wanted to know what he was trying to pull. Poor Huey burst into tears, saying, *Holy crap, Sister, what do you expect? I didn't want to go to St. Kieran's. I want to go to St. Mary's.* Believe it or not, he got his wish.

Larry, a dapper little boy, missed the age deadline for first grade and was enrolled in kindergarten at Sunnyside Public School. Dad was available to take him to school the first day, a walk up steep 56th and ½ Street, through a wooded path, and up a tier of city steps to the yellow brick school. In class, Larry discovered that none of his playmates were there, so he quit school and found his way home. Mom took him straight back. He was so upset that she had no choice but to inform his teacher that her son would not be returning to school. He later learned that his playmates had all turned six in time for first grade at Saint Mary's. *So what*? He wasted no time brooding and found plenty to do on his own until his buddies showed up.

One day he was playing baseball alone on our side lot when a stray dog chased him down and bit him. The Animal Rescue League was summoned, two uniformed officers showed up, and shot the dog dead right in front of Larry. On hearing the tale of horror, his godparents, Aunt Olivia and Uncle Dick, said it was a good thing Dad wasn't there or he would have shot the dog dead himself. Dad greatly feared dogs as a result of being badly bitten as a boy working the milk route with Sam Scott the Milkman. Even so, Sis argued the point: *Dad gets mad, but he wouldn't kill a flea.* Uncle Dick wouldn't kill a flea either, but we had our doubts about Aunt Olivia.

She found our home life below standard and was always ready to leave the minute she arrived. But that day, Mom had baked bread and made vegetable soup and invited them to stay. Dad gave Olivia his seat at the head of the table because she wanted more elbow room. It took her forever to get situated and she fussed over our assortment of tableware the way attorneys fuss over legal documents. Our mismatched plates had more cracks and chips than a geological site and we had not enough knives, forks and spoons to go around. Our guests wanted their vegetable soup strained and Dad grimaced with every spoonful of broth that Aunt Olivia sipped from the tip of her spoon. For Mom's sake, he held his tongue, but everybody knew what he was thinking: *Straining vegetables out of vegetable soup was what had happened to Dick when he married Olivia.*

Aunt Mary had recently married William Marzolf. Uncle Bill worked at Clark's Candy Company on the Northside, and she worked at the Clark Building in town as an elevator operator. She had sold Grandfather Quinn's Aspinwall residence and put its proceeds in a joint savings account. She and Bill owned no car, but being spendthrifts, soon learned that their funds were depleting. In a pre-holiday slump, she reached out to Olivia for a small loan to buy gifts for our family. *No* meant *No*, but not for Mary. On impulse, she went into Olivia's purse and borrowed her Kaufmann's charge card. Olivia got the bill and wanted to shoot Mary but held her aim when the Marzolfs were laid off in an unemployment sweep and received an eviction notice. Our poor relatives begged Olivia to take them in at her big house on Western Avenue in Aspinwall, but *NO* still meant *NO*. Mom couldn't say no, not to her sister.

Dad wouldn't go against Mom and did not interfere but made his feelings felt. He simply did not want the relatives to eat our food or take up our space. Nevertheless, three bedrooms were consolidated into two—Mom on a cot in the front bedroom with five girls sharing two beds and Dad on a cot in the back room with five boys sharing two beds just so that our aunt and uncle could have the private middle room.

Aunt Mary brought along a wooden trunk stamped *Made in Belfast.* In it were photographs of relatives and keepsakes from Ireland, plus a box containing legal documents in the case of *Patrick Quinn vs. American Spiral and Spring Company.* We were not to explore unless Aunt Mary was there, but Sis knew the trunk wasn't locked and went snooping. She thought she heard someone coming upstairs and let go of the lid; it slammed down on her arm and it started bleeding. She found a thick gauze pad in Mom's dresser drawer and wrapped up her wound. No one seemed to notice or even ask what that big bandage was doing on her arm. It felt like two years but was only two months later that the Marzolfs were called back to work and moved out. Under his breath, Dad said, *Good Riddance!*

Mom came down with chest congestion and a fever, but with ten children under fourteen, she knew that if she called the health clinic, they'd send the city doctor and it might take two days for him to get there. Instead, Sis went next door and placed a call to Doctor Noden. He had been to our house before and came that night after his office hours. In his customary way, he removed his black overcoat, folded it over a chair, set his black medical bag on the dining room table and politely asked everyone but Dad to leave so he could examine Mom. He offered an evaluation and wrote a script for an expectorant. His fee for house calls was eight dollars, but he never charged us more than four dollars, even if he examined three or four kids while he was there. Mom's discreet style was to fold four bills, two if that was all she had, and tuck them between the pull-out leaf of the dining room table. After the exam, she pointed to where the doctor would find his fee; sometimes he took it, but not this time. He knew the prescription to clear up her lungs would cost much more.

Everybody in Pittsburgh coughed with the heavy pall of industrial smoke hovering over the city. The Allegheny County Health Department accelerated its efforts for pollution control in public hearings before the County Smoke Commission. The outraged medical community pleaded for anti-smoke laws. Complaints flooded city hall and marchers protested that people made ill from smog were not recovering. City Council passed a smoke-control ordinance but enforcement was postponed due to urgent needs of industry to fill government contracts.

Another ordinance passed banning the burning of garbage in neighborhood dumps. Then the garbage collectors staged a strike for higher wages, better working conditions, new garbage trucks and rodent control. With trash piling up in our back yard, Dad rolled two fifty-gallon metal drums home from the shop to keep our disposal system under control. The strike lasted two weeks but the city's garbage-removal system was still lousy. At first light, garbage trucks roared through quiet streets and alleyways, waking up entire neighborhoods. Like the coal trucks, the garbage trucks often broke down on the road to our hill. That meant no pick up till next week, so our boys hauled our trash to the Homey Hill dump and burned it.

Dad had an adrenalin rush when a pounding rain caused a section of slates to slide off the roof. He took the case to the Major, the real estate's emergency stand-in for our house. He said he'd talk to the owner but the owner might not want to fix anything. Dad got so mad that he said he'd fix the roof himself, if it ever stopped raining. He didn't have to shoot himself in the foot. Schramm's Real Estate informed the owner to comply with the housing code on property rentals. The roof was repaired and our rent was raised to twenty dollars a month.

Disputes between the Major and Dad were show time for our boys. They were at an age when, even as best of friends, they got into an occasional scrap. If Dad was around, he sometimes took a hard line and demanded them to stop—*No ifs, ands or buts, et cetera.* At times, he tended to run on, but his mandate was always clear: *Your rights end where your brother's nose begins*! Bickering among the girls, along with a bit of hair pulling, was tolerated so long as disputes ended quickly. Mom enforced Dad's rules with his same due discretion, but unlike Dad's long speak, she used short speak, like *Stop it*, and put her foot down. Moreover, when idle gossip was brought to the supper table, she instantly suppressed it with *Let's talk about the weather.*

We Scotts had a streak that runs through every family, a chemistry that makes it easy to get along with one and not the other, no name calling allowed. It was one thing to argue in the privacy of our home but intolerable for our disagreements to spill out into the street, let alone the whole neighborhood. Our sibling rivalries could be intense, but there was no fierce competition. We were not expected to inherit corporate Pittsburgh but would need to be prepared to stand up for our rights. We were expected to grow up ladies and gentlemen, solid citizens in a respectable society. We were taught to love and respect one another without comparing and with as little criticism as possible. Our collective interest in pulling together was always there. In that regard, everything was copacetic!

Mom held to her stoic resolve and was always the last to complain, even though she hardly ever sat down to rest and put up her feet. A visiting nurse found her in a state that had to be referred to the public health clinic. The city doctor came and diagnosed her with pneumonia and pleurisy. She was sent to the Lillian Rest Home in Harmarville. Vinny and Sis had to take turns staying home from school so that Dad wouldn't miss work.

Social Services investigated and gave our family high marks, but Huey and Anna were sent to St. Raphael's Orphanage until Mom was well. It was not the first time that Scott kids were sent there. The nun in charge kept on referring to our kids as orphans, inciting the real orphans who lived there to call our Anna *Little Orphan Annie.* It made her so mad that she scrapped with a bully on the playground and put him in his place. She couldn't wait to go home.

Our neighbors, Joe and Mary Monroe, had five daughters at the time and held an altruistic regard for our family of five girls and five boys. Joe would step in when Dad asked for help. What Mom found annoying was when Joe's wife showed up unannounced. As far as the neighbors were concerned, it was understood that Mom liked to keep our family's business to ourselves. But on the day Mom returned from the rest home, Mary showed up bearing a crusty baked potato and cheese casserole which, in truth, was consumed with immense gratitude, even though Mom was too weak to sit at the table.

Ten pregnancies, lack of rest, and inadequate nutrition had taken a toll. Her decaying teeth were beyond saving and had to be extracted. She was sent home from the dentist in pain with her mouth bleeding. DeeDee and Anna doted over her fearsomely, until Mom got up out of bed and declared fearlessly, *You girls stop carrying on like I'm dying. I'll live*! In stages, she was fitted with upper and lower plates at the Arsenal Health Dental Clinic, poor fits that forced her to wear her *manufactured teeth* only when she went somewhere.

Mom depended on Sis more than ever. She had turned thirteen and Mom felt it was time to explain certain things about life and what to prepare for, but Sis already knew what Mom was driving at—the Bible called it a curse on women. This made Sis laugh because Mom had once said that she didn't believe the Bible and that getting hers was a blessing. She slowly resumed her methodical style, managing our household in ways consistent with that traditionally held by women in Irish family culture. Dad supported her decisions, especially after listening to fantastic stories about what went on at our house while he was at the shop. Yet, our parents had miraculously guided our family through the Great Depression and now faced what to do about another world war heading our way.

Hubbard's initiated a graveyard shift that rendered Dad somewhat unavailable on the home front. Swing shifts with days off mid-week drove him crazy and heaven help the kids who woke him up during the day after he worked all night. What do you think he did the day Joe and Skip were playing outfield on our side lot with Larry at home plate and Huey, with eyesight issues, pitched too high and the baseball crashed through the window where Dad was sleeping? He flew downstairs and out the door in his underwear, cussing a wild streak. The boys suppressed their laughter, yet were somewhat warry of his retribution: *Yins kids find somewhere else to play or else.* Where on earth would they go? Over to the Wall, up the Seccy, which we called Wickliff Street, or even the Homey Hill, anywhere in our universe except our side lot when Dad was sleeping.

Our hill was one of the many Pittsburgh hills that created small ethnic neighborhoods, only ours was a collection of ethnic families of Irish, English, and European origins, mostly Catholic. We cherished adventures up and down the crumbling city steps, our stairways to a new heaven and a new earth, a hilly landscape that revealed the signs and symbols of our many struggles. You could not go any deeper into mythology than we Scotts did on our hill.

We were unfamiliar with places like Frick Park with its bike trails, tennis courts and bowling greens; we knew nothing of children who swam in country-club pools or lakes at summer homes. Dad's *shoe-leather express* walked two miles for the regulation swim in the little pool at Lawrence Park on Butler Street, walked four miles to Highland Park to swim in its two big pools, and afterwards go string-line fishing in its man-made lake, or go to the zoo.

The hike from our house to Quill's Hill was an arduous climb through dense woods to its shale-rock cliffs, where before us lay exposed the merciless panorama of Lawrenceville's steel mills and smoke, and the comforting view of our house on Duncan Street.

We explored the quarry and the Indian Caves, where once lived the Delaware Indians before they were pushed deeper into the western frontier, so history believes. Our expedition followed the line of the Allegheny eastwardly along the Indian

Trail, a precarious cliff-side trek up and down seven hills that led to the Indian Spring. There, we quenched our thirst in its pure cold stream, the same spring that flowed down into the yard of the O'Donnells' who lived on a bluff near the Sharpsburg bridge so long ago. It never failed that on our trek back to Duncan Street, a thunderstorm would hit and a hard downpour would flush the pollution out of the air, exposing the glory of a clear blue sky. For the glory of summer, it was impossible to imagine the hardships of winter that lay ahead.

As for Dad, once up, he was up! In between shifts at Hubbard's, he socialized on the barricade corner with men from the hill—steel workers with a penchant to learn everything that technology had to offer, as these were changing times in industry with the rampage of Hitler's Nazi war exploding into another world war in which we would soon be engaged.

1940

On a bitter cold January morning, Dad bundled up for the journey to work. Mom felt well enough to get up with him and send him on his way. Shortly thereafter, Sis placed an emergency call to Uncle Frank at work. He checked out, walked home to pick up his car, scraped the ice off the windshield, spun tires getting up the road to our hill and got Mom to the hospital in the nick of time. Dad blustered with pride when word reached him at Hubbard's that Mom had given birth to another son to be named Richard after Uncle Dick. Most telling about Richie's birth was that Dad declared him lucky number eleven, and he had never claimed a lucky number for the other ten.

Soon after Mom and Richie came home from the hospital, Dad decided to join his cronies at Neid's and share the box of cigars someone had given him. Well, Mom was up with Richie when Dad came home so drunk that he couldn't figure out how to get in the house. He started pounding on the kitchen door, wailing above his own din: *Oh my sweet Rose, my girl, please open the door and let me in; it's cold out here.* Mom knew what to do. She reached for a small pot that she kept on the back stove burner to reheat her tea, opened the door, wacked Dad over the head with the pot, and slammed the door closed. Funny how quickly he came to his senses when the jig was up.

With eleven children ages fifteen and under, Mom turned to the bedrock of social services in Pittsburgh, the Red Feather Chest. They sent us a home-care worker up from Georgia. Evelyn Jones was a shiny-skinned black woman with expressive dark eyes and a grand smile—made grander for every Scott kid she greeted with her subtle *a humm*. She made our lunch but brought her own lunch and shared tales of her life down South while we dined with her.

Huey was spellbound by her every word and every day asked, *Evelyn, what do you have in your lunch bag today*? One by one she laid the contents out on the table, saying in her soothing drawl, *I have a cheese sandwich, a hardboiled egg, a nickel lunch cake and a penny sucker.* A lot of food, not to mention the peanuts stashed in her apron pocket which she generously shared. No wonder he named her *Evelyn Peanut.*

Skip, in fourth grade at St. Kieran's, believed in his heart that our caregiver came up out of slavery to slave away at our house. In his geography book he discovered a photograph of a plantation in Georgia and rushed to the front of the classroom to show it to Sister, exclaiming that the woman in the picture was our maid. Sister reached for her ruler, rapped Skip's knuckles, and said, *Francis Scott, stop making up stories*. Skip wanted to cry but didn't; instead, he responded politely, *Honest Sister, it's Evelyn Peanut; she's our maid.*

Sister detained Skip to investigate what maid he was talking about. He tried to explain that Evelyn was a great help to Mom. Sister accused him of making up stories because the Scotts were too poor to have a maid. Skip was reduced to tears but stood by his truthful testimony and further explained that Mom was grateful to a great woman and the Red Feather Chest for responding to a great family need. Skip was nine years old going on a hundred and nine with the worries of his mind.

At the time, Mom and Dad were concerned about me. I was two and a half years old, in fragile health, and suffering with asthmatic coughing fits that knocked me off my feet. Industrial pollution didn't help, and a blood condition that caused boils and carbuncles made things worse. A visiting nurse came to the house to lance my boils, a terrible thing for the family to watch. I cried so hard that Mom cried with me. Something had to be done, but what? A social worker investigated and filed a report. A stay for a few months at a children's home way out in the country breathing fresh air was recommended. Mom said, *NO!* It was so far away that it might as well be Ireland. Then, carbuncles erupted all over my body and the decision was made. A nurse carried me out of the house and into a white van; Sis chased it down the road, wailing in protest, *They're taking our Patty to a home for crippled children and she isn't even crippled.*

Sewickley Fresh Air Home was founded in 1901 by Mary and Alexander Laughlin as a rest home for ill mothers with small babies, and it evolved into a convalescent home for children of the inner-city poor. In the Thirties it opened its doors to polio victims. Built in the architectural style of surrounding mansions, it rested on lovely grounds overlooking the Ohio valley twenty miles west of Pittsburgh, Pennsylvania.

The April 1940 U.S. Census was underway in Allegheny County. There I am listed as one of thirty-seven children living at Sewickley Fresh Air Home. On the same page, the supervisor, Mrs. Wood, and six attendants are listed as staff-house residents; one Mr. Barr and family are listed as residents of the caretaker's house. Curiously, I am listed in the same census as Patricia Scott, age 2 ½, living with my father, mother, six brothers, and four sisters at 5614 Duncan Street, in Pittsburgh—a real Jesus moment when you can prove you were in two places at one time, at least in my mind.

My earliest memories of living at the Sewickley Fresh Air Home are of Mom and Dad coming to see me now and then. Uncle Frank drove them out there when he could, but getting there on their own was a real hardship. Traveling to Sewickley without a car took at least two hours one way and involved a city streetcar ride into town and a transfer to a county bus for a long ride up and down hills on rough, windy roads. On Sewickley Creek Road, the bus pulled over at Hidden Valley Lane, where passengers got off, crossed an iron bridge, and walked up a graveled road to the Home.

On a visit soon after my placement, Mom and Dad were invited to the Home on a tour of some kind. We were joined by other guests for a meal in the elaborate dining room, and already it was time for them to head home. They started down the road to catch the bus, and it became an idea in my mind that I might never see my mother and father again. I ran after them sobbing hysterically. The attending nurse pried me out of Mom's arms and carried me back to the Home. I resisted and she scolded me; she didn't understand. I was not fighting her; I was fighting for my life. I can imagine now what my mother was going through then.

The Home became my other world with interesting things for a ghetto child to do in a country mansion. The main attraction on the first floor was its well-stocked and spotless kitchen with shiny pots and pans hanging everywhere, a cozy lounge for visitors, a play room filled with amazing toys, screened in porches, and a washroom where we children cleaned up before meals.

Upstairs, the Home was divided into wards of iron beds and foot lockers, as well as two isolation rooms and two lavatories equipped with a shower stall and a bathtub. On the grounds stood a one-room school house well ahead of its times and a playground perfect for little people who loved to swing high and jump low, spin dizzily on a wooden merry-go-round, or splash in the swimming pool installed to accommodate water therapy for the polio kids.

That summer, I turned three years old. Carbuncles broke out all over my body and my vacation home with my family was cancelled. The nurses tried many treatments before taking me to the little hospital on the grounds. A surgeon diagnosed a core of carbuncles wrapped around the base of my spine. I needed an operation so Mom sent Sis out there to be with me for the day. It was a frightening ordeal for both of us, Sis told Mom.

My recovery was slow-going so Mom sent Joe. DeeDee wanted to go with him but Mom said, *No, it's too far but maybe next time.* DeeDee had just been through a procedure to correct a weak eye-muscle condition. Well, I waited all that day for Joe. He found me on the playground, all alone on a swing, and stayed with me until it was time to catch the last bus home. He told Mom that I was too skinny and looked too sad, so Sis returned with Anna to cheer me. They arrived around lunch time and were invited to the dining room, four large square tables with seating on long benches. Sis sat on one side of me, Anna on the other, both amazed at the fancy table settings with white napkins, a pleasant surprise for a children's home. We were served butter bread to dip in our soup, along with an announcement to eat all of our food because children in India were starving. We spent the rest of the day on the playground.

On their way home, Sis tried her best to console Anna, but she could not restrain herself and boldly told Mom, *Patty was all dressed up; she's all better now. Her hair was curled and she looked so pretty in her pink dress. The Home is beautiful too. I wish I could live there. Why do we have to live in an old beat-up house*? Then she remembered seeing the big wound on my backside and broke down in tears. Summer for me had come and gone.

The anticipation of spending Christmas with my family saved me from despair, except for one unexpected incident. Uncle Frank volunteered to fetch me home a little ahead of time. However, a big snowfall hit; he attempted to get on the road and had to turn around because the roads were impassable. Just to be clear, in those days children were informed of visitors arriving in order to be ready. If they didn't show, that was simply another emotional episode to overcome. Well, little me went all to pieces when I was told there was a delay. I feared that I might never make it home again—ever. Two days later, the main roads were plowed, the side roads were cindered, and Uncle Frank delivered me to my family—the Scotts on a Hill in Pittsburgh, Pennsylvania—right on time for Christmas Eve festivities.

Dad always got the biggest tree on the lot and had to cut the bottom off to get it into the house, even though he got it free after waiting until nobody wanted it. With the decorating underway, he let us kids hang our stockings on the mantel and scurried us off to bed with the yarn about Santa on his way to bring our presents down the chimney. It was impossible to believe Dad, bearing in mind that the coal stove pipe blocked Santa's entry.

Christmas morning we bounded downstairs to look for presents, a modest assortment of dime store gifts. Our stockings each held an apple, an orange, and some candy. Everybody bundled up and attended Mass at St. Mary's, where Vinny proudly sang solo with the Slovenian Choir. At home, we played with our new toys, sang Christmas songs, and gathered at the dining room table for a baked ham holiday feast. The big kids cleaned up and looked after the little kids so Mom could rest. You've got to believe that Dad was the happiest drunk on the block.

On New Year's Day 1941, Uncle Frank drove me back to Sewickley, his only free day, but harsh reality does not always spare little people and I made my feelings felt. It seems that I was on a path of risk taking—refusing to speak, hiding in dark places, and trying to run away. I had no choice but to make an adjustment, at least enough to pick up where I left off playing with my newfound friends. But things weren't going all that well elsewhere either.

The Selective Service Act required sixteen million American men between the ages of twenty-one and thirty-five to register for the largest peacetime draft in our history. Over two hundred thousand men from Allegheny County registered to serve in the armed forces, almost ninety thousand from Pittsburgh alone. Air-raid practice drills were conducted in every neighborhood and town across the country.

The Fair Oaks Volunteer Fire Department served the Sewickley Fresh Air Home and conducted air-raid practice drills—all lights extinguished and blinds drawn. Wardens were assigned to enforce the rules. Led by flash lights, we children who could walk were silently filed into the bowels of the mansion and lined up along its stone foundation walls holding our ears against the shrill alarms. Considering that the children of England were living in bomb shelters, we were lucky. Amazing how sensitive our care givers were at the Home. Once all the necessary excitement abated, a fire truck or two would pull up on the grounds and noisy children would pile on back for a ride into town—no seat belts, but we were cured of emotional distress!

My sister Eileen and I were a year apart and were devoted playmates, but every little thing seemed to bother her when I was around. I was home for the summer and no sooner arrived when her heart rate went berserk and she was sent to the Children's Heart House in Oakland. I thought it was my fault. We had gone exploring on the upper realms of the Homey and found a big piece of cardboard. We dragged it up the hillside, jumped

on, took a wild ride down the slope, and landed in a cinder pile. We sustained brush burns that needed attention and had to go home, but she wanted me to drag the cardboard home with us. I said, *No, Eileen. I don't want to, it's falling apart.* She started dragging it herself and suddenly experienced an awful pain in her chest.

The commotion was too much for Mom; she landed back at the Lillian Rest Home for a brief recuperation period. Dad went with Uncle Frank to bring her home. Once she was made comfortable, Sis made tea and asked our uncle to stay. He sat down with Dad to discuss his plan to buy a new car. He inquired if Dad would like to have his old car, and Dad said he'd have to think about owning a car.

At the time, it was almost the only car that appeared on our street. Every other vehicle was a truck. The milk truck, the mail truck, the ice truck, the huckster truck, the garbage truck, the scrap truck, and the coal truck. Uncle Frank figured that once Dad was persuaded to get in the car, teaching him how to drive it would be a cinch. Dad explained that owning a car would keep him broke, and Frank persisted. Dad finally went out to the curb, kicked one of the tires, and got in the car on the passenger side. Frank got behind the wheel and demonstrated how to operate the choke and gas pedal to turn the engine over, and simultaneously operate the clutch and gear shift to pull the car onto the road. He circled the hill, parked the car at the curb and had Dad get behind the wheel.

Reluctantly, he pulled out the choke to start the engine and forgot to push the choke back in. When he hit the gas, a cloud of smoke poured out of the chassis, and the car stalled. After several tries, he got the hang of it, pulled out with a grind and crunch and drove around the road. He approached the bend thinking he had his foot on the brake but it was on the gas pedal. The car accelerated and crashed into the telegraph pole near our house. Uncle Frank, who had never profaned in his life, swore every Irish curse word he knew. Dad cussed for all it was worth and stomped home to get the hammer and chisel with which he pried the fender out from around that pole. Frank got in the car, drove it away, and we never saw that car again. It was bound to be a long, hot summer on Duncan Street with Dad on and off the wagon.

Sis turned fifteen in August and baked a cake for the family. She also cooked, cleaned, and did the laundry. On top of all that, she took care of baby Richie, and he had rickets. She gave him vitamin D sun baths in the back yard two or three times a day, with everything covered up but his skinny legs. He wiggled and cooed when she sang hit tunes she learned on the radio—she knew every word of every song. Once her sweet voice lulled Richie to sleep, she put him to bed and turned her attention on me. The smoky air brought on asthmatic episodes that kept me in bed under a croup tent, and my vacation disappeared in the vaporizing chaos. Summer was gone in a flash, and on Labor Day, Uncle Frank took me back to Sewickley in his new car—a 1940 black four-door Ford sedan with chrome bumpers.

Pittsburgh's schools reopened with Larry spared the demanding journey through the Homey to St. Kieran's. He was susceptible to bronchitis and pneumonia because he had been born a blue baby, a condition that affected his respiratory tract. Mom had appealed to St. Mary's, expressing concern that he would be unduly exposed to the elements if he had to walk to St. Kieran's in the winter. Somehow, Sister Mary Cletus found a way to squeeze him in—the smallest and youngest student in her first grade.

Huey was enjoying a temporary stay at St. Mary's in third grade and showed Larry the ropes. You might say he was a gifted child from the point of view of Sister, who sat him up front and personal, near the blackboard. She loved his Scott intensity, his willingness to learn, his drawn brow that let her know he was thinking, and his reserved manner that told her he'd get along swell in school. One of our house rules was that the younger kids had to do their homework at the dining room table right after school and the older kids do theirs before bedtime. Larry did his homework in bed.

Sis did her homework at school—hands on. Bellefield Vocational's home-economics program was turning out the finest seamstresses, beauticians, cooks, and homemakers. Aunt Olivia had noticed how creative and hardworking Sis was and had invited her on a pre-school vacation. Sis didn't want to stay a whole week but was promised good wages and accepted the offer, an experience of working her fingers to the bone for Auntie O. Uncle Dick felt so sorry for Sis that he helped her when his wife wasn't looking. His wily sense of humor kept Sis smiling or she'd have quit the first day. On her last day, she was anxious to see how much she had earned. Aunt Olivia handed her a bag full of her old clothes, plopped one of her old hats on Sis's head, put streetcar fare in her hand and sent her on her way. She had expected a shopping trip for school clothes at the very least. Uncle Dick walked her to the streetcar stop. The wind whipped up and the floppy straw hat blew off her head, landing on the railroad tracks the other side of the road. He darted through traffic to retrieve it but Sis heard a train coming and cried out: *No Uncle Dick, leave it there.*

Once home, she looked through the bag of clothes and found a tub-sized red and white polka dot dress and a pair of wide-sized white high heels with shoe laces. Her heart sank; she had to wear Auntie O's pitiful donations the first day of school. After school she ditched the whole outfit in the Homey Hill dump, bag and all, and next day wore last year's clothes. Dad felt so bad about chiseling Olivia's stingy stunt that he took Sis to Gimbel's to buy a new school outfit and pick out a nice dress on sale for the upcoming holidays.

Larry was approaching his seventh birthday when Japan bombed Pearl Harbor. Big bold headlines appeared on front pages of every newspaper in the country: *DECEMBER 7, 1941. JAPS BOMB PEARL HARBOR. HEAVY CASUALTIES TO U. S. MILITARY AND CIVILIAN FORCES.* The assault began at 7:55 in the morning, Pacific Time. Nineteen destroyers and battle ships sunk. One hundred and fifty planes downed. Two thousand four hundred and three soldiers, sailors and civilians killed. One thousand one hundred and seventy eight severely injured and badly burned. While the military scrambled for cover and counted losses, Japan attacked our bases in the Philippines, Guam, and Midway, and British bases in Hong Kong and Malay.

President Roosevelt called an emergency session of Congress to declare the United States of America in a state of war and signed the Wartime Draft Act, which extended the draft age to men between eighteen and thirty-eight. The next day, twelve hundred young men from Lawrenceville enlisted. People shook with petrifying ideas and beliefs that it was the beginning of the end of the world.

At St. Mary's, the mothers of boys going off to war blew their noses and wiped their tears all through Father Kebe's wise counsel to keep the faith. He explained that the world for each of us as we know it would end on the day we die. The mood of our household was no less depressing than the mood across the nation; nevertheless, a call went out to stand up and fight and get the war over with. The attack on Pearl Harbor rallied close to four thousand Red Cross chapters and tens of thousands of women volunteers to roll bandages, prepare first-aid kits, and operate blood drives.

How in the world did anyone manage to celebrate that Christmas? Dad took the little kids downtown to see the Santa Claus parade and the holiday displays in the department store windows. The local union hall parties were terrific, with sing-a-long Christmas songs and Santa's arrival on stage. Every child received a *Santa Gift*—a brown paper bag containing a whistle, a comb, a model horse and infantry soldier, a cellophane-wrapped caramel popcorn ball, and a candy cane. We ate the popcorn balls on the streetcar ride home.

Christmas day, Uncle Sam arrived bearing gifts and, understandably, had miscounted. Huey got gypped and wailed, *Uncle Sam, what about me*? Sam felt so badly that he drove all over town looking for and found a store open in Squirrel Hill where the Jewish neighborhood was doing a booming business. Hours later, he returned with a dazzling green dump truck just for Huey, and two freshly slaughtered kosher chickens to roast a delicious Scott family New Year's Eve dinner.

1942 rang in with the raging world war on everybody's mind. People on our hill welcomed in the new year, banging on pots and pans out in the cold, and retreating indoors to warm up and listen to world news. Vinny brought home critical news affecting industry, stories that came in through

Postal Telegraph's lines. He had recently been hired there, a job he got with Dad's help.

It became apparent to Congress that with telegraphic communications vital to homeland security under enemy surveillance, Postal Telegraph and Western Union would have to be merged. Vinny suddenly found himself working the downtown triangle beat for WU. His boss gave him two trolley tokens a day to ride from point A to point B, two tokens to ride from point B to C, and two more to ride back to point A. He walked the last stretch of the triangle to save those tokens for Mom, knowing she needed them to take the kids to the hospital clinics.

Dad turned forty in May and received a U.S. Conscription Office notice to register in the event of a call up of men beyond draft age. In the tone he reserved for real panic, he said, *Time to face the music.* At the recruiting office, he filled out and signed a form and gave it to a registration officer who told him to have a seat. He wondered what was the hold up and began to squirm. Minutes later, he was called forward and told that he was disqualified—too many kids. He breathed a huge sigh, walked up Liberty Avenue at a brisk gait, turned in at the Brass Rail tavern to settle his nerves, and caught the next streetcar home, anxious to report his good news: *Rose, my love, I tried to tell you that eleven was my lucky number and you didn't believe me*! Mom replied, *Crump's sakes, stop bragging, there's a war on and you still have a job.*

Hubbard's comprised a two-hundred-man labor force working three shifts in a stark compound of blackened corrugated tin buildings on the banks of the Allegheny just beyond the Sharpsburg Bridge. Its scant windows allowed for little natural light to alleviate the dreary atmosphere of a dingy work place, an icebox in winter and a furnace in summer, reminiscent of stories about John Scott's experience at Barrow-in-Furness in Lancashire, England.

At Hubbard's, the labor force endured both frostbite and heatstroke but pulled together to bring the shop into compliance with war-time regulations. Parts and equipment not useful for wartime were warehoused. The shop was cleared of dirt and debris in anticipation of government inspections. The Feds observed the neat and orderly mill and took note of both men and women who worked with the concentration of a bee colony, a labor force that boasted: *Hubbard's is the best run shop in Pittsburgh.*

Women employed at Pittsburgh Waterproof Canvas and Awning Company in the Strip District made military hospital tents, a strenuous process of holding onto a heavy olive green canvas with bare fingers while the power pedal pulled the canvas through the machine. They spliced by hand the heavy rope used for bracing tents so that it easily tied into knots to secure tents in position. Production line workers had bleeding blisters and calluses the size of quarters and no one complained. It was a case of the girls wanting to do their part for the boys at war.

CEO John Hubbard created a victory workers program. His employees looked up to him and referred to his company as Hubbard's, never *the Company.* They met quotas that earned them a prodigious measure of bonuses and red, white, and blue victory hats. The community was invited to a rally of speechmaking, picture taking, soft drinks and snacks. Our gang turned out to cheer Dad. He wore his victory hat to work. Sadly, one day it blew off his head in a gust of wind. He chased it down Butler Street, but the wind hurled it onto the flat roof of the forty garages adjacent to the Atlantic Refinery's oil storage tanks. That evening, he made himself a new victory hat with a double sheet of newspaper folded on an angle several times and

tucked in around the edges. Richie cracked up with laughter when Dad put it on; he swiftly took it off and placed it on lucky number eleven's head. The dear lad ran off to locate his comb and wax paper with which to make imitation harmonica music and stomped around the house piping the one-note tune Dad had taught him: *I'm a victory worker for the war.*

The legend of history, Winston Churchill, arrived in Washington D.C. to muster up enthusiasm for U.S. support of Great Britain's defense against Germany. The Prime Minister defined the cause in eloquent language and praised FDR for his leadership in turbulent and dangerous times. Our President, as a proud father of sons fighting in the war, stressed national security. He spoke to the nation over the radio, addressing all Americans as: *My Friends.* A photograph of our president in a wheel chair appeared on the front page of the *Roto* magazine, but the photograph on the inside cover of a boy in an iron lung really disturbed Larry. Dad helped him read the article and, around the supper table that evening, he expressed gratitude that our family was not among the unlucky people riding in wheelchairs or walking in braces with one tall shoe or paralyzed with polio and living in an iron lung.

For a boy of seven, his insights were profound. Ironically, a photo of the Scotts from a Hill in Pittsburgh appeared on an inside page of another issue of the *Roto*, subtitled the largest family in Allegheny County, a statement later disputed by a family with thirteen kids by two fathers. Some twenty thousand people resided in Lawrenceville and over five thousand more commuted from the outskirts to work in our mills. With a strike pending, the union at Hubbard's planned a walkout and was set back on its heels in a big layoff.

Thanksgiving Day approached and what would our family do without a turkey dinner? We never went in for turkey hunting or bringing back the kill for skinning and things like that until that year. The union offered a live turkey to take home and fatten up for the holiday—with no time to get to like the poor creature. It paraded around in a small pen in our back yard, clucking its heart out. Our house full of kids kept the turkey in a frantic state, marveling at how it strutted back and forth, bobbing its head up and down, with never a chance to give it a name.

The day before Thanksgiving, it was time. Dad and Vinny went into the pen and grappled with the ill-fated bird. Despite its calamitous protests, they took the turkey down the cellar, where it was cold, dank and dark, figuring it was the best place to confine the turkey in case something went wrong, but the bird went nuts. Somehow they held on to it and dragged it to the chopping block. The ax was sharpened and ready. Dad and Vinny were sweating profusely and breathing hard and the turkey was getting more difficult to hold down and they had to move quickly. The kids gathered on the cellar steps to watch and wait, wide-eyed. Vinny pinned down the turkey, except for its head, which now bobbed even more crazily. Dad moved into position, raising the ax steadily. The ax came down, made a clean cut, and the head came off, but the turkey reared up in revenge and raced around the cellar. The headless creature seemed more alive than ever before it came to rest on top of the coal pile. It was de-feathered and cleaned and lay in state in a pan of salted water until time for roasting. Happy Thanksgiving Day! Mom shook her head, and Dad carried out his turkey-carving ritual, which began with a raised knife and his boiler-plate doxology: *Bless our poor family and have mercy on this poor bird*. He carved the turkey with precision and the son and daughter who did the best good deed that year received a drumstick. We never had a live turkey again.

We welcomed Christmas, mightily. Gifts, there were few, mostly from relatives, and while appreciated, the gifts seemed not all that important. There was joy because we understood the true meaning of Christmas, which we learned at home, in school, and in church. We sang the holy hymns and holiday songs in harmony, in English and Slovenian; at our house, we kids were always singing. During the holiday season, Pittsburgh raised four-and-a half million dollars for the United War Fund through contributions of commercial businesses and employees. Our mills were recognized for their generosity in the war effort, as well as for being the nation's number-one steel producer. The air was so polluted that people had difficulty finding their way through darkened streets. No one could see the infinitely clear blue sky beyond the smoke cover, but steel workers pledged to honor their *no strike* commitment until we as a nation had won the war.

At Hubbard's, rush orders poured in for war goods like hand-grenade shells and rifle barrels. Tools like picks and shovels, hammers and chisels, screw drivers and pliers—common tools Americans needed—were presently not on sale to the public. The public had learned to make do. Wartime rations made it hard to get razor blades, which had sold in the stores six for a quarter and now sold on the black market six for a dollar.

Old Gold cigarettes, gone from stores where they had sold for nineteen cents a pack, now sold for a dollar a pack on the black market. Nobody questioned Dad on where he got ahold of his *Camel's*.

Mom sent Joe to the A & P on 54th Street with a store list, but without sugar stamps—sorry, no sugar. He packed one bag with canned foods and oranges and put the bread on top. He filled a second bag with the rest of the groceries and took the short cut home. Even when the Homey was buried beneath deep snow, the footpath from 55th Street to Duncan Street was accessible due to heavy foot traffic of people on our hill. Half way through the Homey, Joe's arms started aching; he set one bag down on a big rock to get a better grip, not realizing that snow had soaked through the bottom of the bag. He picked it up and it split wide open. Joe nearly cried when several oranges and two cans of peaches rolled away and down into the ravine. He could think on his feet and quickly removed his jacket, wrapped it around the loose groceries and continued on his journey. It took an hour to get home and Mom raved, *All you shivering saints in heaven, what took so long and where's the sugar?* Joe replied with a twinkle in his eyes, *Mom, maybe we'll get our sugar stamps for Christmas.*

For the first time in its existence, the labor force at Hubbard's worked on Christmas due to the war. Days later, the shop closed to contend with flood waters. With a rubber shortage, there occurred a run on boots. Public works employees, who had to wade through high waters on downtown streets to get to their jobs, paid five or six times their worth on the black market. The enormous amount of coal needed to heat homes and office buildings and fuel our industries and power stations mandated a temporary coal ration and created brown outs, black outs, and candle burning.

Dad begrudged the well-offs who were not suffering for the sake of the war, not this way. He realized that some people lived comfortably and slept soundly in warm beds, with every right. But, who you were and knew greatly influenced how much coal you got. He was convinced that graft was a factor. He couldn't wait for the spring primaries so he could cast his ballot, as he put it, *Vote out the old bums and vote in the new bums.*

David L. Lawrence, the newest big-wheel Democrat on the political scene, had Dad's vote if he ever decided to run for mayor. Like our O'Donnell ancestors, Lawrence was born at the Point, so that made him one of us. He understood the workings of the political machine and enjoyed the support of the rank and file and organized labor. In due time, he would join hands with Richard K. Mellon, a republican industrialist and financier—a merger of common-class political astuteness with upper-class prestige and professional competence that neither could have done on their own to rebuild Pittsburgh. For the present, Lawrence presented himself as a neighborly chap who offered practical advice on how to end the coal shortage and address the pollution problems being ignored by potentates in the Republican Party who owned the mines and mills. He proved to be a shrewd thinker who knew to bide his time until the war ended, when many of the city's problems would be resolved on their own.

1943

It was around that time that the legendary dance of Mom's *Gain-a-Day* began. On wash day, she wore two house dresses, one on top of the other to keep warm and dry, and Dad's old work shoes (which she endearingly called *canal barges*) to keep her feet warm. To keep her abundant head of hair from falling into her eyes, she tied it back with jute twine. She sorted dirty clothes on the kitchen floor, a landscape of bright and dark colors, which she fed into the washer along with a measure of *Oxydol* laundry powder. She fished clean wash out of the hot water with a wooden spoon and fed it through the wringer into a cold rinse cycle. By hand she turned the wash over and over, squeezing out every last drop of soapy residue. On the last cycle, she swung the wringer out over the rinse tub and ran the wash into a laundry basket, a holding area, until everything could be hung up to dry, outdoors or indoors, depending on the weather.

Dad usually set up laundry operations the night before; first he pulled the washer out into the middle of the floor. He brought the galvanized wash tub inside, placed it on a backless chair, and braced it against the washer. He set the oval-shaped copper cauldron on the gas stove and had the boys bail water into both tubs before they went to bed. In the morning, he lit the gas jets under the cauldron to start the water heating and left for work. Sis bailed the hot water into the washer before going to school, and Mom washed clothes when the kitchen cleared.

A day came when she loaded clothes into the washer, plugged it into the only kitchen outlet, and pushed the agitator lever forward to get it going. On the unstable floor, the washer started vibrating noisily. She turned off the agitator, evened out the load, and restarted the cycle. To her amazement, the washer started drifting across the floor. Another big noise when one of the washer's wheels punctured a hole in the floor and wash water splashed out all over the place. She had no choice but to shut down the operation and wait for Dad to come home. She explained that the washer acted up and did an *Irish Jig*. His grin told her that he doubted it.

He assessed the damage, repaired the broken wheel, pounded the lid of a tin can over the hole and restarted the washer. Sure enough, it danced across the kitchen floor right before his eyes. She showed him the dirty clothes piled up in the cellar way, and he said, *Don't worry hon, I'll take care of this problem in plenty of time.*

He talked to a repairman at the appliance store on Butler Street, who wanted the washer brought in. Dad explained his situation in such a way that the repairman came to the house and fixed the washer for free. Anytime a big problem like that was solved at our house made good reason for Dad to drop in at Neid's for a few cool ones. No problem.

A problem came up at St. Mary's when Huey took an epileptic seizure on the classroom floor after learning that he would be re-transferred to St. Kieran's in fifth grade. The mandate also applied to Larry, so Mom re-appealed his case to Father Kebe who resolved it on the spot. He chose Larry to be lead altar boy carrying a lantern in the May procession in honor of the Blessed

Mother. All students were required to bring flowers to decorate the Virgin's altar.

Eileen, in first grade, knew picking tulips and daffodils from neighborhood gardens was a sin, but they were the only flowers she could find. Spring flowers made up for all winter when nothing bloomed and the church looked so desolate. She was first in line for the rosary which we said every evening. If Dad was home, he turned the radio down and closed the sliding doors between the living and dining rooms. We prayed for world peace on our knees, all but Mom who, because of her bad knees, sat at the dining room table and prayed for more ration stamps.

Dad claimed that the government could learn a few tricks from us on surviving the war ration. Cuff-less trousers came in to save cloth for military uniforms, and our boys simply let down the cuffs of their pants and wore them until they were thread bare. We couldn't part with our shoe ration stamps and were able to obtain more by trading our gasoline stamps for Uncle Frank's shoe stamps. We saved our soup and canned milk labels for school coupon drives. Coupons for *Octagon* bar soap earned stars next to your name on the classroom bulletin board. Labels would disappear from our food cans before they were opened. The canned soup we ate for lunch was always a surprise. Everyone saved empty cans for the metal scrap drives and newspapers and magazines for the paper drives.

Every Saturday, our boys cleared these donations from neighborhood door steps and hauled everything to the pickup site on our side lot. Oddly, there was never anything to be found on the doorstep at the house on the barricade corner. Leave it to Larry to go around back and knock. The bedraggled woman of the house opened the door, offered a toothless grin, sized him up and showed him in. She said she had been saving newspapers ever since the last war, and he believed it. The place burgeoned with newspapers, magazines, and old books. It took many trips to haul it all to our side lot; nobody believed where it all came from, and nobody believed the old lady from Europe who drank Irish whiskey and spoke broken English knew how to read.

The local papers advertised community scrap drives and posted scrap metal values:Tin cans three cents a pound. Lead five cents a pound. Iron ten cents a pound. Aluminum and copper fifteen cents a pound. Scavenger hunts in the Homey ravine unearthed metal junk from ditched vehicles to busted washing machines parts, rusty bikes, and baby buggies.The rubber drive paid a nickel a piece for discarded tires and a dime a dozen for rubber boots. The household conservation drive produced gallons of lard and bacon grease to make ammunition and old nylon stockings to make gun powder bags.

Vinny, Joe, Skip, Huey, and Larry sifted through the Homey Hill dump with rakes and shovels and even with their bare hands to unearth a gold mine of scrap. They filled burlap sacks and hauled them down the steep 56th Street steps, setting down the load on every other landing to get a better grip.Their unspoken goal was to make enough money to get as far away from poverty as they could. The Scrappy closed at noon on Saturdays, but the boys made it in time to cash in and treat the girls to the Saturday matinee at the Tenth Ward movie theatre, the Dome, plus a nickel each for a candy bar from the vending machine.

The Dome occupied a deep narrow space between the hardware store and the Allegheny Valley Bank. For a nickel, it offered a stale double feature plus old cartoons and serial clips. Movies were a great way to spend time out from under Mom's feet and, even better, to stay twice through the double feature without having to pay for a second admission, especially if the main feature was Gene Autry and his horse Trigger or Abbott and Costello plus episodes of Flash Gordon and Superman. Re-runs were spliced so many times that the film often broke in the middle of the most exciting scenes. The show crowd stomped its feet and shouted *BOO* until the film started rolling again. If it was delayed too long, the audience tossed popcorn and candy wrappers at the screen. Perpetually interrupted movies never got anybody their money back, not at the Dome.

It happened a Tuesday night when Sis and her girlfriends paid ten cents to see a special re-run of the 1939 Technicolor film *Gone with the Wind*. The film broke right where Rehett Butler *quite frankly didn't give a damn* and the show crowd went berserk. The lanky mustached evening manager of the Dome, dressed in tuxedo and bow tie, turned on the theatre lights and rushed on stage wiping his brow with a big handkerchief. He ranted and raved and shouted threats that if the audience didn't settle down, he'd have to call the police and people would be arrested.

The excitement of going to the Dome kept us motivated to cooperate with family responsibilities Monday through Friday for the pleasure of attending the Saturday Matinee with inevitable broken films. It happened again in the middle of the storming of the *Bastille*. Anna was in attendance with St. Kieran's 7th and 8th grade at a showing of the 1935 Charles Dickens' classic, *A Tale of Two Cities*. The film was damaged beyond repair, and she got so mad that she demanded her nickel back.

Sunday was *Family* Day with little to do besides going to church and the show. All stores and saloons were closed thanks to Pennsylvania's Blue Laws, which were enacted after the state's founding as a colony by Sir William Penn in 1682, as follows: Whoever does perform any worldly employment or business whatsoever on the Lord's day, works of necessity and charity exempted, or practices any game, hunting, shooting, or other diversion whatsoever not authorized by law, is considered to be a law breaker.

Mom worked all day to prepare a fine dinner regardless of the Church's precept forbidding servile work on the Lord's Day. The precept extended to hospital workers, police officers, firefighters, streetcar conductors, radio announcers, and other public servants, including ministers and priests. How in the world did anything get done? It was easy—they did it anyway—we were at war!

Dad and Mom signed parental consent forms qualifying Vinny to enlist in the Navy V-5 Aviation Program in his senior year at Central. Joe wanted to follow in Vinny's footsteps, but at the last minute, inspired by his art teacher at St. Kieran's, changed his mind and enrolled at Connelley Vocational, a trade school in the Hill District equipped to turn out draftsmen, craftsmen, and mechanics. He thought of himself as an artist, and it had occurred to him more than once that he ought not to ruin his artistic hands in mill grease and grime or in dirty dish water, feelings he kept to himself for the time being. He was grateful for the Catholic training that he had received, a heritage that opened for him the universal spirit and great mysteries of the Church.

Skip inherited Joe's newspaper business, the most demanding being Post-Gazette's early a.m. route on Stanton Heights. He asked Huey to sign on and share the profits. *Okay for starters,* said Huey. Payday came, he counted his coins, looked at Skip skeptically and said flatly, *Cheapskate.* Skip said, *What do you mean cheapskate? That's all there is*! Huey wanted to quit but didn't. He saved his choice words for delivering papers through snow drifts. The *Post-Gazette* had to be delivered before school started, an impossible deadline in snow storms. Huey's route crisscrossed the unpaved terrain of the Stanton Golf Course and the Randolph Estate property, later bought up by our Uncle Bart Scott and developed into a middle-class neighborhood, as previously reported. *P-G*'s district manager,

Mr. Gill, who smoked stinky cigars, gave credit where it was due and sponsored Skip and Huey as members of Pittsburgh Newsboys on a fishing trip, a pleasant ride to the upper Allegheny shore in a fancy Hudson sedan. That, and a train ride to Idlewild Amusement Park for the company picnic, highlighted the Scott newsboys' careers to that point.

Larry watched his brothers counting out their profits and recognized a business potential. He asked Mom if it was okay for him to deliver newspapers. She said, *No, not yet.* Instead, she took him along when she shopped on Butler Street and let him carry her packages. One day she took him to the A & P near 40th Street, two miles from our house on the hill. She was already tired by the time they got there, and he could tell her feet hurt.

He hoped she'd cut the shopping short, but she needed one more thing and discreetly slipped a small box of tea bags into her coat pocket. At the counter, she paid for her groceries, but all the way home his mind kept saying, *My mother is a thief, my mother is a thief.* Mom read his mind and said, *Larry, don't worry about the tea bags, I only borrowed them.* His mind told him that the war might be over by the time she could own up. Regardless, he loved her, unconditionally. She had released him from indoor confinement for the summer.

A neighbor on our hill, affectionately called *Sputsie Yuckie*, was our air-raid warden. He wore a tin hat and brown vest, carried a flash light, and went door-to-door when the mill sirens blew in short sequences, reminding the citizenry to turn off the lights and lower the blinds. Dad grumbled *ah nuts* every time his radio program was interrupted and he had to go around the house drawing our dark green roller blinds, which were so full of holes that the lights in our house shined like stars in the night. When the street lights came back on, he walked to the barricade corner to watch our hill's petty gamblers play card and dice games, but he seldom bet more than two bits on a crap game because he never won.

It was an exciting time to be part of history. In a revival of patriotic spirit, the great lady of song, Kate Smith, toured the country singing songs she had made famous in World War One, generating national enthusiasm to invest in war bonds. It was all people talked about: Buy and save war bonds. Miss Smith sold over thirty-six million dollars' worth of Victory Bonds through payroll savings plans. "Praise the Lord and Pass the Ammunition" became the number one hit on the music charts. Theaters featured war movies and ran promotionals for the war effort during intermission. In our community, we seldom had to travel downtown or to Oakland and the Northside or Southside to enjoy the revival.

Everything was right there in Lawrenceville. Bowling alleys, pin ball and slot machine hangouts, the Dome, the Model, and the Arsenal movie theaters, little theater playhouse, and churches on every other side street. Catholics were cautioned to avoid Protestant services or risk damnation, but curious Scott kids occasionally visited the Methodist Church on Holmes Street, the Baptist Church on McCandless Avenue, and the Presbyterian

Church on Stanton Avenue. We sang the Protestant hymns with gusto. If Mom knew that, she might've killed us.

In June 1943, Vinny graduated from Central; he had met all V-5 requirements for the aeronautical engineering program and prepared for enlistment in the Navy. Mom asked if he had time to go out to Sewickley and bring me home. *Sure, Mom,* he said. I was being released from the Fresh Air Home, permanently. I would turn six in August and start first grade in September. I would miss my teacher at the one-room school house, Miss Venezia. She was small in person and great of stature, generous, kind, sypathetic and patient; she taught me how to print my name and count to one hundred.

I would miss my friends, the fun we had on the play ground and the children's March of Dimes parades in Fair Oaks in the springtime. I would miss the gardener, Mr. Barr. I followed him everywhere just to watch him cultivating the landscape, planting flowers, and watering everything with his gigantic watering can on wheels. I would miss Raymond, a polio boy confined to bed. He built aircraft from an aeronautics kit and let me fly his planes around the room. And I would miss *Laughie* (Mrs. Laughlin) who taught me how to wash up and sit properly at the dining table. Three years of early childhood memories in the Home would never completely leave me. Sometimes, I had felt like I didn't know where I belonged, but I was thrilled to be going home for good.

Vinny held my hand the whole way home on that rickety bus ride through boroughs, small towns, and on the streetcar from town to Butler Street. Halfway up the city steps to Duncan Street, I started coughing, and he carried me the rest of the way. As soon as I saw our house, I ran breathless into the backyard. There was Mom leaned over the washing machine feeding a sheet through the wringer. The washer had been moved to the alcove outside the kitchen door for the summer, which made it easier to hang wet wash on the clotheslines stretched across our vacant lot.

When Mom saw me, the wooden spoon fell out of her hand, and she squealed, *Oh my little girl, how you've grown, and you look so pretty in pink.* It was my good dress. She picked me up and I buried my face in her warm bosom for some moments before she had to set me down and undo a sheet that had wrapped itself around the wringer. The washer suddenly made a terrific grinding noise and the wringer gears popped. She instantly pulled the electric cord that ran through the opened dining room window to an inside wall plug. Even though incidents like that made her shake, she always held her ground. She took me into the kitchen, set me on the side of the sink, and wiped my face and hands with a cool wash cloth. After a grilled cheese and

tomato soup lunch, Vinny brought his red bike out of the cellar and took me for a ride to the Wall and back, then steered onto our side lot where I fell off the bike, screaming. He felt awful about it, but other than my wounded ego and brush-burned knees no harm done. That day was the first time I saw Vinny cooking supper—a Slovenian dish of potatoes and sausages—the last supper he would serve our family for quite a while.

Days later, he headed for basic training at a Navy boot camp east of Buffalo in Sampson, New York, the farthest that anyone in our family had traveled outside of Pittsburgh, except for Dad who attended the 1933 World Fair in Chicago. Our whole family rode the streetcar into town to see Vinny off at Penn Station, a scene both sad and jubilant. Hundreds of draftees were boarding trains heading for all parts of the country and the world, none we felt more proud of than Vinny. His orders were to report to boot camp by midnight. He had barely found time to reorient himself and say goodbye to his friends. No one can put words in Mom's mouth—she said so few—but surely she felt a deep agony when they embraced and said goodbye. No one save God knew if he'd be injured or killed in action, or if Mom would ever see her first-born son again. Dad trembled and held back tears; he gave Vinny a slap on the back and wished him safe journey.

After boot camp, Vinny was to report to the Naval Station in Pensacola, Florida. Instead, he was sent to the Brooklyn Navy Yard and assigned to radar and fire control training on the *USS Blue Ridge*, a radio command ship of the Seventh Amphibious Force assigned to the Pacific Theater. Starting wage for a radio technician was ninety dollars a month. He was given the choice of how much of his wages to be put in a savings account or to be sent home. He chose to keep ten dollars for personal use, the rest to send home. The ship sailed south through the Atlantic and west through the Panama Canal bound for Sydney, Australia, with short stops in Bora Bora, Tahiti, and New Caledonia, an endless sea journey of war games with little rest and no sleep.

By the light of day, talk of war fascinated me and in the dark of night terrified me. One night I awakened from a nightmare that *Japs* were breaking into our house, and I woke up screaming. Dad came in the room and told me to *cut it out*, my racket was disturbing the whole family. Mom came in, pulled a chair over to the window, and held me in her lap. We leaned on the windowsill, looked out into the night and counted headlights of cars rolling over the Sharpsburg Bridge. Soon the rumble of freight trains down along the river bank lulled me to sleep and Mom put me to bed.

Her sensitivity to restless children inspired Mom to give Sis a quarter to take me, Eileen, Larry, and Huey to the Dome, enough money for admission but nothing left over for candy. Sis kept her fingers crossed that we wouldn't ask for any, but when we passed by a candy store, we begged. She didn't have the heart to say no and let us select a few of *these, those, and thems*, as we called penny candy.

At the Dome, she boldly stepped up to the ticket booth, placed the dime and nickel she had left on the counter and asked for five tickets. The fat and bald headed afternoon manager, chewing on a soggy cigar and talking out the side of his mouth, accused Sis of trying to chisel our way in to the show. She got so nervous that she gave him the *what-fors* and a hard time that finally wore him out. He screamed *Never Again* and let our crowd in but we had to double up in the rear seats. Sis was burned out by the time we reached home but felt good when Mom said she had actually rested. She knew we were starving and told us to raid our victory garden until supper was ready.

The Department of Agriculture encouraged planting victory gardens to supplement produce absent from grocery shelves due

to the war. Free government seed packets motivated families to plant corn, tomatoes, lettuce, onions, carrots, radishes and beans—lots of beans. Dad made a "V" for Victory sign, painted it red, white and blue, and mounted it in our garden. Turning over the resistent yellow clay and planting seeds in all those rocks took faith, but by some miracle our garden produced. Skip did most of the cultivating but Dad set Sunday aside to work the garden as a family event—mainly to pull weeds.

Normally, Eileen was a late riser but awakened early on her birthday. She came down to the kitchen looking for something to eat, looked out the window and thought she was dreaming. Sure enough, there was a cow in our garden eating an ear of our corn. She ran through the house sounding the alarm, but no one believed it until Skip rushed out back and saw it too. He knew who owned the cow, ran all the way to the far side of the Homey, and pounded on Mr. Trontel's door. He had just come in from feeding his chickens and, on hearing Skip's frantic report, followed him back to our house and lured his cow out of our garden—corn and all—a cow of great worth to the Trontel's; it gave good milk.

We got our milk from Whiteside's, a family-operated dairy in Butler County. They delivered on our hill Monday, Wednesday, and Friday. Mr. Whiteside let us run up a bill month-to-month on Dad's promise to *rob Peter and pay Paul*, an excuse that earned extended credit, to a point. Mrs. Whiteside added a free bucket of lard to one of our orders, more than we needed, so Mom and Sis tried to make soap out of it to save money. It turned out to be a big laugh, a big mess, a big failure, a big waste of time, and a dangerous process to begin with.

A little danger seemed a thing Scott kids were occasionally lured towards, like the day Eileen got hold of the wooden matches. It was my birthday and Sis baked a cake. She set it aside for later, but Eileen saw where she put the candles and matches.

After supper, Eileen and I went outside to play and she asked if I ever saw a match burn twice. She struck a match on the side of the box and it ignited. She blew it out and, in the breeze, it re-ignited. She was thrilled that her experiment worked. She blew on it again and, thinking the flame was out, tossed the match aside and it landed on my good dress, which went up in flames.

DeeDee was on K.P. duty and saw from the kitchen window what she said looked like me going up in flames. She rushed to my aid with a wet towel, smothered the flames, carried me into the house, doused me with cold water, stripped me down, and set me on the table to assess my condition. She did all this with such calm that even though I was an emotional child, I didn't cry. She let me see myself in a mirror—singed hair, eyebrows, eye lashes—and I remained calm. Lucky for me, she had first-aid training. I said, *Thank you, Dee*, because she had turned fifteen and announced that she was no longer to be called DeeDee. She intended to pursue a career in nursing after highschool.

A few days ahead of St. Mary's re-opening, Dad took me and Eileen down to the main drag to buy new shoes. Wagner's in the Ninth Ward sold a better quality product but Book's next door sold more affordable shoes. There, we picked out brown tie oxfords with high hopes that they would hold up. Mom took us shopping for school clothes at the Goodwill down the block. We had a wonderful time rooting through bins and picking out pretty colors of clothes that fit. Mom, with Richie in tow, walked us to school on opening day. We felt well off in our outfits until we got to class and Sister Mary Cletus opened the windows against the moth ball fumes.

At this juncture, we could have used a session with Larry showing us the ropes, but he was an upperclassman in Sister Mary Wilhelmina's third grade. Sister Mary Cletus directed Eileen and me to share a double desk at the back of the room and Eileen objected, *What the heck do you mean first-grade side? I'm in second grade*. Sister was quite short but stood tall and calmly replied, *Eileen Scott, didn't anyone at home tell you you've been held back*? Eileen retorted, *What the heck would they tell me a thing like that for*? Sadly, she learned that she had to repeat first grade; she had missed too much school because of her bad heart. As far as I could tell, my sister had a good heart. She showed me the ropes and looked out for me when the visiting school nurse was in the building.

The Allegheny County Health Department required all city schools to participate in the visiting nurse's program. Miss Ruth Becker's office was on the second floor of our school. All students were given an annual physical. It came time for my first exam and Miss Becker told me to open my mouth and stick out my tongue. Eileen, in line behind me, watched attentively as Miss Becker held my tongue down with a wooden tongue depressor and looked down my throat with a flashlight. She examined my teeth and next up was Eileen; she refused to be examined. Miss Becker had previous experience with Eileen and simply wrote something down on a piece of note paper and told her to give it to Sister Cletus. Sister, in turn, told Eileen to tell our mother that Miss Becker would be taking me and Eileen by taxi to the Health Department's dental clinic the following morning. Eileen got off with a hygienic cleaning; I got two teeth pulled, a miserable experience.

It took some time for me to figure out what *the ropes* really meant—striving for the good, always upward, vertically, like climbing a rope. Mom and Dad taught us how to take care of our things and how to put up with things like pulled teeth. Eileen was presently in a fix. She did not appreciate the picture of Pope Pius the Twelfth hanging on the wall above Sister's desk. His swarthy look and haunting eyes gave her the creeps, and she told Sister, who seldom lost her patience, to take it down. Sister was forced to explain that no one held more power than the Pope except God and Father Kebe.

God's truth—Sister Cletus held the reigns. She introduced the class to the theology of the devil's work shop, a notion that the devil took advantage of the idle mind to perform his evil deeds. Both Eileen and I got the idea that if we let our minds wander from prayer and school work, the devil would gather his weapons and set up shop inside our heads the way Dad set up shop with his tools at Hubbard's, a notion that troubled us.

At home we asked Sis about this. She was as level-headed as she was intelligent and put us straight, explaining that the only time our minds could idle was if we were sleeping, but then our guardian angels took over. That night, Eileen and I knelt together at the side of the bed to say the night prayer we learned in school: *Now I lay me down to sleep. I pray the Lord my soul to keep. If I should die before I wake, I pray the Lord my soul to take.* Eileen was afraid to die and afraid of the dark. She would make me look under the bed to see what was under there. I'd look and say nothing was under there but dust balls, and she didn't believe me. Mom took her every word to heart and encouraged her to be brave.

Sis had taken on a posture of maturity and more of Mom's ways, especially when they worked together. She loved radio, didn't own one, couldn't afford to buy one, invested in a ten-cent raffle ticket, and won a Motorola table radio. She put it on the shelf above the kitchen sink and listened to hit tunes and the soaps to take her mind off household drudgery.

One afternoon, the banjo-strumming *Arthur Godfrey* show went into a loud commercial break: *Let Oxydol put the sparkle back in your clothes. Get rid of that tattle tale gray.* Sis looked out at what was drying on the clotheslines and hollered, *That's enough already, what do you know? Tattle tale, battle tale, we have it all.* She ignited the stove jets to heat more wash water in the cauldron and suddenly realized that it was pouring down rain. She scrambled to bring the laundry inside, tossed the tea towels on a rack above the stove and, while her back was turned, the towels caught fire. She opened the door to let out the smoke and hollered *help help* when she saw our neighbor, Mr. Chirico, arriving from his shift at Union Steel. He rushed to her aid, shoved the burning towels into the unlit oven, closed the oven door to smother the flames, and went home.

Sis was at school the day the washer took its next fit. Larry, Eileen, and I rushed home from school famished and lunch wasn't ready. Mom was in a panic with the washer rocking and the floor flooded. She struggled to bring the washer under control, crying out, *Christopher Columbus, Crime-a-nently Crime*—the worst cursing we had ever heard from her. She tugged the washer back into position to finish the cycle, placed a bucket under it to drain the water, then pushed the washer back into its corner, where it stood when not in use like a sentry at the cellar way door.

The cellar way was a place where we were not allowed to hang around—too dangerous. Dad had installed hooks to hang up the mop, broom and dust pan and had built shelves to store scrub brushes, scrub rags, scrub buckets, cleanser, bleach and laundry soap, name brands like *Clorox, Old Dutch, Oxydol,* and *Rinso,* and hand soaps like *Fels Naptha* and *Lifebouy.* A long string attached to a short chain turned on a light bulb above the top step so we could see what we were looking for in there. Ten narrow steps led into the bowels of the cellar, a spooky place made even spookier when Huey reminded me that the boogie man lived down there.

The last straw with the *Gain-a-Day* was upon us when, a few days later, wash water started leaking into its motor while Mom and Sis were washing clothes. They had put on their boots and worked frantically to get the load through the wringer before something blew up—and it did—a crackling sound and they started yelling at each other to be careful. Electricity was in the bucket under the washer. It was in the mop and on Sis's elbows, sparking and flashing and next thing she knew it spiked her hair. The more soaked she got the wilder the electrical storm in the kitchen became—until Mom did something smart; she pulled the plug.

That evening, Dad listened to the electrifying story of why supper was late and why piles of dirty laundry were still sitting on the floor. To calm everybody down, he offered his reliable line, *I'll buy a new washing machine when my ship comes in.* Sis bravely asked, *What ship, Dad*? She was busy at the sink when a large flap of wallpaper slid off the wall above the sink and slapped her in the face—no laughing matter. Moreover, the kitchen had absorbed so much moisture that a large section of plaster had to be replaced. Dad had to build a fire in the *Kalamazoo* to dry things out. It's oven door had cracked in two or we would have had Mom's homemade bread by then.

Sis was late for school a few days over that chaos. Once a week after school, she took a streetcar to the Strip District to buy *Tip-Top* day-old sliced bread for a nickel a loaf at *Ward's Bakery*. Dee and Anna shared this job. It was easier to buy bread than bake all day as family life was going. The wind was up the day Sis started up the 56th Street steps with two arm loads of bread, and the bags split wide open. She salvaged most of it and continued on home dreading that Mom might kill her because the bread got squashed in transit, but all that Mom had to say was, *We can make stuffing with it.* In school, Sis learned innovative ways to prepare meals with stale bread, like French toast with sautéed apple slices on the side and baked bread pudding with cinnamon and raisins. We marveled at her secret-recipe for rice pudding with nutmeg. She also managed our food coupon budget and the store list.

We were out of everything the day Mom gave Skip the last money she had in her purse, a ten dollar bill, and sent him to the A & P. An hour later, he came home empty handed—he had lost the ten dollars. She sent him back out to find it. He came home two hours later, dreadfully pale and shivering, to tell Mom the ten dollars was really lost. She sent him out a third time, saying not to come home until he found it. He retraced every footstep through the Homey to the A & P and returned home, tired, hungry, and scared to death. He just could not find the ten dollars. Sis felt so sorry for him and the whole sorry story that she said, *Forget about it, Skip, the Society for the Improvement of the Poor will give us more food.*

She liked to bake in the gas stove oven and had learned in school that pre-heating the oven increased her baking success, but each time she struck a wooden match to light it, it went BOOM. Skip showed her how to strike the match before turning on the gas jet, and she showed him how to make a good pie crust. Her culinary skills were becoming a vital family resource, but she held onto a dream of becoming a professional chef so that she would not meet the fate of girls who had to drop out of school to help out at home.

In the summer heat, Dad still expected a hot meal and seated himself at the head of the table. I was unsure about where I fit in or where to sit—*this seat, no, not that seat*—something that had been going on ever since I came home, although it was impossible to speak up about it at six years of age. Dad took the matter in hand, saying, *Patty, you sit by me. You're no orphan.* My brothers and sisters were honest-to-God not used to me being home. In disbelief, I watched them stake their claim to a seat at the table—a bit of a hungry mob scene with grace said at lightning speed. *Bless us oh Lord and these thy gifts which we are about to receive from thy bounty, through Christ our Lord, Amen!* It was an experience for me like seeing my family from outside the world and at other times seeing them from the inside looking out—one little girl living between two worlds.

Our meals were portioned sparingly to assure enough to go around. Mom served Dad first, and he started dousing his food with black pepper. Eileen raved, *No Dad, don't do that. Patty has asthma.* Pepper dust went up my nose and down my throat. Mom settled me down and served my plate, but I was not hungry. There and then, Dad dove into one of his dogmatic lectures, *Patty, you listen up. Don't be so proud. Be humble like me and learn to eat crow. Put a little salt and pepper on your food and it will go down easier.* I guess no one ate more crow than Dad did, but Iwas too naive for his speech; and when he said, *Stop playing with your supper and start eating or you'll be stuck in the house the rest of your life*, I cried. He finished his meal, and when he went to the living room to read the paper, Mom let me go outside to play; she understood that I was a poor eater; she ate little herself.

Dad found it necessary to take Sis aside and explain that she was needed at home. Actually, he came right out and told her that she'd have to quit school. She shook for three days over his dire proclamation before uttering a word. She understood that Mom was overwhelmed with stress and distress and that her health suffered, but still, Sis cried her heart out. She had hoped to graduate and pursue a career. Dad felt so bad for asking her to make such a sacrifice that he said he was sorry. Sis was greatly torn, but as it turned out, we kids were extremely grateful to have her at home. It comforted Mom on her bad days to have Sis there making sure that we looked nice going out to school and were bundled up when the weather turned cold.

The coal ration had ended, but the gasoline allotment was cut back forty percent. People who owned cars couldn't buy enough gas to drive to work. Bus and taxi services were curtailed, and our aging transit system couldn't handle the overflow of commuters crowding onto streetcars. There were mishaps, break downs, and trolley disasters. Scandal erupted when Cornelius Scully, in his second term as mayor, was arrested for violating the gasoline ration after driving to West Virginia, three hundred miles round trip, on a family vacation.

On top of all this, the city garbage collectors staged a strike. Twenty thousand tons of garbage accumulated during a twenty-day walkout. City Council had about enough of the rebellion and passed an ordinance transferring municipal garbage disposal to private contractors. Dad spoke sternly to our boys about keeping our back yard clean and hauling our garbage to the Homey dump as soon as our trash drums were full. Skip told him not to worry about the garbage; he and Huey would handle it. Huey was a sweet boy with an honest face, an honest heart, and a steady purpose in his eyes. He loaded trash into the wheelbarrow; Skip wheeled it to the dump to be burned and let his comrade carry the matches to keep him motivated.

Huey loved a good fire; it guaranteed no trace of our garbage and nothing left unburned for the rats to enjoy. It was not uncommon for conflagrations that charred the Homey Hill to be blamed on Huey, although he was nowhere in sight when those fires raged. Fire was still the worst threat to the city's survival even though the Pittsburgh Fire Department had modernized its fire-fighting equipment and fire fighters had radically improved fire-fighting techniques.

On our hill, brush fires were already out by the time the fire trucks got there because neighbors would pool their resources and put blazes out with brooms and garden hoses. False alarms were a nuisance with anonymous culprits setting them off.

The fire alarm on our hill was mounted to the telepole at the barricade corner. If it went off, a firetruck soon roared onto Duncan Street, and Huey was blamed even though he wasn't tall enough to reach the fire alarm, unless maybe Skip gave him a boost. No one would believe a story like that although Larry was usually around when the Homey caught fire; he loved firetrucks. The suspected arsonist could have been anyone!

It is known that when the Homey caught fire, the firetruck's siren and the smell of burning grass drove Huey upstairs and under the bed. In fact, he hung around the house so much that Mom encouraged him to spend more time outside, saying, *Go outside and play you house plant.* That made him so mad that he stomped his feet and left in protest, *I'm not a house plant, I am not. I'm a boy*! And BANG went the screen door.

Nothing felt more invigorating to Larry than being outdoors. Even when his ball team had no bat or glove, they played on our side lot and ran all the bases—nine full innings—which highly amused Dad. He called Larry *short stop* and sometimes *runt*, which really bothered him. One day, he complained about it to Mom. *Oh, my dear boy*, she said, *it's what's in his head and heart that makes a man.* That gave Larry ambition. He and his buddies built a shed at the far side of our lot with lumber borrowed off the city steps. They needed ten-penny nails, so Larry figured Chandek's tool shed was a safe place to swipe from because Dad would cover for him if he got caught. Maybe it was raw envy on Dad's part. Mr. C was a college graduate who made good wages as a high-girder man for American Bridge. Dad criticized his articulate style and opined that *he acts like an on-high and talks like he just swallowed a dictionary.* Anyhow, the stolen nails busted right through the shed's rotten wood, and the first big rain caved the whole thing in. Larry ended up rebuilding it single-handedly.

These were great days for me hanging out with Richie. He was two and a half years younger and inches taller than me.

He had been through a procedure similar to what Dee went through to correct weak eye muscles, first wearing a patch over one eye to strengthen the other and vice-versa before being fitted with round-wire glasses. They had to be the smallest pair ever made, and he was to wear them at all times. He seemed forever to loose them, and I wondered how he was supposed to find them if he couldn't see.

One morning on Dad's way out to work, Richie appeared sleepy-eyed in his underwear and said, *Wait up Dad.* It was the bond between them that made Dad close the kitchen door, pick Richie up and give him a big hug. Dad noticed that Richie was not wearing his glasses and asked where they were. Richie said he didn't know and Dad gave him an ultimatum: *Son, you better find those glasses before I get home or else.* Everybody in the house tried to help Richie find his glasses, and he fretted all day long. He couldn't tell time yet, but had an instinct for what time Dad would show up. The trick for Richie was how to get on Dad's good side before he went into an uproar.

Dad showed up right on time and found Richie parked at the back door, staring down at his bare feet, twirling his cowlick, and biting his fingernails. Dad observed his son's fretful stance and said, *Well, I guess you couldn't find your glasses, and I sure hope you do by the time you are old enough to go to school or you'll never learn how to read.* Richie said with the conviction of his soul, *Dad, I'll learn to read, I promise, even if I never find my glasses.* After supper, Richie thanked Dad for letting him go out and play. He couldn't find his socks but put on his shoes, and we took a walk over to the barricade near the Wall to look for smoothe, flat stones; they sailed the farthest over the hill.

Summer's end and the onset of an early winter was depressing for all of us, especially Larry. He came down with bronchitis, and Mom had to keep him home from school against his will. He had, like all the Scott kids, survived the childhood diseases—chicken pox, measles, mumps, and head lice, too. Keeping sick kids home was not Mom's favorite idea because they loved school. But Larry hated being stuck in the house.

He was easily bored, so he waited until Mom was resting on the couch and tip-toed down the cellar stairs to play on the coal pile. She felt a draft, got up to close the cellar door, and realized that he was down there. She hollered for him to come upstairs; it made him so mad that he slammed the cellar door, and the *King's Funeral Parlor* calendar fell off the nail holding it in place. Mom made him hang it back up and sent him to bed with a hot mustard plaster compress slapped on his chest and that really made him mad.

He got out of bed and under it found Dad's shoe shine kit and, in it, a tin of Kiwi Cordovan Shoe Paste, an applicator, and a polishing cloth. To wit: he polished every pair of shoes he could find, regardless of color. Being stuck in the house in cold weather got him imagining that he lived in sunny California. He loved any place warm because he was always cold. But once recovered, Joe bundled him up and took him for a sled ride in the Homey.

A letter from Vinny cheered us, one and all, but he was sorry to say that due to the war he would not be spending Christmas at home for the first time in his life. Us kids decorated the downstairs with red and green streamers and tinsel, and someone hung a bouquet of mistletoe in the kitchen doorway. Dad showed up late Christmas Eve with a caravan of drinking cronies and a tree too big to fit through the front door. His friends gave him a hand cutting it to size, and Larry held the door while they carried it in. He thought it was his tree because it was his birthday and helped them to set it upright in a tub filled with bricks. Dad's friends annoyed Mom, but Sis got a big kick out of their pseudonyms—better names than the *Three Stooges,* she said: the O'Malley brothers, Beans, Shoots and Jumps plus Doo Balls Astridge, Big Ed Kelly, Bad Eye Reese, Lard Ass Mullen, and Banana Nose Flynn—you get the idea. Funny thing, we never knew what else they called Dad, except Scotty. His friend Skinny-Bones Schmidty, who worked at Hubbard's and boarded at Besal's, gladly gave us a hand because he respected the Scotts.

Dad actually had a gift for decorating the tree once us kids were in bed. Proof of it came Christmas morning when we scampered downstairs to behold the splendor of our holiday tree. It dazzled with bright lights and ornaments hanging from every limb and dripping with meticulously hung icicles.

There was always a feeling of apprehension that Santa Claus might not have made it, but beneath the tree lay wrapped presents, one for each of us, except for Eileen and I who, that year, had to share a baby doll. (I always wondered where it disappeared to after its eyes went missing.) Larry was first to open his gift, a pair of ball-bearing roller skates from his godparents, Uncle Dick and Auntie O, a gift that had to serve as his birthday present as well. He may have been thinking he deserved two gifts, but when asked how he felt about it, he said, *Who's counting*?

Everybody anticipated the big snow of January 1944, and it just kept falling—dazzling white snow turned gray before it settled on Pittsburgh's productive earth. Our factories operated around the clock and recruited women to fill an urgent need for wartime positions. Sis was hired at the Spring Works on the site of Grandfather Quinn's old house on Butler Street. Mom and Dad weren't happy about her decision to work outside the home because she had a million things to do before work, then work on O-rings for bombers on the assembly line all day, and do another million things after work. By her reckoning, Sis worked three jobs.

Dee was doing most of the laundry by then, and Dad trusted no one more to iron his good shirts. The boys stood in line waiting for theirs hot off the ironing board—a bit of spoiling—but they learned how to iron their own shirts when she was unavailable. Saturday was house-cleaning day, time to *redd up*, as they say in Pittsburgh; that is, put everything in its place. In our cramped household, you couldn't just walk in and drop your stuff down someplace; it might not be there when you came back for it. With a measure of slack, we created a cozy *lived in* look, and Dad was satisfied as long as the house smelled nice. Once the washer was put away, Anna lugged the kitchen chairs to the dining room and scrubbed and waxed the kitchen floor on hands and knees, let it dry, and spread a layer of newspapers to protect it from foot traffic. On Sunday morning, she proudly removed the newspapers so the family could enjoy a spotless floor on the Lord's Day.

Anna and Dee cherished breaks from housework to play street games with their girlfriends. A favorite was jump rope and Dee was a champ. When it was her turn to jump, one girl would take one end of a long rope, Anna would take the other, and chant: *I like coffee, Dee likes tea, I like the boys and they like Dee.* They were learning to cook, Eileen and I to do the dishes. We bickered constantly over whose turn it was to wash or dry and put away mountains of dishes, pots, pans and tons of mismatched knives, forks, and spoons. We tried to work out our disagreements under our breath when Dad was around, but he had sonic hearing and regularly stormed into the kitchen to tell us to *pipe down, or else.* We were at that stage in life when his idle threats passed over us like the rush of water over Niagara Falls. Sis appreciated our efforts and rewarded us with an occasional trip to the Enright Theater in East Liberty, which we called *Sliberty*, for the Saturday morning live radio broadcast of the Amateur Hour, or the Sunday matinee at the Regent Theater to see Oscar award films.

Sis and her girlfriends attended the Dome's Tuesday Jackpot Night, and Mom didn't like that, even though Sis won free tickets for its Thursday Drama Night. The 1935 film *Mutiny on the Bounty* was showing and her girlfriends went gaga over Clark Gable. Sis wanted to tell Mom all about the movie, but when Sis said Franchot Tone was a better actor, well, that didn't go over. Mom let her know that she was concerned about slacking off on housework to accommodate her social life and offered a few words on the risks of late-night gallivanting. Sis burst into tears and said, *Geezmaneez Mom. Stop nagging about the housework. I'll get it done when I get to it.*

Mom told Vinny about it in one of her letters. He understood her reasons to fret but never questioned Sis because she had taken over a central role in the family. He had little room to dwell on things back home with the *USS Blue Ridge* leading an assault on Hollandia, New Guinea, a major Japanese base where huge forces were entrenched. Intense operations in that area, today part of Indonesia, were in preparation for MacArthur's *heroic return* to the Philippines. Eventually, Vinny wrote back asking Mom to try not to worry about him; he was concerned about her, too.

After some type of very personal surgery, Mom returned to the Lillian Rest Home. We kids felt doomed, but no one was sent to the orphanage this time because Sis took leave from the Spring Works to stand in at home. The weather warmed and Uncle Frank brought Mom home; we were all there lined up at the curb to greet her. She was wearing her good dress, the black crepe with a fancy white bodice. She appeared a bit feeble getting out of the car, slowed down by her heavy arms hugging her body swollen with water weight, and her oxfords tied loosely to accommodate her swollen feet. As one advancing towards an unchosen destiny, she shuffled her way up the sidewalk to the backyard and finally smiled at us kids. It was spring again!

St. Mary's second graders were in training to receive the sacrament of First Holy Communion. Eileen and I learned of our divine origins and the need to seek divine solutions to our problems. On the First Friday in May, we sought Sister in school to find a divine solution to our problem. We had no communion outfits or shoes and no money to pay for the accessories, because we had failed to sell our share of chance cards and raffle tickets. Sister put our troubled hearts at ease, giving us white leather purses, white-beaded rosaries, and gold bound white prayer books. She had discreetly borrowed communion dresses from a Parish family with older children in the school, beautiful lace dresses and veils, which we gratefully accepted. Dad took us down street to buy white buckle shoes; Mr. Zugell was truly sorry, but all he had left were black patent leathers. We didn't care; we were thrilled with our shiny-new shoes.

Sunday morning, our big day had us jittery. Mom, although she did not feel well, helped us into our communion outfits, fixed our hair, kissed us goodbye, and sent us on our way with Sis, Dee, and Anna for moral support. Eileen had concerns about how she would swallow the host. All the way down the road, she prayed incessantly, *Dear sweet Holy Jesus, precious Jesus, please don't let the host stick to the roof of my mouth.* I obsessed on how it was possible to consume Jesus in the form of not only a dove but a flame and a spirit, three persons residing in a tiny piece of bread, philosophical notions all too perplexing for a child to contemplate.

At church, we were taking our places in the processional lineup and were suddenly jolted into stark reality. All of the other girls' communion dresses were bright white and ours were faded yellow. They were wearing white patent leather shoes and ours were black—a disastrous emotional experience for two innocent first communicants—but we got through it in resiliently superb Scott family style, stoically proceeding down the aisle to kneel at the altar for Holy Mass. As it turned out, Eileen had nothing to fear. When it came time to receive the host, she swallowed it without incident, as did I.

That afternoon, we gathered blossoms growing along the neighbors' fences and returned to church that evening for the May Procession in honor of the Blessed Mother. Our Holy Communion class, led by altar boys holding lanterns, scattered blossoms down the center aisle, creating a floral path along which Father Kebe, dressed in a gold trimmed, white satin vestment, delivered the Holy Eucharist enclosed in a gold monstrance to its sacred place on the altar. He raised the censer, a bronze vessel of incense, which he ignited and stirred until the sanctuary was filled with perfumed smoke to keep demons away. The censer was swung three time in a series of blessings as the congregation chanted the *Asperges Me.* The ritual concluded with the crowning of the Blessed Mother's statue and the children singing a classic May hymn to the Virgin. Our First Holy Communion would remain for years to come a ritual to keep us inspired to listen to our conscience and walk uprightly and boldly.

Sister handed out final report cards, and students were not to open them until they got home. On the way up the city steps, Eileen said a prayer and opened hers. I asked what she got and she showed me, so I showed her mine. I must have said the wrong thing. She flew home and told Mom that I thought I was better than she. She gave Mom her report card, as did I. Mom sent Eileen upstairs to change clothes and sat down with me at the table. Kindly, she said, *Patty, you are never to share your report card with your sister again.* I didn't understand why, but it felt like the right thing to do. Later on, she talked to both of us, saying, *You are not to compare, you are both equal. Your father and I love all of our children exactly the same.* My sister and I never shared report cards again; we were growing up.

Thereafter came a persistent rap at our front door. Mom had just sat down to sew buttons on shirts. Sis rushed to the window and peered through the curtains to see a tall thin woman in a beige suit standing like a sentry on our front steps; she was holding a black briefcase in one hand and a black umbrella in the other. Mom asked who it was and Sis said she didn't know. Mom told her not to answer the door. The rapping persisted, and Mom asked Sis to send the woman away. Sis, sensing redemption near at hand, showed the woman into the living room, offered her a seat in Dad's chair, and invited her to make herself comfortable. Mom's grimace was profound, though there was no real cause for alarm.

We were regularly visited by representatives of agencies around town, some who helped and some who annoyed. The woman started to explain why she was there; she had become a volunteer to get out of the house as a cure for depression. She wanted to brighten up our lives and started asking questions like, *How many children do you have, Mrs. Scott*? Mom knew it was none of a perfect stranger's business and was on the verge of telling the woman to leave, but Sis carried a chair in from the dining room and sat down, as if on the brink, spellbound by the woman's every word.

Mom looked weighted and confounded by the deliberations being propounded. It soon became apparent that the woman was from the Allegheny County Birth Control League and Mom ordered her out. Sis cried, *Don't go dear lady. Mom doesn't mean it. Mom, please don't send her away. Listen to her. She knows what to do*! The woman stood up in chagrin, not knowing how to respond. She apologized for disturbing the family and went her way. Tears fell like diamonds on Sis's face. She begged Mom to call the woman back, a sobbing plea never heard as Mom fell into a dirge of her stress song: *Yelp us, oh yelp us. We need thy very help. The Lord he does know, He does know it all.*

June 6, 1944. D-Day. Seven hundred ships. Four thousand landing craft. A hundred thousand troops, American, English, Welsh, and Scot—a mighty allied force had survived the invasion, and ten thousand soldiers lay dead. The beaching of Normandy had begun at three o'clock in the morning U.S. East Coast Time. *The tide is turned*, said our Commander-in-Chief, President Roosevelt. *Free men of the world are marching together to victory*.

The Fighting Sullivans, a movie about five brothers who joined the Navy and were killed in action the same day on the same ship, was playing at the Dome and the whole town went to see it. Many good films were being produced with excellent casts portraying real men and women out in the trenches fighting for our country. War movies inspired the kids on our hill to stage more intensified war games in the Homey with many accidents and minor injuries. Huey got hit on the head with a gigantic earth sod, but Larry sustained a shot in the throat with an arrow and was rushed to the emergency room.

Eileen sustained a hole in her knee, a deep wound Mom stuffed with bread to stop the bleeding, but it was not because she was injured in battle. She was only watching the war games. What happened? Mom had given Anna a store list and a few dollars to go to the A & P and told her to find Eileen and take her with her. She found Eileen but forgot to hold her hand going through the Homey. Eileen tripped and fell on a sharp rock that gashed her knee. Anna took the brunt of Mom's anger for the accident and trembled until Eileen's bandages came off.

With school out for the summer, Eileen and I underwent surgery to remove our tonsils and were kept overnight at the hospital. Joe brought us home in a taxicab and a few hours later, Eileen hemorrhaged and was rushed back to the hospital for further treatment. Then Joe cut his hand on a piece of rusty metal at the J & L Steel mill on the Southside where he presently worked a summer job. He wiped the blood off with his shirt and kept on working. The next day he saw a red streak up his arm. He went to the J & L first aid station and the nurse cleaned up his wound and bandaged it. She took his temperature; he had a fever, a fever much higher than when he had scarlet fever in fourth grade. At the company hospital, he was treated with penicillin. The drug was a new release for treating infections, and Joe was one of the first patients in the city to receive it and be cured. How's that for Irish luck?

He was home the day I took a bad fall. Mom had started supper and I was hanging around just to be near her. She discovered there was no bread in the house and Dad had to have bread to dip in the stew gravy. She gave me a quarter to run to the store and said keep the change for candy. With pennies to spend, I sped across our side lot, tripped on the flapping sole of my shoe, and fell flat on my face, sustaining a gash in my nose from a broken beer bottle.

Joe heard my screams and carried me inside, stretched me out on the couch and, when Mom saw the big hole in my face, she fainted. Sis quickly revived Mom and applied pressure to my wound with a big towel to stop the bleeding—blood everywhere—and she was crying, *Oh my God* like it was the end of the world. Joe knew what to do. He wrapped me in a sheet, carried me down the city steps to Butler Street, intending to carry me all the way to St. Margaret's Hospital on 46th Street. A streetcar showed up and he got me to the emergency room to receive many stitches. It was enough already—a nasty scar and time to move on. Our dear mother and father could absolutely not wait for school to re-start.

First day back, Sister Mary Cletus took one good look at me and asked, *Patty Scott, what happened to you*? Father Kebe walked into the classroom, and as always, dressed appropriately in black cassock and Roman collar. Sister prompted us to stand and greet the pastor in our sing-songy chorus: *Good morning, Father*! He nodded approval, clasped his hands behind him, paced in front of Sister's desk and, with a yawn in his speech, said, *Good morning children, you may sit down now.*

He cleared his throat and began the customary quiz from the Baltimore Catechism: *Who made the world? God made the world. Who is God? God is the Creator of heaven and earth and of all things. Where is God? God is everywhere. Why did God make you? God made me to know Him, love Him, and serve Him in this world, and to be happy with Him in the next*....and so forth and so on.

He praised the class for our knowledge of the faith, then shifted his stance and emphasized our duty to obey our parents at home and Sister in school. He stepped up to the blackboard, pointed at a big crack down the middle of it, and explained that the crack was there to remind us of the importance of good deportment in school. To assure that we would not forget this, he directed us to take a closer look, saying that it was where a boy got his hard head cracked a few years ago. Terrified, I imagined any one of my brothers sustaining brain damage had they not complied. I came forward to examine the crack, a crack wider than the divide of the hemispheres pictured in the Catholic Geography Text Book. After school, Eileen and I raced home to spill out our concerns.

All grown up at eighteen, and so Irishly pretty, Sis listened attentively and said: *Oh no yins kids, don't ever believe that story. Father Kebe handed that same line to our class when I went to St. Mary's long time ago. That blackboard cracked the day it was installed and that smart priest must still be trying to get his money's worth out of the deal. He's just doing his job. It's tradition!*

The Church frowned on the pagan feast of Halloween but, every year in the fall, we prepared for the big trick-or-treat take. Our boys dressed as vagrants, covered with soot from the coal bin. They headed out into the light of a harvest moon, each with a pillow case slung over a shoulder. Mom crossed herself; her boys were on a mission. Her girls, dressed as peasants in long skirts and babushkas, were on our own mission and could hear in the distance our brothers chanting: *Noots Noots, Noots Noots.* The chant originated in the old world as a beggar's chant for a share of nuts from the harvest. In Italy, the chant took on a special meaning on All Hallows Eve, the evening before All Saints Day, when children in costumes paraded through the streets of Rome chanting for the release of souls from Purgatory.

In our times, people of diverse beliefs knew nothing about the ancient purgatory chant, but on our hallowed journey, we Scott kids chanted for treats in exchange for no tricks. It seemed everyone cooperated, except the old woman from Europe who lived in the house at the barricade corner and an old woman from Europe who lived alone in a house at the corner of Celadine Street and the upper incline of the 56th Street city steps.

Sis dressed in the tattered trench coat Dad wore to work in rainy weather and a babushka to disguise herself in order to supervise the little kids. It was my first Halloween trick-or-treat adventure. She never let go of my hand until we were safely back home with our sacks half full of oranges, apples, popcorn balls, and penny candy. The boys arrived way late, exhausted and exhilarated—their sacks weighty with the good stuff collected in rich neighborhoods—dried provisions to last half the winter. *Nice work kids*, Mom said.

It was considered inappropriate for older kids to go trick or treating, but Joe hoped to squeeze the last drop of fun out of the privilege. In his junior year at Connelly Trade, he was studying illustration and graphic design. He also studied classical dance as an extra-curricular under the direction of his physical education teacher, Frank Ekl, at his studio above the Garden Theater on the Northside. At home, he practiced ballet positions and danced for us. For Halloween, he wanted to be a swashbuckler in pantaloons brandishing a sword. He created a colorful coat from remnants of cloth that he sewed together with needle and thread. He applied black shoe polish to his eyebrows, a circle of red lipstick to his cheeks, and crowned himself with a black fez made out of cardboard. He slung a pillow case over his shoulder and danced out the door with his cardboard sword raised and his magical coat billowing in the wind. *Noots Noots*, he chanted, *Noots Noots.* Only he could have imagined the countless souls in purgatory being released into the glory of the universe.

He had planned ahead to do his bidding in the affluent community of Shadyside, well beyond the limits of Lawrenceville, and arrived home near midnight, sack brimming with high-end candy bars, and at the bottom of the sack, many coins—nickels, dimes, quarters, and several half dollars. Mom was impressed, and no one was more pleased than he to receive all that loot. That was the year he took a Charles Atlas course to show off his muscles and erected a horizontal bar in the back yard to keep the glory going. Dad was not impressed.

Mom's patience with Dad evaporated a night when our stabilizing force didn't come home for supper. She fretted over bills and war-time wages frozen, a predicament that had the labor force upset. She surmised that a union meeting may have held Dad up. The union had purchased an abandoned church near Hubbard's office building, a convenient walk from the shop, where they socialized and could get a load off their chests out of ear shot of *blue tails* and *stool pigeons*, as they called company spies. Dad's binges and lost wages were a deep concern for Mom in her letters to Vinny.

His letters home, though infrequent, spoke of how much he missed us and how sorry he was that he would not be home for Christmas, again. We learned that the *USS Blue Ridge* had successfully led assaults on Leyte Gulf, the Liugayan Gulf, and Bataan. That early November, his ship docked in Manila.

There, Vinny learned that he had been awarded a Navy bonus and arranged for a wire transfer of the full amount to Mrs. Rose Scott, 5614 Duncan Street, Pittsburgh, Pennsylvania, with a note suggesting that Mom should do a little personal shopping for herself. She hadn't given herself a day off in ages but went downtown in her old coat and came home in a trendy black wool Chesterfield coat and a fancy black hat. Dad, feeling a twinge of envy at number-one son's generosity, still complimented Mom on how she looked—like a million bucks. She made her feelings felt; she intended to buy us kids a new coat, one at a time.

Department store merchandise went on sale the day after Christmas. Mom took Skip shopping at Gimbel's downtown.

He had earned it. Once a week he dug dirt out of the corners of the hallway stairs and shined the stair pads, a job nobody else wanted, and he had done other chores to please her. All he had to wear that day was a rag coat, but he picked out a reversible corduroy trench coat; it fit perfectly. From there they went by streetcar to visit Aunt Mary and Uncle Bill on the Northside, where they were served a delicious meal.

A stone's throw from the apartment was the Western Avenue Bird Sanctuary. Skip could not believe all the birds of every color flying from tree to tree chirping so beautifully in such cold weather.

There seemed no reason to be anywhere else, but it was time to go home. Aunt Mary sensed this and, on the way to the streetcar stop, made a detour to the Northside Market House, where she bought a dozen doughnuts to send her sister and nephew on their way with best wishes to the Scotts for the New Year.

1945

The day after New Year's, Dad absent-mindedly left for work without gloves and boots. Way late for supper, Mom put us on detail, two at a time, keeping watch at the front window. We wiped circles in the steam to look out into the darkness—still no Dad. The beak-billed weather bureau cartoon mascot for the *Pittsburgh Press*, adequately named *Donnie Dingbat*, had reported clearing weather. It snowed fifteen inches that day. Radio programs were interrupted with reports that streetcars, taxis, and automobiles were stranded, and commuters were trying to make it home on foot, except for those who could afford to stay at the downtown hotels, which were filled.

To our relief, Dad arrived around ten that night with a shopping bag full of groceries; he was covered with snow and singing the one tune he knew in a jovial tone. He had gone to the store after work because he knew we might be stuck in the house and out of food for a few days and was sorry it took so long; he had stopped at Neid's on the way home.

The storm reminded him of the good old days delivering messages for Postal Telegraph in snow drifts and food shopping for his mother. It was freezing then, too. Sis gave Dad a hand unwrapping and served up one of his favorite suppers—beef stew. He could tell by Mom's expression that she was grateful he had made it home in once piece. She was sitting beside the coal stove with her feet up and with Richie sound asleep in her lap. He had been waiting up for Dad to tell him he wore his glasses all day and was learning to read.

On February 8, 1945, Eileen and I went to school feeling confident that Sister Mary Cletus would forgive us for being late. There, we found Sister Mary Amatore, the convent housekeeper, delivering the terrible news that Sister Cletus would not be teaching school. She had died in her sleep and was taken by God. We never knew Sister had terminal illness. Maybe she didn't know it either; she worked so hard. It was impossible to imagine a dead nun, let alone one as immortal as Sister Cletus. She had seemed youthful compared to Sister Amatore, who had taught parochial school for over fifty years, only to be pulled out of retirement to teach a frantic first and second grade class. Parish women stepped in to assist at the convent, cooking and cleaning so that Sister Amatore could focus her attention and energy on the children in school. The body of Sister Cletus was to be laid out at the Sisters of Notre Dame Motherhouse on Troy Hill.

Eileen and I wanted to pay our respects and Mom wouldn't let us go. She said it was too far and too dangerous for two little girls to be walking in snow and ice all the way to the Strip District, crossing over the 31st Street Bridge, and then climbing steep Rialto Street, known as Pig Alley, to get to Troy Hill. Furthermore, our boots were no good. We were consoled to be singing with the congregation of St. Mary's at the funeral mass. The Parish grieved the loss of a wonderful woman who died at age fifty-six after serving the Catholic Church for over forty years. No one would ever or could ever fill the shoes of Sister Mary Cletus. People who loved her shed tears of sorrow, saying, *Let us never forget her.* The Parish mourned all through the forty days of Lent, and at last we entered into the high holy days of our beautiful religion.

On Holy Saturday, Dad dressed up to go downtown on his traditional Easter shopping spree. He gave Mom a peck on the cheek and told her he'd be back in a couple of hours, unless a good movie was showing. With his great brain, he trumped up ways to motivate us to clean the house while he was out. He admonished us to have our chores done when he returned or the Easter Bunny might not make it. Everyone had an assignment, and we put our hearts into doing a good job in anticipation of the goodies Dad would surely bring home.

He arrived carrying many bags and set them down to inspect our work. He saw flaws like swirls of dust on furniture tops and smears on the windows, but Mom told him how hard we worked. We sighed with relief when he said the house looked beautiful. After supper, he took the box of last year's Easter grass down from the closet and set up his traditional nest on the dining room buffet. We were not to touch it, and as Eileen put it, we had to keep up our hope and wait for Jesus to come out of the grave so the Easter bunny could pass the candy around.

Easter Sunday morning 1945, the chaplain aboard *USS Blue Ridge* was saying Mass when General Quarters sounded: *Gentlemen, tend to your duties; I will stay here and tend to mine.* The ship had been hit by a *Kami Kazé*. Among the casualties was Vinny's buddy, Johnny Shibble of McKees Rocks. The ship sailed to Pearl Harbor for repairs, where Vinny ran into one of his friends from our hill, Connie Kogovsek—you can bet they missed home!

Unexpectedly, on April 12, 1945, President Roosevelt died at the Little White House, his vacation retreat in Warm Springs, Georgia. He had been working at a card table for a few hours, dipping his gold-tipped fountain pen into indelible ink and signing official documents. He had complained of a terrific headache and then collapsed, never to regain consciousness. The Nation mourned the enormous loss of its beloved leader, lowered flags to half mast, suspended commerce, and the government and schools closed.

Vice President Harry S. Truman was hastily sworn into office. People said he looked dreadful and dazed when he placed one hand on the Bible and raised the other. His sharp features revealed shock at being swept into the overwhelming duties of the presidency, and feeling so completely unprepared, he prayed he would measure up to the task. Afterwards, he spoke to the Nation over the airwaves and everyone tuned in:

I will serve this high office to the best of my ability. I am a common, everyday man. With humility, I call upon all Americans to help me keep our Nation united in defense of the ideals so eloquently proclaimed by Franklin Roosevelt. I shall not shirk my duty. Our goal in this horrible war is unconditional surrender.

On April 25, 1945, Berlin fell. Hitler had fought his insane war to the bitter end. His fanatical fantasies had been shattered by news of the desertions of his top officers. In his bunker beneath the chancery he and his bride, Eva Braun, ended their lives. On May 8, 1945, V-E Day, the war in Europe ended. German high command signed an unconditional surrender in a schoolhouse at Reims, headquarters of General Dwight Eisenhower, Supreme Commander of the Allied Forces. Prime Minister Churchill broadcasted the news to the largest radio audience in the history of the world, saying, *I only wish President Roosevelt had lived to see it. We have victory but we're only half won. We call upon Japan to surrender and we promise that the Japanese will not be exterminated or enslaved.*

In downtown Pittsburgh, Pennsylvania, a hundred thousand people turned out for a ticker tape parade to celebrate victory in Europe, V-E Day. Sixty-four enlisted officers from western Pennsylvania who had returned home highly decorated led the parade. Next day, President Truman flew to San Francisco for the signing of the U.N. Charter. A million people turned out to cheer him. Americans were expressing confidence in our new leader with high hopes that our Pacific operations would succeed and our boys would come home.

Our hillsides burgeoned with pastel blooms, a sight glorified by the leafing of the stately poplar trees that lined St. Mary's convent property on 57th Street. The sidewalk was covered with worm-like buds that dropped from the trees by the millions when the leaves opened. On our way to Mass that Monday morning, we had to tramp through an inch-deep mess and peel sticky crusts off the soles of our shoes before entering the church. After Mass, Father Kebe invited the student body to be seated for a few moments before we proceeded to the school. He usually did this to announce good news, such as the date for the school's annual picnic at West View Amusement Park.

That morning, our pastor delivered horrifying news that death camps had been discovered in Europe and that Pope Pius the Twelfth had instructed the faithful to pray for the dead, the dying, and the persecuted. At home, we listened to horrific stories on the radio. Men, women, and children of Jewish faith had been executed in gas chambers. Edward R. Murrow, an overseas CBS broadcasting journalist, had walked into a death camp and was describing the appalling tragedy live over the airwaves. The whole world would soon learn of the Holocaust.

Sis still worked at the Spring Works, making hardly any money. She had heard about a better-paying job in East Liberty and applied. At Wiggins Welding Company, she was trained to do spot welding, a position she filled to replace a man drafted into the army, although she was not invited to join the union—no women allowed. The guys she worked with called her *Rosie the Riveter*. She was a good sport, kept her nose clean, did her job, and on breaks joined co-workers for a smoke—Lucky Strikes, acquired on the black market. She knew that Mom didn't go for her cigarette smoking. It was bad enough that Dad inhaled three packs of Camels a day. Sis had to figure a way out of upsetting Mom.

After work, she'd stop at the East Liberty A & P and spend her own money on groceries. If she got home late, Mom had her supper plate waiting, but it was not like they were communicating well. Sis worried about Mom's next verdict on her social life. She thought she had earned the privilege of doing whatever she wanted to do because she was paying her way. Mom thought she was spending too much time with friends and wished she'd stay home more, but Sis needed her friends. Though she was always proper, her trustworthiness and classic wit made her a very popular girl.

Sis wished she didn't have to get up early on Saturday to do housework when she came home late on Fridays, her roller skating night, and wanted to sleep in. On one of these occasions, Mom tried to rouse her and she resisted. Mom took off her shoe and aimed it. Sis couldn't believe she'd throw it and boldly announced, *I'll do the housework on Sunday. I don't even care if servile work is a mortal sin; it's a dumb rule.* Mom's shoe just missed. A new annoyance surfaced when Sis and Joe started going to the Saturday night polka dances at the Slovenian Hall—the *Slovenski Dom*.

The baroque, three-level brick structure was erected at the start of the 20th Century to serve the civic and social needs of the Slovenian community settling in western Pennsylvania. The auditorium on the top floor of the hall accommodated political rallies, holiday parties, live shows, a movie theater, and the dance hall. The first floor served private parties and business meetings, and the basement housed a bowling alley and lounge. The hall was a popular hub for socializing—a great place to congregate just to get out of the house for a while.

When he could, Joe stayed out all day to avoid housework, even crawling out the cellar window sometimes to avoid unwelcome encounters over his share of responsibility. On a night when he walked in the house after midnight thinking he was in the clear, he discovered a sink full of dirty dishes and a note from Dad to do them. Tired and frustrated, Joe started swearing under his breath.

Mom heard it from the other room and asked what was wrong. *Mom*, he said, *I can't clean up this mess. I can't put my hands in dirty dish water. I'm an artist. Someday my hands will be worth a million dollars.* She grabbed a wet dish rag, slapped him across the face with it, and said, *If you are going to be so smug and proud, I don't want anything to do with you*. He was never so humiliated in his life, but her admonition opened his eyes to the stark reality that he had been preoccupied with everything else going on in his life.

Between school and work, he invested time at the Carnegie Museum and Library in Oakland, took voice lessons downtown and dance lessons on the Northside. Dad did not understand or appreciate his passion for the arts and said so. This saddened Joe but, undaunted, he devoted free nights to cleaning the kitchen after supper, entertaining us girls with *do re me fa so la ti do* up and down the scales in his high-tenor voice with his million-dollars hands submerged in dirty dishwater, then drying all those pots and pans to the Donkey Serenade. At one point, Dad charged into the kitchen declaring he was in no mood for opera racket with a war going on. Joe's eyes lit up and he did a dervish twirl right in front of Dad. *Hmmmph*, said Dad. It was obvious he had reservations yet to be defined.

Nothing like a surprise visit from Vinny to lighten things up. The Navy sent him home on a classified assignment at Carnegie Tech involving radar and coding components. Mom nearly fainted when he walked in donned in full Navy Blues. We celebrated, meaning the dining room table was expanded to accommodate mother, father, and eleven children, all of us together for the first time in ages, all squeezed in to share the joy of our eldest and his homemade cooking. Mission accomplished, Vinny headed back to high seas; a stroke of Irish luck might have kept him with us a bit longer.

August 6, 1945. Mom turned forty-four years old. On her mind, along with a million other things, was the exact whereabouts of her Navy boy. She prayed for his safety, wondering what detail he might be working and where he might be—almost anywhere and in grave danger. It was on that day that news came blaring over the radio that the United States had dropped an atomic bomb on Hiroshima, Japan, causing total destruction and killing eighty thousand people instantly. Truman went on the air, begging the Japanese people to leave all industrial zones immediately. Three days later a plutonium bomb was dropped on Nagasaki, killing seventy thousand more people. Emperor Hirohito had no choice; he told his Supreme Council to bear the unbearable and surrender. He already knew that Truman would rebuild Japan as he was rebuilding Europe—a compassionate gesture considering we were the world class United States of America and that it was expected of us.

It was a few days afterwards that Mom took me by the hand and we went for a walk; she was still very upset over the atomic bombings. She looked so sad, but so beautiful with her thick dark hair blowing in the wind. We circled the hill and came home. The bucket she used to bail water was sitting in the yard.

She located the shovel Skip used in our garden and filled the bucket with dirt. She murmured something to the effect that we needed to share our dirt with Japan because they didn't have enough dirt to plant a garden. I don't remember what she did with that dirt. She was just not herself, that's all.

V-J Day—August 14, 1945—victory in Japan. Everywhere bells tolled, whistles blew, and across America millions poured into the streets in a carnival spirit. Paper debris swirled through the air and covered the landscape. People flocked to churches, mosques, and synagogues to thank the Almighty that the war was over.

In the mid-August heat, Pittsburghers held their biggest parade in memory amid joyful screams, horn honking, beer drinking, and plenty of horsing around. On our hill, the neighbors organized a block party, with plenty to go around of European cuisine, Mr. Radanovich's home-brewed beer, and Mr. Balkovec's home-fermented wine. In a festive mood, we gravitated to the barricade corner to watch hundreds of balloons sailing high above the city's smokestacks and tree tops and then floating away, a celebration that lasted well into the night.

Next morning, Mom shuffled Eileen and me off to Fresh Air Camp in Mars, Pennsylvania. By my lights, it might as well have been the planet Mars. The summer camp operated from June until the end of August. The last two weeks were reserved for the less fortunate sponsored by the Red Feather Chest. Huey and Larry had pre-warned us to look out for snakes under the beds and good luck sleeping on the stinky peed mattresses. Mom kissed us goodbye and told us to be good.

Once on the road, Eileen said that Mom sent us to camp to get rid of us, but I said no, she had told us to have a good time and not worry. Worry my eye! All the way to camp, Eileen complained that it was too hot on the bus. She kept getting out of her seat to ask the driver how much longer, were we there yet, and what country was he driving us to? Mars was a long way off as our universe went, but I loved every minute of that bus ride into the splendid countryside.

The campsite was lovely; its cozy white cabins with green shutters warmed the landscape. Leave it to Eileen to have a meltdown when we were assigned to different cabins. There, our counselors taught us how to make our beds military style—sheets tightly tucked and corners squared. At breakfast in the dining hall next morning, my dear sister loudly propounded on the absurdity of making a bed that way because at home the sheets didn't even fit the mattresses. Oh how she wailed—sleeping on a hard cot freezing under a thin blanket with snakes under her bed. I didn't understand what she was talking about; I had the best night's sleep in a long time.

Right off, she told every girl in the food line that she was starving and that our mother would never torment us like that. We were served buttered toast, scrambled eggs, and orange juice, which I thought was delicious, but not Eileen. She complained that her food was cold and didn't taste right. It was beyond me why she asked for seconds, only to feel rebuked when she was told *no seconds*. After breakfast, we were marched around the camp for exercise before being let loose on the playground. Eileen wound up with blisters and landed in First Aid. That was day one, and for all concerns, she admitted she had a good time. Two stimulating weeks of fresh air out in the country flew by.

We hiked, played games, roasted marshmallows, sang songs around a camp fire, and came home with head lice—a small price to pay for a terrific childhood experience—but no money in the house to buy soothing blue ointment at the drug store. Mom sent Skip to the gas station for kerosene. She massaged it into our hair and tied rags around our heads, stink rags. Our scalps burned, our eyes burned. Dad arrived in a boisterous mood and said he could hear our wailing all the way down at the wall. He didn't want to hear any sob stories and told us to be thankful for a free vacation.

I was Mom's first volunteer to climb on a chair at the kitchen sink and have my hair washed with Octagon soap and rinsed with Heinz white vinegar. Eileen next and the fumes went up her nose and in her eyes. Dad told her to stop screaming, but she couldn't help it. Her beautiful blonde curls had to be cut because of all the knots. Mom was sorry, but it wasn't the only problem disturbing her weary mind. Vinny was still out there somewhere in the Pacific.

September 2, 1945, Japan signed an unconditional surrender and *USS Blue Ridge* sailed from Okinawa to the Port of Tsingtao, China, on leave. Vinny said it was a fascinating place and that the Chinese people treated our American servicemen with dignity; his Navy wages were still keeping our rent paid. Ten days later, a hundred eight million American working women were handed pink slips and dismissed from their wartime production jobs. Sis was laid off but Dad's job was spared for the time being, and we kids were back in school.

Larry joined the Pittsburgh Newsboys delivering the *Post-Gazette*, beginning in a blue-collar neighborhood on Camelia Street and ending in the white-collar neighborhood of Stanton Heights. The middle class felt about right to him, and sometimes he wished he lived there. His route tracked through the golf course to the Randolph Estate, then zigzagged through McCandless Avenue and back to Camelia Street.

When winter came, he pretty near froze, and it dawned on him why Mom didn't want him going out in the cold because it affected his health. His last stop was John Coco the Shoemaker's shop, where he warmed up by the coal stove and Mr. Coco gave him a hot chocolate drink for a free paper. Larry was far from home at seven-thirty a.m. and barely made it to school on time.

The district supervisor, Mr. Gill, came to the house to pick up customer collections and pay Larry his share of the profits. Larry recounted his earnings and came up short. Guided by gut instinct, something didn't feel right. Honesty meant everything to him, and he had to work up the nerve to speak up: *Mr. Gill, you cheated me.* Mr. Gill was getting up in years; it was an honest mistake. In school, Larry told Sister all about it. Her charge to him was this: *God will give you only the trials you are able to bear.* He was, after all, a popular newsboy, and his route kept expanding.

The experience inspired him to get a second job, taking over Rudy Zupancich's piece of the lucrative Butler Street paper route. The Sunday paper weighed a ton and had to be delivered Saturday night, using a wagon or sled depending on the time of year—three or four hours of hard work for fifty cents. Next he landed the Union Steel route handed down in the family and about thirty houses near the mill, good money that caused him to be hours late for supper on a regular basis. Papers sold for four cents. The guard at the gate, a tall Italian fellow named Krist who smoked Cuban cigars, made the men pay a nickel, leaving a penny change for Larry. This meant money to go to the show and hog up on Black Jack chewing gum, candy cigarettes, penny candy, and nickel packs of Juicy Fruits. He loved candy and said it ruined his teeth but the Navy would later save his teeth. He confessed that the paper routes exhausted him and that sometimes he was too tired to eat a re-heated supper or do his homework, but no one ever took it away from him—Larry knew the ropes, on the job, in school and in church.

One Sunday after church, Sis made a rare exception and took Larry to see his godparents in Aspinwall at their request. Uncle Dick played deck cards and Chinese checkers with Larry while Sis gave Aunt Olivia a hand in the kitchen. At dinner, there was so much food, and Auntie O kept saying *have more.* They tried to tell her that they were stuffed, but she was trying to fatten them up.

It was time to go home, and they said *thank you.* On the way to the streetcar stop, Larry sat down on the curb with a bellyache, threw up in the street, and slept on the streetcar. Sis said over and over, *Never again, never again.* Larry knew he'd be going back. His godmother was fond of him and said so. Even with her odd disposition, she dug his jokes. She always admonished him to get good grades so he'd get a good job when he was older. Homework gave him a hard time, he confessed. He thought Sister Mary Theolinda gave out too much of it and didn't do it; his excuse—the newspaper business.

In third grade, Eileen and I went into the school's fund-raising business. We were not sure how to go about it and got so discouraged that Anna stepped in; she wanted us to succeed. She had been seeing to our needs forever and taught us how to take care of ourselves. She loved combing our hair and always told us how beautiful we looked. We came to a house on Camelia Street where a lady screamed at us for knocking on her door. We ran so fast that I took a fall on a cinder path and limped to school the next day with hopes dashed of seeing a star next to my name on the bulletin board.

In a sullen mood, I complained to a new boy in class who sat behind me that at our house we ate Campbell's soup for lunch and I didn't like it. What else could he do but pull my pigtails and invite me to lunch at his house? The Burkharts lived in the tall square house at the intersection of Christopher Street and the 57th Street city steps. Mrs. Burkhart wasn't sure why I was there but was kind; she served hard boiled eggs with buttered toast and hot chocolate. I thought that her home was a palace, three floors of large, high-ceilinged rooms, one room per floor—the opened concept. I wished I could live there.

Mom sent Anna out to find me, and she knew where to look. At the bottom landing of the city steps, she started calling for me, loudly. I heard and, feeling guilty, tried to ignore her, but Billy's mother said I better go home, that my mother was probably worried about me. I suddenly felt a rush of fear but responded like I'd been dining out all my life and took time finishing my hot chocolate. Covered with toast crumbs and my face smeared with chocolate, I emerged from the scene of my crime and fell into Anna's worried embrace. *Don't cry, little sister, don't cry*, she kept saying on the way home, *I wish I could have lunch with that family, I hate canned soup and hate boiled oats even more. I dump that stuff down the sink drain; I'm an expert at it, but don't tell Mom.*

Out of nowhere came my dear mother, pounding on my head with her fists, tears pouring down. *Don't you ever run away again. You'll eat our soup like everyone else. Who do you think you are?* She pounded a few more times for good measure and I couldn't believe she had hit me. I never saw her strike anyone and didn't even believe she was capable of mortal sin, but the sting of humiliation taught me to never do *that* again. It was not a sad time for me. The war was over and Vinny would be home in no time.

In November, David L. Lawrence was elected Mayor of Pittsburgh. After years of being tried for political impropriety and cleared, the brilliant and feisty Irishman said he felt humbled by the victory; he had good lawyers. The Irish had been in leadership roles in city politics ever since the days when our Scott-O'Donnell and Quinn-Grant ancestors of Ireland settled here. Their offspring were now among its business professionals, educators, doctors, and lawyers. Second and third generations of European descent did not want to spend their lives in the mills. They were completing their education, moving up in the ranks, and entering politics. Cornelius B. Scully, in his last official act as Mayor, signed an ordinance setting the highest real estate levy in our history.

U.S. post-war industrial manufacturing came to an almost abrupt halt. Hubbard's laid off half its work force, Dad among them, and our landlord raised the rent from twenty to thirty dollars. Dad got so mad that he went out and got drunk. Days later, Mom notified Uncle Frank of a family emergency—nothing new to him, and he knew where to look. There had been times when he had to lift Dad's pay envelope before it evaporated on a binge. This time, he found Dad slumped over the bar at Neid's and took him home to sober up. Dad was called back to work right before Thanksgiving and the union gave us a free turkey, already plucked and cleaned, thank God.

Mom could not hide her dire straits. She was without the luxury of a nervous breakdown or time to rest up, and she was always trying to get warm. Anytime she covered up under blankets on the living room couch, she invited me and Eileen and Richie to squeeze in with her. Presently, she was on and off the couch, leaning against the coal stove trying to assuage a foreboding pain in her side. Her body had taken on a form that both awed and frightened us. The word *pregnant* had never been uttered in our house, and it was difficult to understand what made Mom so ill. All that I could figure out was that God created Adam and Eve, the stork delivered babies, and Uncle Frank showed up in time for something or other.

Early on the second day of December 1945, Mom was shuffling from room to room, talking to herself, arranging one last thing here and clearing one last thing there. Dad attended to her intermittent needs, fueled the coal stoves, and announced that there was a pot of hot oats on the kitchen stove, that Sis was in charge, and that Mom was going to the hospital to get her sprained ankle fixed.

With no blizzard to impede progress, Uncle Frank arrived and heard Dad's remark. In an unfamiliarly harsh tone, he told Dad to wise up and tell us the truth—our mother was going to the hospital to have a baby. We must have looked stunned until Huey burst into laughter, saying, *Yeah Dad, I remember the last time you handed us that line and we got Richie*!

All that day, the established routine prevailed with everybody pitching in. Sis kept the kitchen warm and inviting with mouth-watering aromas wafting through the house. That night, she brewed tea with honey and lemon and let us hang out in the kitchen—waiting and waiting. The very second Dad showed up, we assailed him with anxious questions, and he responded, *Your baby sister is cute as a button. Martha is the spitting image of your mother and has the glory of Ireland written all over her face.* He began singing off-key his merry old tune about eighteen long years living in a flat and abruptly shifted to an announcement: *Yins kids listen up. I have a new lucky number; it's lucky number twelve*! And he wasn't even drunk. Of one thing we were certain, Divine Providence had come through, and our new baby had made it into the world safe and sound.

Dad noticed that the wood and coal bushels were filled and thanked the boys. He noticed the supper dishes done and the kitchen floor clean and thanked the girls. He removed his tossle cap and its under-wrapping, the upper-half of an old nylon stocking that kept his head warm, and hung everything on hooks in the cellar way. He sat down to take off his boots, and with his breathing labored, announced that he wasn't a spring chicken anymore; he was forty-three years old.

We were at the height of our Christmas excitement when Mom and the baby came home. It was the longest hospital stay of Mom's life so far. She looked so pale and fragile. She held Martha close but barely had the strength to smile and say hello. She went straight to the living room, sat down on the couch, and asked Sis to take the baby.

Sis was used to Mom's get-to-the point directs, but when she said a second time *take the baby*, Sis started shaking and said, *Mom, I can't take the baby. Who needs a baby with all this*? Sis was thinking of Vinny and Joe and Dee and Skip and Anna and Huey and Larry and Eileen and me and Richie. Mom understood and knew what to do. She lifted the bunting away from Martha's wee face and told Sis to come see. Our newborn sister opened her eyes and smiled and stretched and yawned, as though her sixth sense knew to put on a little Irish performance to win Sis over. Well, that did it.

Sis took Martha into her arms and said, *Mum, I don't even know what to do with her. She doesn't even have a bed to sleep in.* With everyone in a state of wonder over Martha's arrival and with no bed prepared for her, Joe pulled the bottom drawer out of the dining room buffet, dumped its contents, set the drawer on the dining room table, and said, *Here Sis, here's a baby bed, put Martha in here*! While Richie hopped up on a chair to investigate, I scurried upstairs, grabbed my pillow, and gave it to Joe. He fluffed it up, tucked it into the drawer, and Sis bedded our baby down. Baby Jesus in the Manger could not have received more love than the love we felt for Martha.

In the excitement, Mom started coughing, a rattling cough. Dad threw a blanket over her but she couldn't get warm. He threw a few more lumps of coal into the stove and slid the mahogany door between the dining and living rooms closed, telling us kids to try to keep it down. Shortly, he came out to check on Martha; she was sleeping soundly under the bright light of the chandelier, the prettiest baby we had ever seen. Dad glowed with pride and smiled, then dished out the usual orders about who was to do what and when and instructed Sis: *As soon as the baby stirs, give her to Mom.*

He went to the cellarway and grabbed his coat, saying he had the *heebie-jeebies* and was going out for a while. We thought we knew what that meant, but this time he wasn't gone long. He returned with groceries, merrily announcing that kids were cheaper by the dozen. Hard to argue that line. He had been present for every one of our births, so why wouldn't twelve be his lucky number?

He had to work on Christmas Eve and brought the tree in at the eleventh hour and a half. We kids had gone to bed wondering if there would be presents under the tree come morning. We expected little, having already received the gift far greater than anything imagined, the gift of Martha. As it turned out, Santa came through with gifts for one and all, including a bassinet for Martha, thanks to the relatives!

Lawrenceville's stores did a brisk business that 1945 holiday season in spite of factory layoffs. Jewish proprietors who owned grocery stores, drug stores, clothing stores, and novelty shops had put their trusted Catholic clerks in charge during the Hanukkah and Sabbath Days so the Christians could get their shopping done. Irish, English, Polish, Russian, Croatian, Serbian, Czech, German, Slovakian, and Slovenian proprietors had stocked their bakery shops, butcher shops, and provision stores and had catered in a true holiday spirit to the diverse culinary tastes of the locals.

Ours was a culture of diverse peoples of mixed origins, a happy sort not so poor as to have had the joy of life ground out of them and never with sufficient affluence to give up the struggle. People lived payday to payday and bought their groceries before anything else got paid.

Dad spent his pin money to take us shopping, but shopping with Dad was not expensive, it was priceless. He took us window shopping on Butler Street and let us warm up in the toy department of Autenreith's Five and Ten sales basement. With few coins to spare, he always let us select a nickel or dime item and never took us home empty handed; he was no cheapskate and made no excuses, except to remind us that he would buy us more expensive stuff when his ship came in.

Vinny's ship out in the Pacific was two days at sea, heading for Japan, when it engaged a typhoon in one hundred-thirty-five-mile-an-hour winds—his fifth typhoon in two years. All that while, he was mentally preparing for his last critical months of Navy service before discharge. Imagine his gratitude when the *USS Blue Ridge* reached Port Naha, Japan in gorgeous weather. There, a message came in from the *USS Tolland* which was docked there; it would be leading a convoy carrying critical materials and needed a tinker mechanic. By an act of fate, Vinny found himself promoted to petty officer rank and aboard that ship on its way to Seattle to pick up radar and communications supplies—a shock to the system, from the tropics to the frostics.

1946

A bitter cold January morning. Dad stuffed a jumbo baloney sandwich in his overcoat pocket, gave Mom a peck on the cheek, and headed out. In the yard, he encountered dagger-like icicles dangling precariously from the alcove overhang. He went to the cellar to get the ax, cussing in his frustrated way when problems arose. It took many swings to knock the icicles loose—a sound like thunder when they crashed to the ground. He put the ax away, grumbling that he'd be docked when he punched the time clock at the shop; he'd lose a half hour's wages for being late.

Mom herself was not in the best of moods but made sure everyone went out bundled up. Eileen and I put on our blue wool coats and flowered babushkas—cotton print head squares we wore folded on an angle and tied under our chins. Joe followed us out the door, but Mom held him up, asking if he had time to build a fire in the upstairs coal stove. She had work to do up there and wanted it warm for Martha and Richie. Joe did as told and continued on his way. Suddenly, there appeared many birds, mostly starlings, he thought. They swept down over the snow and landed on the fence. He beckoned Mom to come see.

She peered out and heard the birds chirping, a sound sweet as larks rising up in the crisp air. Where did they all come from and why were they there? It was too cold to linger, but Joe would never forget that day. It was for him like trying to understand one of the great mysteries of life that could never be fully understood.

That afternoon, the agent for Metropolitan came to collect on our life insurance policies. Mr. Harris had been our insurance man for twenty years. He had turned completely bald and was wearing new horn-rimmed glasses and his same old brown suit. Poor as we were, it was impossible for us not to wonder why our insurance man didn't look more prosperous. Seeing Mom with an infant in her arms, he started taking down information on the new addition and adding up the amount due. Dad, when he had the money, would set an envelope aside containing the exact amount for the insurance man. Mom had to tell him to come back some other day. Dad's agitation over this, and being down to our last lumps of coal, stressed the whole family.

Skip and Huey had been instructed to have shovels handy after school and wait for the delivery of our emergency coal supply. The coal truck arrived with Dad sitting up front directing the driver to back up as close to the house as possible. The roar of a ton of coal hitting the side of our house shook everyone and everything in it. Dad grabbed a big lump of that coal, brought it into the kitchen and dropped it in the coal stove's fire door, setting off a flurry of burning embers for the amusement of his greatest admirer's sixth birthday. *Thanks, Dad, for the fireworks!* said Richie.

Over the next days, the pain in Mom's side made it difficult for her to get upstairs. A cot was placed against the chimney wall in the dining room where she could rest during the day. We kids would come home from school and find her there with Martha and Richie tucked in beside her. Even with the good news we had to share, she would doze off in the middle of the conversation. More perplexing was why she was too weak to sit at the supper table.

She was in such distress one morning that Dad sent Sis next door to call Doctor Noden. It was past eight o'clock that night when he arrived. Everybody else we knew drove a car, but our doctor drove an *automobile*. Even so, it could not make the ice-slicked road to our hill, and he had to park in front of the church on 57th Street and walk up. He set his medical bag on the dining room table, hung his coat over the back of a chair, and in his polite manner asked everybody but Dad to leave the room.

Mom shifted to the edge of the cot, sitting quietly with her bare feet on the floor. Beads of sweet collected on her brow and chills ran through her. He examined her, raising questions as he went along, to which she nodded yes or no, too embarrassed to talk with no teeth. He recommended bed rest, a mild laxative, and a change of diet. Drink plenty of cold water and warm tea. Eat fresh fruits and vegetables. Mom didn't eat that way because she didn't cook that way. She cooked food that stretched and would go around, food that would stick to our ribs; no use explaining that she was barely eating. He told Dad to keep an eye on her and bring her in if she didn't feel better in a day or two. She was up late that night with abdominal distress when Joe got home. He could see that she hadn't combed her hair all day and that told him she was really sick. He fixed her a glass of water with a spoonful of bicarbonate of soda, her antidote. She drank it straight down, thanked him, and told him to go to bed.

February 7, 1946. Nothing unusual going on for a Thursday morning. Sis left for work, making a run for the Stanton Avenue bus to East Liberty. She had been delayed helping us kids and knew her boss at Wiggins would be standing at her work station tapping his pocket watch when she got there. The city steps up to Celadine Street were blocked, so she took the path through the woods to McCandless Avenue and lost footing on the ice. By the time she reached the bus stop, the bus was pulling away. She ran after it, shouting *STOP* and waved it down. Out of breath and exhausted from running, she took a seat and fell asleep. The driver knew who she was and woke her up at her stop.

I had been kept home from school that day with respiratory misery. Mom treated me with a Vick's VapoRub chest compress, tucked me in on the cot with Richie and Martha and, believe it or not, crawled in with us under a pile of blankets. A while later, the dining room window started rattling; the wind had blown it off its track. It took her many minutes to get moving and I watched her struggle to line the window up with the track. She stuffed newspapers in the cracks with a butter knife and put a few more lumps of coal in the stoves.

She went to the kitchen to do the breakfast dishes and discovered the water pipes were frozen. She heated the iron, went to the cellar to apply its heat to a connection on the frozen water line, and it burst all over her. Drenched and shivering, she hollered for help over Besal's back yard fence, and Dolphie responded. Even though he stuttered, an impediment that made it impossible for him to speak in unobstructed sentences, his compassion made it possible for him to dot every ***i*** and cross every ***t*** of her instructions to get Mom the help she needed.

He called Schramm's Realty, who contacted our old landlord, the Major. He arrived carrying a knuckle-buster pipe wrench and, with a grunt, went down the cellar to shut the water off. The water valve broke off in the wrench, so he went out to the curb, shut off the main, replaced the broken valve with a piece of straight pipe, turned the water back on and went home.

Dee and Anna arrived from school to find Mom disheveled and shivering on the cot and we little kids huddled together on the couch in the living room. Anna piled blankets on us and rebuilt the fire in the coal stove. Dee made vegetable soup for supper. Mom took but a few sips. After supper, Anna took Martha, Richie, Eileen and I upstairs, put us to bed, read us a story, kissed us good night, and turned off the lights. It was six o'clock in the evening and pitch black outside.

Sis got home from work a little ahead of Dad and saw that Mom was having a difficult time, more than just being cold; her color was off. Sis meditated on how Mom could possibly breathe under all those covers and lifted some of them aside, saying, *Mom, the only time you are not cold is in July and August.* Even in her weakened state, Mom chuckled. After a cup of tea and a slice of soft toast, she appeared to be doing better and dozed off. Sis and Dad ate a late supper, talking about nothing, she said, then he took over with Mom. The house felt quiet and everything seemed fine, so Sis grabbed her radio and went up to bed. She tuned in the pop music station and Doris Day's big hit Sentimental Journey was playing, one of Sis's favorites, which she often sang to us in her sweet voice. She not only sang it to us; she gave us an artistic performance: *Gonna take a sentimental journey, gonna set my heart at ease. Gonna take a sentimental journey, to renew old memories.* Sis fell into a deep restful sleep.

February 8, 1946. Sometime after midnight, Dad stoked the coal stoves and went to bed. Dee stayed downstairs with Mom and rigged up a bed on two dining room chairs. She covered up but couldn't get comfortable, so she sat in the dark thinking about nursing school. When she opened her eyes, it was getting light outside, the house felt cold, and Mom was not on the cot. Dee found the kitchen door wide open and Mom, still in her two housedresses, walking in the snow in bare feet, completely oblivious to the cold. Dee tried desperately to coax Mom inside but when she started walking out of the yard towards the street, Dee screamed—screams so piercing that everybody in our house was right there.

Sis rushed next door and called Doctor Noden on his home telephone reserved for emergencies. He answered the call and instructed Sis: *Get your mother to West Penn Hospital, she'll be all right.* We all sensed a feeling of dread as Sis combed Mom's hair and helped her into her shoes and coat. Her murmurings sounded like she was memorizing where everything was, what we were supposed to do, things to do for the baby, what we needed from the store, and what to cook for supper. Uncle Frank was already there and helped Mom and Dad into the car. Sis, with tears streaming down, waved and cried, *Mom, I'll come see you on Saturday; I'll bring you something nice.*

It was a year to the day since Sister Mary Cletus had died and St. Mary's student body was required to attend the anniversary mass. It had just started snowing when Larry, Eileen, and I headed for church. Dee stayed home to take care of Richie and Martha. She also cleaned the whole house and made macaroni and cheese for supper. Everybody was hungry and really enjoyed it, though we ate in silence, each feeling our own terror. Joe cleaned the kitchen and Skip cleared a path through the snow from our house to the street. Dad was still at the hospital with Mom.

Sis was nineteen years old and it was her Friday night out. She and her friends had planned to go to the midnight skate at the Lexington Roller Rink. Raye Green was going to be her skating partner, the only boy she ever brought home that Dad liked. Sis knew that Mom was in a good place and thought it might be okay to go out. Sometime after ten o'clock, she bundled up and walked to McConnell's house on Camelia Street to meet her friends, wall-to-wall kids hanging out at that small house and some partying going on. Right around eleven thirty, they headed out to catch the bus to East Liberty. It was in that exact moment when they reached the corner of McCandless and Stanton Avenue that something came over Sis. She had never felt such a strange feeling before and said she could not go roller skating. She told her friends about Mom going to the hospital that morning, and Raye Green walked Sis home.

It was just after midnight when she got there and found Dad slumped at the kitchen table, still in his tossle cap and overcoat. He looked so sad, so alone, so abandoned, she thought. He looked at her through a blur of glassy-eyed tears and said, *Mom's gone.* Two words that Sis felt like a lightning strike. Her long silence, and then, *Oh no, Dad, oh no. What happened*? Shaking like a leaf, she helped him out of his heavy outer wrappings and lit a fire under the tea kettle. He forced himself to sit up straight, and barely able to get the right words out, said, *They did everything they could do for her. She just kept slipping away all day.* Sis shriveled up in a heap of anguish, crying, *Oh no, Dad, oh no.* She sobbed uncontrollably, yet mustered up the courage to ask, *Did Mom say anything?*

He pounded his fists against his head, coughing and choking, and finally answered, *Yes, yes, your mother was saying the names of yins kids, one by one from beginning to end. Vinny, Sis, Joe, Dee, Skip, Anna, Huey, Larry, Eileen, Patty, Richie, Martha—Martha, Martha, Martha. Your mother told me to tell all of you that she loves you. Then she was gone. She's gone, Sis, your mother is gone.*

Joe awakened to a loud pounding sound. It was Dad crawling up the stairs pounding his bare fists, one hard pound on each of the fourteen steps to the landing. He was groaning a horrible groan, and he kept on repeating over and over with every step he reached, *She's gone kids, she's gone. Your mother is gone.* Terror filled Joe's mind when he remembered the bicarbonate that he had given Mom the night before. All he could think of was that he had caused her to die. Anna heard the frightening racket and turned on all the lights. Tremors of an undefined horror filled every room of our house.

Mom was gone and we would always wonder what she may have said in a personal way to Dad at the end. No one had the courage to ask, and it would remain a very private matter for him. Perhaps she recited the prayer of the dying of her dear Ireland: *I am going now and I am very thankful to you and grateful for everything and when I see God I'll ask him to be good to you.* With that, Mom could close her eyes and go straight to her glory. Dawn broke and the news of her death spread like a wildfire in the Homey Hill. Neighbors came in tears, all bringing trays of their best fixings; all wanting to do something, anything, for us.

Later in the day Uncle Frank arrived all bundled up against the cold. He had driven Dad home that late night and had returned to the hospital with Aunt Grace to attend to details that Dad was in no condition to handle. Our uncle explained that he had to walk from his house on Keystone Street through the snow-bound Homey Hill because there was too much snow to get his car up the road to our hill; he was carrying his tool box and a functional pipe wrench. He turned the water off at the curb, went to the cellar to install a new water valve, turned the water back on at the curb, adjusted the water pressure and returned to the cellar to turn on the new valve and bleed the air pressure from the line.

Before going home, he offered uplifting words to us kids, but he had walked in on a heartbreaking scene, so disturbing that even he cried. The owner of the Leo P. King Funeral parlor, a somber looking man in a dark suit, was in the living room with Dad and Sis, discussing arrangements for Mom's funeral. Dad had pulled himself together enough to turn over Mom's five hundred dollar Metropolitan Life Insurance policy, instructing Mr. King to do a good job.

We were told the funeral would be delayed so that Vinny could get home. We were also informed that Mom died of yellow jaundice, which made no sense to a child, let alone twelve children. Perhaps it was the only way to tell us a thing like that, but for Mom it had not been quite that simple. The autopsy report of Coroner William D. McClelland, M.D. stated: *Rose H. Scott died February 8, 1946 at 11:25 P.M., twelve hours after admission at West Penn Hospital. Cause of death—Hepatitis and Encephalitis—inflammation of the liver and brain.* Mom never drank a drop or swallowed a drug and we would always believe it was poverty that killed her. Mr. King gathered the signed papers, extended his sympathy, and left; Dad was right behind him.

Eileen stared out into a world all her own and began to flail and weep and lament, *I tried to tell yins and no one believed me. I knew all along it was coming because Mom didn't look right and she didn't talk right, so I asked her: Mom what's wrong? and she said: I am going to die tonight and they're going to put me six feet under.*

I thought Eileen had lost her marbles and we all trembled with concern for her. *You don't understand,* she cried. *Dad doesn't believe in the afterlife. He always said that when you die you got nowhere else to go but six feet under. I had a terrible nightmare of Mom six feet under.* Nine-year old Eileen was put to bed with her heart trouble, in bed with Anna. I was eight years old and put myself to bed with a library book.

Dad came home drunk and stayed up all that night drinking one beer after the other, wallowing in a gloomy dirge. It was impossible to sleep in that despairing atmosphere. Just past dawn, a Western Union messenger rapped on our front door to deliver a telegram from the Red Cross. Dad, sound asleep on the couch, bolted to his feet and somehow snapped out of his stupor. He gathered us at the dining room table, where he read the message aloud: *Mr. Vincent P. Scott, Sr. We are in the process of notifying Vincent P. Scott, Jr. U.S. Navy of death of mother Rose Helen Quinn Scott. Arrangements being made to send him home. Our Sincere Sympathy.*

I shivered just thinking about how Mom, with her bad knees, had prayed evenings at the dining room table for her son's return, while the rest of us on our knees recited the rosary for the war to end. Mr. King returned to take Sis to the funeral parlor to pick something out to dress Mom's body in, a depressing ordeal. No sooner back home, Sis was summoned next door to take a telephone call from Joanne McConnell. Sis picked up the receiver and said, *Hello, who is this?* All that her best girlfriend had asked was how our Mom was doing and Sis broke down, screaming into the telephone, *If you want to know how my mother is doing, why don't you go down Butler Street and ask Leo P. King.*

Same day—out in the State of Washington, Vinny was on board the *USS Tolland* in port at Lake Union Shipyard in Seattle scheduled for departure to Okinawa. The ship's boilers had failed a test or the ship would have already been sailing high seas. Same day—the Red Cross transmitted *shore-to-ship* a message not to be given over the phone. Vinny was summoned to captain's quarters and ordered to go ashore and report to Red Cross headquarters with no reason why. He saluted in acceptance of the order, shook to the marrow of his skinny bones, and was on his way.

At the Red Cross office in downtown Seattle, the nurse on duty asked, *How are things going at home?* Vinny frowned but cheerfully said, *I just got a letter from my mother yesterday. Everything is fine. She had a baby about two months ago.* The nurse seemed to have no compassion in her tone; she just stared at him coldly, and bluntly said, *Your mother is dead.* He returned to ship, where the captain handed him travel orders and called Boeing Field for flight reservations at Seattle Airport. There, he waited hours for a cancellation that got him as far as Billings, Montana. The aircraft hostess looked surprised to see Vinny on board and asked what he was doing there. *A twist of fate*, he replied. He had just met that whole airline crew a few days before at a party for his best shipmate's brother. The plane's copilot told Vinny to stay aboard;

he would be flying east to Detroit where he would transfer to Pennsylvania Central Airlines.

In Detroit, one Mr. John Lovelace of Wilkinsburg, Pennsylvania, had given up his seat so that Vinny could get home. In the last phase of the journey, his mind seared with images of growing up at Mom's side. The shock of her death devastated him and he had no one to talk to, so he wrote in his pristine hand on the blank back page of his orders: *Here was one of the finest women ever created by God. She bore twelve children, not because she was a good Catholic, but simply because no two people in this world ever loved each other more dearly than did our Mom and Dad. They gave us something far beyond all riches. They gave us the gift of love.* These thoughts would sustain Vinny all his days.

Somehow Mom and Dad had managed the basics. Beyond that, Catholic Charities and the St. Vincent de Paul Society had added important extras, including visits to the hospitals. Mom loved St. Mary's and Father Kebe, and she adored Sister Mary Cletus; it was they who had provided wise counsel and got our family so much of the help we needed. After the death of Mom's devoted friend, Father Doyle of St. Kieran's, the priests there had seemed aloof to her. Now, she was being buried from there.

Vinny, handsomely dressed in formal Navy attire, arrived home two days later, only to feel outrage when he learned that Mom's funeral mass would be at St. Kieran's. He asked his godfather to help him get the funeral transferred to St. Mary's. Hoping to quiet Vinny down, Uncle Frank went with him to see Father Kebe, who had to apologize and explain rules and regulations of the Catholic Diocese regarding births, baptisms, marriages, and burials—sacraments to be performed only in the Parish of ethnic origin. We were Irish and Vinny surrendered to the mandate.

On the first night of *the viewing*, our Quinn and Scott relatives arrived at the funeral parlor right behind us. We hadn't seen some of them in years. A heavy scent of perfume and cigarettes overwhelmed the atmosphere. In the *viewing* room, opulently furnished and brightened by crystal chandeliers and soft wall lighting, Huey spotted a black woman in a black overcoat and feathered hat sitting in a far corner and instantly realized it was his beloved *Evelyn Peanut*.

Two at a time, we kids were escorted to the casket where Mom's body lay, a casket surely meant for a person of wealth. There, we kneeled and made the sign of the cross. On each side of the casket, on marble pedestals, sat polished brass urns flourishing with tall ferns. Ornate vases and wicker baskets, overflowing with fresh cut flowers, surrounded the casket. A lavender evening dress had been chosen, all that was available. Mom had never worn an evening dress in her life. Her powdered face was swollen from the autopsy and makeup she never wore had been applied. At the foot of the casket lay a single red rose and a note on a card signed in Dad's hand: *To my dear Rose, my girl.*

Eileen came upon the scene and fell apart. Aunt Grace's sister Marty Reynolds lived a few blocks away and took Eileen to her house for the night. Richie and I stayed close as instructed but were both experiencing something akin to a trance with everything flying by our sheer innocence and a parade of unknowns approaching the casket to kneel and sign themselves.

Aunt Mary, ever so kindly, walked us away from that scene to a room decorated with wood-framed art and steel folding chairs. We sat beside each other, swinging our feet to and fro for something to do. I surely looked like a worried little woman in my pink dress and blue sweater, Richie like a worried little man in his green sweater and tan trousers. He began twirling a piece of his yellow hair with his fingers, and I began scratching my blonde head, habits that we had both developed early in life to assuage Scott family anxiety. There commenced between us an odd conversation. Richie said to me, *Patty, did you see anything in that other room*? I said, *I think I did. Did you see anything*? He said, *Yeah, I think I seen it, too.* We kids were, of course, profoundly affected by Mom's death, a tragedy too absurd to comprehend. We had never seen a corpse and it terrified us, not to mention that it was our mother.

Second night of *the viewing*, the funeral parlor overflowed with mourners greeting each other in strange and awkward ways. Father Kebe appeared in solemn attire and approached the casket to bless Mom's body with holy water and recite a prayer from his breviary. The school sisters of Notre Dame of St. Mary's, standing in the back of the room, began the recitation of the five decades of the sorrowful mysteries of the rosary. All had come out of deep respect for our mother, and in that oppressive room, a woman was heard saying, *Having twelve kids is what killed her; I wonder how they're taking it.*

Tuesday, February 12, 1946—everything frozen, snowy, and cold, and no streetcars running. Our neighbor Mary Monroe came over to help me and Eileen dress for the funeral. At that point, she didn't care what anybody thought of her intentions; she brought two of her daughter's nicest outfits for us to wear, after which she bundled up Martha and took her home.

Uncle Frank drove half the family to the funeral parlor and was scheduled to pick up the rest of us. Dad had instructed us to start walking just in case of a delay. We started walking, bundled up to the hilt, hoping to meet our uncle along the way. Ice glazed the naked trees and brush; the hillsides shimmered like diamonds. We reached the bottom of the road, where Uncle Frank was kneeling on the frozen ground fixing a broken tire chain. He told us to go on ahead, and we walked the rest of the way in the blinding glare of early sunlight on the frozen snow. Wind-smitten and shivering, we arrived at the funeral parlor, which already burgeoned with mourners at eight o'clock in the morning.

Grandmother Mary Scott, Uncle Sam, and Aunt Rose walked in, and like everyone else, felt the shock of a wonderful woman who had so bravely born twelve children and died so unexpectedly. For two days and nights, mourners had streamed through King's funeral home; people seemed to come from nowhere, everywhere. We hardly realized the many acquaintances Mom and Dad had, perhaps because raising our family had not allowed them much time to socialize. People gave Mass cards and money and offered assistance. Dad had shaped up and dressed up, responding in gratitude.

Father James Gilmore, the pastor at St. Kieran's, arrived to escort Mom's body to the church. He appeared a dark figure in black cassock and white surplus beneath a black overcoat with a purple stole draped over his shoulders. The aged and stooped priest with darting eyes and wind-blown white hair stood at the casket praying from his *Breviary*, Psalm One Hundred Thirty: *Out of the depths I cry to you O Lord; Lord hear my voice! Let your ears be attentive to my supplication. If you O Lord mark iniquities, Lord, who can stand? But with you is forgiveness that you may be revered.*

He blessed Mom's body with holy water, faced the people, and blessed us too. Mr. King directed everyone to assemble in the front parlor according to which car we would be riding in. I held Eileen's hand and we stopped dead in our tracks, shuddering when the casket lid closed with a loud thud. She was still nine and I was still eight years old, but we felt ancient. We were first out onto the sidewalk to board one of the flagged funeral cars, some thirty or more, as happens when the death is a shock. There, we encountered seasoned *prayers* among the many strangers who huddled together on porches and door stoops watching the cortege passing by on its way to the church.

At St. Kieran's, the procession of mourners passed through the heavy oak doors into the vestibule of the church; a stooped woman veiled in black wailed in an eerie tone: *For shame, that foreign priest on Fifty-Seventh Street turned her away. She loved his church. For shame, that poor woman left twelve kids behind. Wonder what will become of them? Families like that usually break up.* It was hardly possible for Dad to come to grips with such an unpredictable loss, all too soon, all too soon.

In the diffused light of the church, we filed down the center aisle followed by our relatives and friends and took our places in the front pews, there to behold the massive stained-glass windows depicting the lives of saints and the glory of the heavens, reflections in cobalt blue, deep green, ruby red, glowing amber, and earth tones. Beautifully carved statues of Jesus, Mary, and Joseph, and the Irish saints were shrouded in purple cloth because the season of Lent had begun. St. Kieran's school children sang from the choir, backed by the deep fugue sound of the tremendous pipe organ. The pall bearers had been assigned. Vinny in formal U.S. Navy attire, Joe, Skip, Huey, Uncle Frank, and Uncle Dick, in dark suits and ties. They escorted the casket to the Nave of the church and placed it in position outside the sanctuary.

Father Gilmore began the Miserere. Psalm Fifty-one, the prayer of David: *Miserere mei Deus secundum magnum misericordian tuam. Have mercy on me O God, in your goodness...in the greatness of your compassion wipe out my offense. Thoroughly wash me of my guilt and of my sins cleanse me, for I acknowledge my offense, and my sin is before me always. Against you only have I sinned and done what is evil in your sight.* The priest entered the sanctuary. His altar boys, Skip and Huey, followed behind. Huey took his coat and Skip helped him into a black satin vestment, which was embroided front and back with gold crosses. At the foot of the altar, the priest bowed three times as he entered into the solemn funeral rite, the Requiem Mass.

He turned to the people, motioned them to stand and said, *Requiem aeternam dona e-is, Domine.* The choir and congregation responded, *Et lux perpetua luceat eis.* The priest said, *Liberame Domine de morte aeterna…tremenda. Quando caeli movendi sunt et terra…Di-es illa, di-es irae…calamitatis et miseri-ae…et lux perpetua luceat e-is…libera me Domine, Tremens.* With his back to the people, Father Gilmore bowed at the foot of the high altar, paused until a coughing spell subsided, and continued the Mass, chanting in his weathered voice: *Kyrie ele-i-son,* and the school children on the choir loft sang the Kyrie: *Kyrie ele-i-son, Kyrie ele-i-son, Kyrie ele-i-son. Christe ele-i-son, Christe ele-i-son, Christe ele-i-son. Kyrie ele-i-son Kyrie ele-i-son Kyrie ele-i-son. Dominus Vobiscum,* the priest said. *Et cum Spiritu tuo,* the people responded.

Father Gilmore motioned everyone to be seated. He came down from the altar, sprinkled us with holy water, and took his seat in a high-backed oak chair off to the side of the sanctuary. Skip and Huey took their seats, one on each side of the priest, and the choir chanted the Sequentia: *Di-es irae, di-es illa, solvet saeclum in favilla. Teste David cum Sibylla, quantus tremor est futurus, Quando judex est venturus, cuncta stricte discussurus! Tuba mirum spargens sonum, per sepulcra regionum, coget omnes ante thronum… Rex tremendae majestatis, qui salvandos salvas gratis, salva me, fons pietatis… Huic ergo parce Deus: Pi-e Jesu, Pi-e Jesu, Pi-e Jesu Domine. Dona eis Requiem, Amen.*

The priest ascended the stairs to the elaborately carved oak pulpit, pulled a handkerchief out of his sleeve, blew his nose, adjusted his glasses, and read the Epistle in Latin and in English. The people stood. He said, *Fratres* and read aloud the Gospel in

Latin, then in English in his accomplished brogue: *A reading from the Gospel of Luke, Chapter Sixteen:*

There was a rich man named Dives who dressed in fine purple and linen and feasted sumptuously every day. At his gate lay a beggar named Lazarus who was covered with sores and who longed to eat the scraps that fell from the rich man's table. Then one day poor Lazarus died and was carried by angels to rest in peace in the bosom of Abraham. Likewise, Dives the rich man died and was taken to Hades. He cried out from the abode of the dead, O Father Abraham, send Lazarus to dip his fingers in water and cool my tongue for I am in torment in these flames. And Father Abraham said from afar off: A great chasm has been fixed which no one can cross...

At the conclusion of the reading, the priest wiped his wet eyes for he too had entered into our sorrow. He folded his hands in prayer, shifted his gaze our way, and spoke to us in his moving Gaelic tongue, *You children, try not to weep. Your mother is in heaven. She is looking down on you and she is well pleased.* A well of sobs rose up as the priest descended from the pulpit and returned to the high altar to begin the Offertory. At the Consecration we kneeled, the priest chanted and the choir sang in the language of the dead: *Sanctus, Sanctus. Sanctus Dominus Deus Sabaoth...Pleni sunt celi aeternam, gloria tuo...Hoc est enim corpus meum...Per ipsum, et cum ipso, et in ipso...Ecce Agnus Dei, quitolis pecata mundi...Dona eis requiem...Per omnia saecula saeculorum, Amen.*

Together, we stood, we knelt, we sat, we stood and knelt again, and there was Dad slouched in the pew, a widower lost in grief, enduring an unbearable ritual. At the end of Mass, the priest incensed the casket and blessed it with holy water as a woeful lamentation reverberated through the church. Mr. King then directed us out of the pews and up the aisle in procession from the church to the funeral cars, followed by six pall bearers escorting the casket, as the priest recited the *In Paradisium*: *May the angels lead thee into Paradise; may the Martyrs receive thee at thy coming and take thee to Jerusalem, the Holy City. May the choirs of the Angels receive thee and mayest thou, with the once poor Lazarus, have rest everlasting.*

The sun's blinding glare on the windshields protected our privacy from the stares of the curious who huddled on porches and sidewalks watching the purple flagged cortege move slowly through the streets of Lawrenceville, Garfield, Bloomfield, Shadyside, and Squirrel Hill. At the edge of Hazelwood, the funeral cars abruptly stopped. Two men in black overcoats came out of a stone building and waved the cars through the spiraled wrought iron cemetery gate with its great arch on which was engraved in large Old English lettering: *CALVARY*. We didn't need a sign. We knew it was *CALVARY*.

The cars circled up to the third level of the nearly deserted cemetery and pulled in at the side of the narrow, snow-covered road. From that precipice we could see through the naked trees the heavily populated industrial district of Hazelwood and far below the Monongahela River. On that slope, a grave had been assigned—the plot that our mother's body would share with her mother and father, Patrick and Margaret Quinn, in Section M, Lot and Row 610, where also rested their sons, James and Joseph. So much irony to reflect on going all the way back to our venerable ancients, some of it stranger than fiction just thinking that when Dad's time would come in 1972, he would be buried in this grave, as if fate had planned it all along to give us a sign from beyond the grave, *All Is Well and at Peace Here.*

At the graveside we huddled together, shivering through the solemn burial rite. The pall bearers set Mom's casket in place over the opened grave. In the high wind, Father Gilmore's vestment beat about like a ship's sail on a rough sea. He offered incense, sprinkled the casket with holy water, and gave the last blessing. At the priest's side, Skip and Huey responded through chattering teeth. In the final ritual, the priest sprinkled a handful of dirt over the casket as graveside attendants lowered it into the ground. The concluding prayers would forever impress upon our minds the true meaning of life and death, *earth to earth; ashes to ashes; dust to dust…May the Lord receive this good woman Rose and may her soul, in the spirit of the martyrs before her, go forth now into eternity, Amen.*

It didn't feel fair for the sun to fall out of the sky on twelve children who loved their mother with their whole hearts and souls. Two men with shovels came up the side of the hill and started shoveling dirt into the grave. Sobbing, we returned to the funeral cars, circled back down the hill, and out of the cemetery. Sis looked back one more time at the great arch on which was engraved: *CALVARY.* The journey home seemed endless, like a journey between time and eternity bearing a sadness that changed our perspective forever. Sis couldn't believe it could get cold enough for the whole cemetery to freeze solid. *Even the dead people, all frozen, cold like Siberia. Then it was over. done. gone,* she said, and she could not stop shaking.

Uncle Jim and Aunt Marty invited us for lunch at their house. She wanted to do this part for us. She said it felt too sad going to church because the organ music was sad. She was not our real aunt; she was Aunt Grace's sister, but she was a very real aunt to us kids. She served us a feast of nourishing food, and we ate and ate until there was nothing left. It was time for us to go home and we didn't seem to know how to show our appreciation. It was nothing that could be articulated, only felt, and we were starting to wonder where Dad was. He was supposed to take us home but had slipped away, and where he may have gone was disturbing. Sis thanked Aunt Marty and went to her girlfriend Angie's house nearby, a refuge for Sis. She didn't stay long; she had to pick up a pair of shoes at the shoemaker shop and stop at the Monroes to pick Martha up.

The sun had gone down by the time we got home. We were greeted with huge icicles dangling from the rain gutters and downspouts; the house was in total darkness and so bitter cold that it gave us a deserted feeling. The boys built fires in the coal stoves and we all went straight to bed, coats and all, way down under the covers. The ice-coated windows had been stuffed with newspapers to prevent them from rattling, but they still rattled, and the wind rattled the streetlight all night long—so hard to sleep with the house feeling deathly cold.

Death, when it visited our house, struck with the mighty power of God. We beheld its great sorrow, its stripping away, but we didn't know the first thing about death or how to act or what to do. We knew we were Irish and that life had broken our hearts. Fate, like nature, had dealt its cruel blow; we were living as if under a spell. Mom's last illness was for us a going forth that in her passing left her invisible foot prints across the cold floor. The attitude of illness for the poor of the times was that if you could not be well, you might as well die and give those you leave behind relief from a burden. It was not that our mother wanted to die, though she surely suspected she was going to. We would never know what beckoned her out into the cold in the early dawn of the day she died.

The Sunday after the funeral, a friend of Father Kebe's drove him to our house to pay a visit. He noticed that Dad was conspicuously absent but apologized for not making it for the Epiphany blessing. He had curtailed his rounds, saying that it was becoming too much of an ordeal. Funny thing, the cryptic legend that he had written in white chalk "*19 C + M + B + 38*" though blurred was still visible on the woodwork above the kitchen door. He had come bearing an envelope containing cash donated by his Parishioners to help with our funeral expenses. He offered condolences, crossed and blessed us with holy water—*In nomine Patris et Filii et Spiritus sancti.* You couldn't get more blessed than that; but it was not God's fault that bearing up was becoming more difficult for us.

With very little time left of his leave, Vinny recruited Uncle Frank to deal with Dad and set to work putting our house in order. He rounded up the laundry, pulled Mom's washer out of its corner, got it going, and found himself wrestling with it when it started drifting across the kitchen floor. Perhaps he saw in his mind's eye the dance of the *Gain-a-Day* when Mom washed clothes and sang *Oh Yelp us, Oh Yelp us.* He couldn't believe that

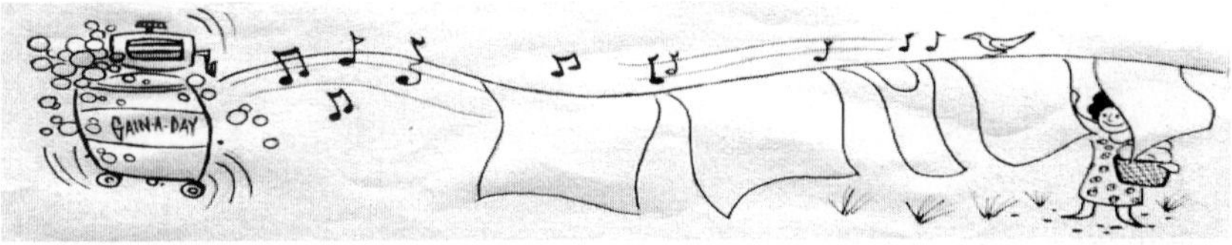

old washer was still running. It ran all day, all week for that matter. Wet wash was hung on clotheslines stretched through the kitchen, the dining room, the upstairs hallway banister, the bedrooms. In retrospect, Mom's washer symbolized the kind of patient, enduring love and devotion she had imparted to each of us every day of our lives. But she was gone and it felt really eerie to have Vinny leaving too. He reported to the Sampson Naval Base in New York, where his Navy adventures had begun, to complete his tour of duty.

So much of what we lived through in the following weeks was experienced in a daze—the big kids sharing days off school and work to take care of the little kids the way we had done to keep social workers at bay when Mom went to the rest home. Now, it was all beyond the understanding of a young family with an absentee father. We were losing our sense of direction.

Sis was missing too many days of work with things at our house reeling out of control. Her boss at Wiggin's wanted to fire her and she had no defense. She didn't belong to the union—no women allowed—but the guys at the shop went to bat for her. The foreman explained that he had to let Sis go because the man she replaced during the war wanted his job back. Sis's friends told the boss to fire another woman who was goofing off on the job; he did, and that saved Sis's job.

Sis was twenty years old. Her hours at Wiggin's were 7:00 a.m. to 3:00 p.m. She came home one day thinking she could catch a little shut-eye before making supper. Instead, she found Dad slamming his body against a wall, railing incoherently, and going crazy right in front of her. It looked to her like he was trying to do himself in. This was just too much; she could no longer deal with the personal pain of the loss of our mother, and she left home. Sis was close friends with the Heinricher girls, Tess and Aggie of Camelia Street, ever since their grade school days at St. Mary's; they and their mother took Sis in. Mrs. Monroe was aware that Sis had moved out and never said a word but offered to keep Richie and Martha during the day while everybody was at school and work. We were grateful.

Word got around as to where Sis was and a few of us kids went to see her; I know I did. While Sis was with the Heinrichers, perhaps a few months, her friends kept her informed of what was going on at 5614 Duncan Street—and then the big story broke. Allegheny County Social Services sent an agent to our house to investigate. Visitors from that agency had been making suggestions all along regarding good families who had the means to take in a few of our kids. Dad said, *Leave our family alone; you'll split us up over my dead body*.

However, a formal report was filed and it was determined that Richie and Martha would have to be placed with foster parents. The news reached Sis. She blasted into our kitchen through the back door and there was Martha sitting in a high chair wearing my old dress, which hung nearly to the floor. She reached her arms out to Sis and said, *Mama.* That was it. Sis knew what she had to do. She quit her job and stayed home to take care of our family and keep us together.

Dad, a man deeply troubled in mind and body, had lost weight and was skinny to begin with. We could almost tell when he was ready to hit the bottle by the banner case of hives that erupted on his forehead, and by the way he drummed his fingers on the armrest of his chair and smoked his cigarettes. With Mom gone and without a twelve-step program to shore him up in the way Mom had, his life caved in around him. In the valley of the shadow of death, we could tell Dad feared evil. If only he could reach out and grab hold of a rod and staff to give himself courage. We, his children, took it all in, confused and fearful, not knowing what to do or how to behave to please him.

He went to work every day but was becoming increasingly late for supper and Sis did not criticize him for it. She saw that in the state he was in he easily slipped into a dark and sullen reverie. Sometimes he would come to the supper table, and just as we started passing the bread and oleo margarine, he would leave the table saying he wasn't hungry. He'd say he was going to the living room to read the paper. We would quietly finish our supper, go check on him, and he'd be gone.

One day, Sis told Dad that she was making a baked meat loaf supper with all the trimmings, a meal he really enjoyed. He assured her that he'd be home on time and didn't show; she sent Larry out to find him. The private tears of a boy on a quest for manhood were Larry's own business as he journeyed down the 56th Street city steps to Neid's. He knew full well that he'd find Dad slumped at the bar and would have to help him home—a struggle for the boy and the man. Dad looked like a bum—disheveled, unshaven, and drunk—and it took forever to get him home. In shame, he stumbled in the front door to avoid Sis in the kitchen; Larry helped him upstairs and into bed.

Larry harbored a resentment towards Dad for teasing that he was the *runt of the litter.* Then he remembered Mom's insight, *What is in the mind and heart is what makes the man.* He decided to sit on the side of the bed and have a talk with his father: *Dad, I'm old enough to know that you need help. I'm not mad at you or anything like that. I just want to talk sense to you the way Mom used to talk sense to me. I want to be clear about how I feel. Maybe you ought to wise up, you have twelve kids now. Christ's sakes, I'm only twelve myself.* He wasn't sure that Dad even heard him.

Joe observed everything that was unfolding as a holy experience, and even in the face of Dad's gloom, uttered no word of criticism to magnify it. He expected to be drafted into the Army when he graduated from Connelley, but his callup was delayed and he felt compelled to get on with his life. He took a good look at Pittsburgh with its aging buildings, scorched factories, and smoke, and packed his belongings, all he owned in the world, and left town. He didn't go far. He and a buddy traveled to Somerset, Pennsylvania, where they found summer work in the home construction industry, installing a couple of roofs and a few other odd jobs. Joe counted his earnings, reflected on his sorry fortune, and returned home. His basic training orders were waiting for him; he had ten days to sign in at Fort Knox, Kentucky.

Vinny returned with his honorable discharge and registered at Carnegie Tech, but enrollment could not be assured for two years, so he enrolled at Allegheny Valley Tech, a television and electronics school. Every day he came home to a hot meal that Sis prepared. She also packed his lunch because he had to go right back out to work on the night shift at the Spring Works. Sis had worked there when the hammer press mill was temporarily converted for wartime defense making O-Rings for Bombs.

Vinny's job was to load steel bars into a heat-treating oven to bake and then unload them for molding into industrial springs for railroads.

Dee had graduated from high school and worked at the Craft Paper Factory in East Liberty. She found a new job and got Anna her old job there. The manager asked Anna if she planned to quit school to hold down the job. She said, *Yes.* The job involved placing boxes on a conveyor belt and filling them with wrapping paper and ribbon. She just couldn't keep up with those boxes speeding by, so the boss put her upstairs doing the same job manually and put her in charge. Time came to return to school and she quit the job. The manager was furious and called her a liar. Anna replied, *I guess I lied.*

Skip returned to Central, Anna and Huey to St. Kieran's, and Larry to St. Mary's along with me and Eileen. She had a serious absentee record and was afraid she might be held back, but we were promoted to fourth grade. The best we could do to stay together was for me to help with her homework so she wouldn't flunk. She was frantic on the first day because she had to iron her own clothes. Somebody had given us an electric iron, she didn't understand how to use it and scorched her white blouse.

Seven months after our mother's death, even though it seemed like yesterday, it appeared that we kids had returned to some semblance of normalcy with God's grace. We just hadn't had a whole lot of idle time to feel sorry for ourselves and, besides, Dad had come through. Beyond grief was the rattle of his lunch bucket, which sat on top of the ice box next to his Big Ben alarm clock that no one was allowed to touch. He took it upstairs at night and brought it downstairs in the morning. He cooked breakfast and called from the foot of the stairs for everybody to get up. We resisted the call; it grew more persistent, and he blasted another call, but it was his last call that got us moving, *Get up, get up, get up*! *Get up, get up, get up*! *Y'up yet*? He was already halfway out the door cursing a streak when we got to the kitchen. *Damn it yins kids; if I get docked for being late, you'll pay up!*

In the peace-time economy, wages were stagnant. Jobs made vacant were jobs available to new recruits because the unemployment office had three workers ready, willing, and able to fill each and every position with men who traded in their military uniforms for steady employment in the mills. Hubbard's told its labor force that their jobs were at risk if they walked out for a pay increase. Dad advised Sis that if he lost his job due to a strike, a non-union job awaited her. Sis said she didn't need any bright ideas.

The weather was nice and Dad started taking Martha for walks in the neighborhood to show her off—his baby girl—*the spitting image of her mother with the glory of Ireland written all over her face.*

He stopped at the barricade corner to watch a few rounds of dice, before bringing her home for Sis to feed, bathe, and put Martha to bed. At eight months, she had outgrown her bassinette. The family highchair had disintegrated and, her godmother

Aunt Marty had provided a new one plus a crib too large to fit into the small back room where we girls slept.

Dad figured now was a good time to adjust our sleeping arrangements. He moved into the front room with the boys and moved me and Eileen into the middle room that he had shared with Mom. He was satisfied that Martha's crib fit nicely into a corner. All he asked me and Eileen to do was keep the room clean, so I kept my stuff off the floor and made my side of the bed, because sooner or later he'd show up to investigate. When he did, Dad gave me but a smile, sent me downstairs, and talked to Eileen.

Eileen had trouble settling down at night, but once asleep, she snored. Sis would wait until Martha fell asleep downstairs before bringing her upstairs to put her to bed. To my joy, she sometimes woke up after Sis left the room. In the glow of the streetlight, I watched her wiggle out from under the covers, pull herself up by the crib bars, and start cooing, my perfect opportunity to do something good. I put her in bed with me until she was soundly sleeping and put her back in her crib, hoping that I had done the right thing.

Richie had started first grade at St. Mary's, and Dad had him fitted with high-top leather shoes called clodhoppers to support his weak ankles and high arches. During the breaking-in-new-shoes phase, the shoe laces became untied, and he tripped and fell off the curb and into the street. Dad had me keep an eye on little brother after that because he had gotten pretty banged up. Dad said he was sorry for not having Richie's feet reset when he was an infant. Fortunately, he was not wearing his glasses at the time of the accident.

Sis helped him get ready for school and, with Martha in her arms, escorted the little man-boy in a fancy shirt, short pants, and round-wire specs to class. Sister Mary Lauda had replaced

Sister Mary Cletus. She gave him a front row seat so he could see the blackboard. First thing he noticed was the big crack down its middle that he had heard about. He planned to consult Sis as soon as possible. School sometimes made him feel like he was drifting into another universe. The joy of walking home after school with his friends snapped him out of it, and he was happy that Sis was home when he got there.

The season changed and the middle bedroom with no direct heat source was chilly. A night late in the fall, the temperature dropped into the teens. I snuggled up with Martha in my bed and she slumbered in sweet stillness. I wondered if babies dreamed. Sis peeked in on her way to bed. She must have been satisfied or she would have put Martha in her bed for the night. Martha was a good baby; she comforted all of us.

The holidays came and went, like Labor Day, Halloween, Thanksgiving, Christmas, and in a heartbeat it was New Year's. Everybody at our house was accounted for through all kinds of that insufferable winter weather. Our house was warm and cozy and we felt a sense of security just being together—all for one and one for all—awaiting the return of spring. At last, our windows were opened to let in fresh air—the doors, too, and the flies. Sis aimed the broom, not in defiance of her surrogate role, but only to sweep out of our house the pure city dirt that we tracked in every time we crossed the threshold. Like Vinny, she wanted everybody to get out of the way so she could clear the deck.

Richie stalled in the kitchen doorway, awaiting recognition, but Sis was mopping the floor and gave him her *didn't-you-go-yet* look. He said he was thirsty and she, being a problem solver by nature, opened the ice box, chipped a cup full of ice off the ice block and gave it to Richie, saying, *You can cool off outside*! He obediently left the house, accidentally slamming the screendoor shut behind him; he came back in to say he was sorry about that—irresistible, our Richie.

It was not uncommon for the boys to get kicked out of the house so the girls could clean it. Huey would round up his wacky friends on the hill like Herky, Speedy, and Billy, and go for a swim in the Allegheny River at their secret watering hole called *Bare Ass Beach.* Sometimes Skip and Billy's brother Willy would go along, for the walk, not the water. They thought the *BAB* swimmers were nuts. Their dipping and diving point was along a small sandy section where a nearby creek flowed into the river. Train conductors going by blew their whistles and shook their heads, but the boys had a blast. Why they called it the *BAB* is a mystery; they wore their swimming trunks and went home wet.

A day came when Sis was trying to get odds and ends done around the house and told Eileen, Richie, and me to go outside. Richie already had his glasses on but went back inside to find his prize possession, his green felt hat that Larry had decorated with his prize pop bottle caps. We walked over to the wall at the bend of the road and waited for something to happen. Usually kids on the hill would be playing there, but not that day. We hopped on the wall, and Eileen suddenly broke down over how much she missed Mom. Sympathetic little brother in his dandy hat right away responded, *I wonder why Mom died.* Eileen said, *She was sick and tired, that's why.* And I said, *Not of us, though, Mom loved us.* As

we tried to comprehend our grief, we began to weep. Richie simply could not endure it and scooted off the wall, saying, *Let's take a hike up Quill's Hill and look for some good rocks.* Eileen said, *No we can't do that. Sissy would murdalized us; we better go get permission.* On our way back to the house, we discovered Huey on our side lot up a chopped off stump of what we called the invasive Sumac tree.

All of a sudden, the four of us became engaged in the idea of what could be done about chopping down trees. I picked up a branch that was laying on the ground and suggested that such a tall branch could be a cross and maybe we could have a procession for Mom instead of going on a hike. Eileen wanted to be the priest and Richie said he'd have to be the priest because he was a boy. Using child-like logic, our argument settled. Since the procession was my idea and mine was the largest branch, I should be the priest. With Eileen and Richie relegated to altar boys bearing pretend lanterns, we assembled for the procession with Huey looking on in sheer disbelief. He scooted back up the bared tree trunk, spread his arms wide and proclaimed, *I'll be Jesus on the Cross*!

Our procession proceeded along Duncan Street, where we came upon Richie's pal, Sonny Boy, whose mother had just died, another Rose. It seemed appropriate to invite him to join us, as well as his sisters, Bootsie and Wootsie, my playmates. They lived with their father, Ross Lacata, in the big square house near the barricade corner; it had served as a police horse barn early in the century. It was a great place to play in out of harsh weather, especially when Mr. Lacata was at work and we had the run of the place—nothing dangerous, of course. Our procession reorganized and headed up the Seccy, a short trek from the barricade corner.

There, we ran into Johnny Boy, another of Richie's many companions. Johnny's father, Angelo Chirico, was propped in a wheelchair behind an easel where he was painting a fresh landscape. His oils on canvass flourished with color and depicted scenes of villages in Italy, where his mother and father were born. We knew Angelo's wife, Vee, was down back cooking her famous pasta sauce. The enticing waft of her garden tomatoes simmering in a large pot flavored with olive oil, garlic, onions, and spices, made our bellies growl. Every so often, she invited kids on the hill to partake of a generous plateful of her homemade *spagetts.* The cellar adjacent to her kitchen was stocked with large cans of olive oil imported from Italy, and her kitchen table was spread bountifully. Her garden salad was drenched in imported olive oil and balsamic vinegar, which she served with chunks of her homemade crusty bread dipped in olive oil. Imagine how proudly she glowed as she chanted: *Mangia, mangia. Eat, eat!*

Next door to the Chiricos, Grandma Yuckatich was sitting on a bench in the shade, wearing a babushka and praying the rosary. With narrowed eyes, she watched us regroup to accommodate a few stragglers and a filthy mutt with a wagging tail. Our commotion brought out a slew of neighbors, who convened for the purpose of interpreting the deep meaning of it all. Our procession circled up steep 56th and ½ Street, which ran a short distance to a dead end at the Celadine Street steps. We turned and marched back down the road to the bend where our procession dispersed, but not before we sailed our branches over the wall, and went home. We also participated in a few pet funeral processions in those heydays on our hill. But about those branches, Richie felt compelled to inform us, *They are called Tree of Heaven, not Sumac. Sumacs grow in low clusters.* Heaven help us!

Schramm's nailed a *For Sale* sign on our house! Vinny saw not only impending disaster for our family because Dad didn't believe in owning property, he saw a window of opportunity and made an offer the owner could not refuse. He made an appointment with the Veteran's Administration and applied for a mortgage through the Allegheny Valley Bank on Butler Street. He invested in 5614 Duncan Street not because he had to, but because it was the character of the man.

Vinny made a deal that restored our sense of security and offered us more hope than ever. We never knew that our nextdoor neighbors were renters until Dolphie Besal bought their house. Ironically, the closings on the sale of 5614 and 5612 Duncan Street occurred on the same day—August 6, 1946—Mom's forty-fifth birthday. Vinny paid five-hundred dollars down and had the deed transferred into his name. The mortgage was set at fifty-dollars a month and Dad agreed to pay half. Owning a home of our own gave our family a sense of personal esteem and pride. Property ownership does that to you—a feeling of confidence and stature, a feeling that all is well even in the face of concerns like how to pay for and maintain your property and how to beautify a house that had been neglected for years. We vowed to take care of it and keep it clean.

1947

Everywhere, people were buying old and neglected houses and fixing them up. Not since post World War One had our city seen grassroots efforts to improve neighborhoods, a movement largely credited to revised lending laws and the fine example of political leadership on both sides of the aisle in the planning phase of Pittsburgh's Renaissance. Our renovation began with the help of home-building contractor, Uncle Bart Scott, who brought in his big equipment and jacked up the back of the house which sat on a crawl space. In preparation for excavating the earth beneath the kitchen and erecting concrete block walls to support the structure, Vinny recruited Joe, Skip, and Huey to help carve out a passage from the cellar through the stone foundation to access the abyss of clay and rocks. Dad was first to strike a blow with his picmatic, work that got harder with every swing. The crew filled wheelbarrow after wheelbarrow

with the heavy diggings, wheeled it across the cellar floor, and one shovelful at a time shoveled it out the cellar window. A huge mound of earth and rocks accumulated in front of our house. Neighborhood kids sat on the curbstone under the trees on the other side of the street, watching in amazement as huge heaps

of hard clay and rocks went flying out that tiny window. Every evening, the boys hauled one wheelbarrow load at a time and dumped it over the embankment across the street.

The *Kalamazoo* was scrapped and the kitchen floor was ripped out, leaving no floor for a while. Dad forgot this one night coming home from the bar. He opened the kitchen door and fell into the hole. No harm done, apparently, and Huey couldn't stop laughing, nor could Skip—the funniest thing to have happened during the big dig. Vinny shook his head, not seeing anything to be amused about in the hard work ahead. Everyone wondered how much longer his chain link work crew would survive without a break, considering their clothes were coated with mud, and man did they ever sweat!

In the last phase of the big dig, somebody complained that the Scotts were dumping on private property. Vinny called a work halt and Dad went out for a few beers. It must have been a Friday because Sis made macaroni and cheese.

After supper, the boys went back to work; no one knew or dared to ask how the dumping issue was resolved or if it was ignored. Joe, home on leave, did most of the detailed digging to prepare for a Bilco entrance from the back yard into the cellar. Two big truckloads of concrete blocks and sacks of mortar were delivered, and it took long, hard hours to erect the concrete block foundation.

While it cured, Vinny started rewiring the house. He asked Larry to be his apprentice, a position to be taken seriously. He worked alongside Vinny, replacing the fuse box in the cellar, ripping out old wiring and rewiring the house. The light socket that dangled from the kitchen ceiling was replaced with a modern fixture and wall plugs were installed. Hardest working was Vinny, an astute supervisor with refined skills and ability.

He was rewarded with good news that the Allegheny Valley Bank had granted him an equity loan to pay for home remodeling and a central heating system. A coal furnace would be installed in the cellar and vented to the dining room chimney. The living room chimney would be torn down because it was unsafe. Starting on the roof and working down through the attic to the second floor, the chimney bricks were removed and the gaping hole in the roof was closed. With extreme caution to look first, the bricks were dropped one by one out the middle bedroom window to the sidewalk below.

I was not to go near the job site, but curiosity got the best of me one day. I went upstairs to watch Vinny work. He looked so funny with a work hanky tied around his mouth and covered with soot. Dust billowed up around him when he pulled a loose brick from the chimney. I asked if I could help and he said, *What are you doing up here?* He realized why, of course, and said, *How would you like to do me a favor and throw this brick out the middle bedroom window; don't forget to look twice before you drop it. When you're finished, go downstairs and ask Sis to let me know when lunch is ready. You stay out of here, okay?*

I felt so proud for being asked to help that I carried the brick to the other room and dropped it out the window—without looking—and then it happened! My brick hit our iceman on the head and knocked him cold. Fate in that moment had placed him there to deliver a fifty-pound block of ice for our icebox.

In panic, I rushed down to the kitchen only to learn that I had probably killed the iceman. I hid in the cellarway bawling my eyes out. I later learned that he would survive, but I had convinced myself that I had gotten away with murder and felt burdened with guilt. In my despairing state of existence, Sis took me shopping in East Liberty. We boarded the Stanton Avenue bus and couldn't believe our eyes. The iceman was sitting on the bus all dressed up in a suit and tie; he tipped his cap and said hello. We had never heard him say a word or seen him wearing anything but grubby clothes. Relief overwhelmed me when Sis whispered, *See Patty, I told you not to worry. You cured the iceman*!

The remodeling progressed in stages as money came in. Joist beams to support the new kitchen floor were installed, but we had to cart the dirty supper dishes across a plank board from the dining room table to the kitchen sink. Joe was uncomfortable with this precarious operation and took over until it was time to report back to Fort Knox.

Joe's Army division received orders that they were being shipped by train to the west coast in a holding zone on their way to Japan for six-month post-war duty with allied occupation forces. The train was scheduled for a layover in St. Louis, so Dad wrote down an address and asked Joe to look up Sam Scott. Joe did and, when our *grandfather* opened the door, the first thing that went through Joe's mind was, *Wow, he looks like my Dad.* Even in their brief encounter, something stirred in Joe's being that made him feel that Sam Scott was his real grandfather, despite the travelling Irish song and dance team story.

Days later, his division reached the Presidio in San Francisco. The first thing Joe did was walk the length and breadth of the city exploring its breathtaking views. He visited the cultural sites and attended a performance of the San Francisco Ballet. He was so inspired that he signed on with its choreographer, who went by the name Christopher. So, we can say Joe danced with the San Francisco ballet, if only for a few days. Dad started brooding over the loss of an extra breadwinner, even with Joe sending money home. Perhaps Dad had given up hope that his ship might come in.

The neighbors thought our ship came in when the Davis Sand and Gravel Company's truck rolled onto Duncan Street and poured wet concrete down a chute through the cellar window. Like the great concrete artisans of old Rome, our boys shoveled and wheeled, hoed and raked, trialed and broomed, smoothed and finished, and let the concrete set up. Vinny announced that the cellar was no longer to be called a cellar; it was the *basement*. Limestone and concrete block walls were now the solid foundation on which our kitchen rested, and a new phase of renovation was underway.

The filthiest job of all was tearing out and replacing the crumbling fiber plaster walls in every room in our house. A professional contractor re-plastered the kitchen walls after the wall sink was replaced with a cabinet sink and a new kitchen door and window were installed. New stairs to the basement and laundry facilities were installed, including a hot water line, a hot water tank, laundry tubs, a flush toilet, a steel and cement shower stall. A hot air furnace was on the agenda. The family of one of Vinny's buddies was having a gas furnace installed and told Vinny he could have their old coal furnace if he dismantled it. It took many trips with Uncle Sam's truck to haul that galvanized octopus home and many days to install it in our basement.

One day, Dad invited Richie down to the basement to show him how to sweep the floor *properly,* as he put it. *First you take a whisk broom and brush off the work bench and shelves—careful to lift things, like Vinny's inventions, and set them back in place. Then, you start at the edge of each wall and corner and sweep toward the center of the floor. You don't move to another spot until all the dirt in each sweep has moved forward. Once it's piled in one spot, you get the square-edged coal shovel and sweep the pile onto it, then dump it into a bucket. And always do good work no matter how big or how small the job*, said Dad. What a remarkably fine work ethic to hand down in the family!

On the first cold evening of the season, Dad built a gigantic fire in the furnace. Hot dusty air roared up through the floor vents, heating the house to a comfortable temperature and causing a night long episode of sneezing, coughing and hacking. It seemed no one minded Dad's first call to get up the next morning, nor his second or last call, for that matter. When we jumped out of bed, our feet hit a warm floor; we knew we had arrived in the modern world, with time to relax and prepare for the upcoming holidays.

Sis had seen the 1934 film *Imitation of Life* starring Claudette Colbert, which returned to the Dome for its final run. Sis wanted to see it again and took Eileen and me with her. It is a story of a widow with a small child who takes in a black housekeeper whose child looks white. The child wants to be white and rejects her black mother. Together, the two women succeed in a business venture making pancakes, and all that the heart-broken housekeeper wants in return is a big send off to heaven with a fancy funeral when she dies. The day came, and everybody at the Dome cried through that last scene. It was no wonder why Sis, Eileen, and I fell apart over the heart-breaking memories of our mother's death.

In the aftermath, I was sitting on the curbstone in front of our house feeling an overwhelming sense of loss. One of my playmates came upon the scene and asked why I was crying. I said, *I want to be with my mother.* She bluntly said, *You don't have a mother; your mother is dead.* I screamed, *My mother is not dead. She's alive in heaven.* My playmate said, *No she's not Patty Scott; your mother is dead.* I rose to my feet and knocked her down; her dear mother pulled her out from under me and took her home. It seemed I was heading down a path of rebellion.

The 1948 film *The Big City* came to the Dome and Eileen and I went to see it on our own. In it, Danny Thomas and two other male actors adopt a foundling played by child star Margaret O'Brien, who has to fend off meanies who taunt her with comments that she has no mother—a gentle story compared to *Imitation of Life*. Some showgoers were annoyed by roles Miss O'Brien played, but her portrayals reflected for me who I then thought I was, a sensitive and anxious little girl. I probably should have seen a specialist, but who knew?

Our family still believed in God, attended Mass, and tried to fulfill our sacramental obligations, all but Dad, of course. As we matured, we would be exposed to diversified beliefs and broader thinking which was at the heart of our spirituality. Skip and Huey were well integrated into the community's social and cultural life, both taking voice lessons, performing in musicals, and trying their luck at the Catholic high school dances, where *the most beautiful girls in the world awaited*, so they said.

Even though Dee and Anna had long since attended St. Kieran's School, they never missed teen dances in its church basement, which also served as a gym, a popular place for kids to get together with their friends. One evening Dee and Anna got dressed to go to the dance and Vinny questioned where they were going. Dee did not wish to explain this, so she simply said, *To the gym.* To which Vinny replied, *Jim should come here.* She understood. Vinny was just looking out for his sisters.

School girls routinely walked Richie home and would later called on him to come out and play. Cassie Frank lived with her Grandmother Zupancich in one of the three houses at the bottom of the footpath that connected Duncan Street to the Keystone Street extension. Cassie, a pretty lass, liked to invite Richie to her house for supper. Her attention impressed him, but he soon learned to use diplomacy and say no thank you, because Cassie's grandmother served cabbage soup. He couldn't get the insidious smell of it out of his nostrils—it lasted forever and permeated everything—the house, the walls, the clothes, a summer day. From the Homey to the Seccy, the smell of cabbage soup knew no bounds. It was as unwelcomed by Richie as was welcomed the waft of Mrs. Chirico's fresh garlic and imported olive oil tomato sauce.

Richie's thirst for adventure knew no bounds under the influence of library books that his older brothers and sisters brought home from school. He looked forward to the greatest adventure of all, receiving an education. After all, he had been looking at those big books since he was a baby; sometimes taking them to bed and reading them upside down, with or without his glasses. He had imagined racing through St. Mary's school corridors with the works of Fyodor Dostoyevsky and Charles Dickens tucked under his arm. He had dreamed of going to the school library on Tuesday mornings to exchange *Crime and Punishment* for *A Tale of Two Cities*. Imagine his shock on the first day of the new school year, an experience for Richie as dull as the opening scene in the Dickens' classic, *Hard Times*:

Facts. Teach these boys and girls nothing but Facts. Facts alone are wanted in life. Plant nothing else, and root out everything else. The scene a plain, bare, monotonous vault of a schoolroom with a plane of little vessels then and there arranged in order, ready to have imperial gallons of facts poured into them until they were full to the brim.

The scene for Richie on the second-grade side of the classroom was plain and monotonous, but he learned that one plus one makes two, two plus two four, three plus three six with nothing left over. Learning to write in cursive scourged him, even though Sister Mary Lauda tried to encourage him with *Practice makes perfect*. He gave that up in favor of printing on a slant to give his penmanship that cursively look. The problem was how little of what went on in class stimulated his curious mind. Sister's voice would trail off and he would gaze out the window, watching Father Kebe feeding the birds in among the trees on the hillside.

Sister would prod him out of a daydream with the pointer, and he would try to keep his mind from drifting by watching what the other kids in class were doing. His fascination with humanity would prove to be his main school distraction. His charisma would enlist a sortie of friends, allies, buddies and even pals to reinforce his self-worth in spite of blotches that would appear on his otherwise glowing report cards. Of these marks, he would ask: *How did that get there?*

St. Mary's got a new principal that year, and Richie already sensed what might happen to him next. Sister Mary Hubertha felt that the children sat at their desks too long and asked Father Kebe to allow a period of fresh air and exercise outdoors. He said it would be too risky with cars zooming up and down the street ever since the war ended. A neighborhood child had recently been killed by a car right in front of the school. The principal was sorry about the tragedy but went over the priest's head. God granted permission for her to release one class at a time for brisk marches on the Parish grounds.

Father Kebe, out behind the school raking up fall leaves one afternoon, noticed the first and second graders marching around the church. At first, he was amused but, on second thought, halted them and asked their teacher what they were doing out of doors. Sister Lauda explained that the principal made them conduct a procession in honor of the elevation to sainthood of Mother Frances Cabrini. Though born in Italy, the Mother had served as a missionary to Italian immigrants in New York City and had founded schools, hospitals, orphanages and child-care centers in the U.S. and elsewhere. Our pastor appreciated this but had to advise the principal that the church did not need more Italian saints and that we ought to pray for a Slovenian saint.

The principal agreed and proceeded to distribute holy cards to all students of our school, holy cards depicting an image of the new saint, instructing we children on how to advance a case for a miracle. We were to look at the holy card, stare into the sky and blink three times, then gaze at the image on the holy card, resume staring at the sky and wait for the face of Mother Cabrini to appear in the heavens, a sure sign that a miracle might occur.

Eileen and I, in fifth grade, were on our way home with our book bills; she halted me on the city steps and said we better take out our holy cards and pray for a miracle that Dad will pay up. She stared at her holy card and up at the sky and had a vision. She told me to do likewise. I stared at the sky and a painful glare blurred my vision. I refused to put up with eye pain and put my holy card away. At home, Eileen told Sis that I lacked faith in miracles, and I told Sis that Sister in school was nagging about the book bill. Sis sent us to Dad with our sorry story.

He set aside his newspaper, asked what was on our minds, and we spit it out. Beads of perspiration formed on his brow, hives erupted on his forehead, and he started scratching like he was going after a tick. He lit up a cigarette, took a few puffs, flicked a hot ash into his lead ashtray, and invited us to come closer so we could hear what he had to say. In Dad's august presence, we boldly stood tall, arms crossed and wide-eyed. He started drumming his fingers on the arm rest, raised his brow, and shifted into one of his long-speak diatribes.

Now listen up you two, there is something that you should know and are old enough to hear. I earn a hundred fifty dollars a month, barely enough to keep a roof over our heads and pay the bills. We have a big family and that means lots of groceries. Food costs money. We cook with gas and gas costs money. The house gets cold and we burn coal. Coal costs six-fifty a ton these days and we go through fifteen or twenty tons every winter. The house gets dark and we don't just turn on one light. Yins kids turn on every light in the house and probably won't learn to turn the lights off until you are old enough to pay your own light bill. And girls, you know we need clothes and shoes, and that costs money. I have to buy the things we need on credit using my good name. So listen up, I want you girls to hold onto your good name and your pride, and by God, when my ship comes in, I'll go down to St. Mary's and pay the book bill myself.

Sis heard it from the kitchen and hollered in short speak, *Pay up Dad.* Vinny was at the dining room table absorbed in his problem solving mind, which at times made him seem aloof, but once we had his full attention, he entered wholly into our concerns. He had been through similar hard times and couldn't help but overhear Dad's admonition. He asked us how much was owed on the book bill, turned to a clean page in his notebook and wrote it down. A buck fifty for books and four bucks tuition apiece for Larry, Eileen, Richie and me. Vinny multiplied by four and took out his wallet, counted out twenty-two dollar bills and asked Sis for an envelope. He printed *Book Bill Money* on the outside of the envelope and put the money inside, sealed the envelope and gave it to Eileen, instructing her to put it in her book bag and turn the miracle over to the principal first thing in the morning. Eileen said, *See, Patty, I told you Mother Cabrini would give us a miracle if we asked for one.*

Dad opened an account at a new grocery store at the corner of McCandless and Stanton Avenues, *Heinricher's Market*. The Heinricher brothers operated the store, which included a full-range of produce, a deli, fresh fish and poultry, and a butcher shop. Their prices were higher than food stores on Butler Street but you couldn't beat the quality and deliveries were free. Our whole crew attended opening day and came home with free goodies. Every other day, Sis sent us kids to Heinrichers with two store lists, one with a few things to bring home that she needed right away, like milk and bread, and the other a list of groceries to be delivered. Relief from the burden of lugging groceries through the Homey was appreciated by everyone on our hill.

Dee, in her new job at Rosenbaum's Department Store downtown, earned enough to pitch in at home. She bought a sewing machine, sewed most of her own clothes, and dressed stylishly for work. Her manager took note; actually, he had a crush on her and took her home in a taxi on nights she worked late. He wanted to date Dee, but she was too busy. As a jurist she had earned recognition by prosecution and defense attorneys alike and served both civil and criminal trials. Court cases then were not tried with the technical complexity they are now. Cases were explained in layman's terms; jurors reviewed evidence and rendered verdicts with a clear conscience. The system was not perfect but Dee said it worked. Seeing the stable juror she was, the jury commissioner kept calling her back, even though it was apparent that she spent many an idle moment writing provocative poetry.

Dad created a *federal case* over Uncle Frank's and Aunt Grace's move to a house on Fourth Street in Aspinwall with their son Bucky, protesting that travelling across the river to see them created an inconvenience for the Scotts. Moreover, Marty and Jim Reynolds moved into the upstairs with their four kids. Both families switched from the Democratic to the Republican Party, seeing it as a more unified party with a practical ideology for the middle class. We were invited to their house-warming party with plenty of tasty food and sweet drinks. Our die-hard Democrat Dad drank beer all day and made his feelings felt, calling our relatives *Traitors*. They usually ignored Dad when he ranted like that.

The year rounded out in good form with our Aspinwall Uncle Dick and Aunt Olivia hosting a holiday celebration at their house on Western Avenue. She made the biggest bowl of potato salad in the world and served sliced baked ham on fresh bakery buns. Dad drank beer with Aunt Mary and Uncle Bill and no one seemed to mind that—after all, we were in the season. Uncle Frank made two trips to drive us all home. It made for a good time, and we cherished the trouble our relatives went to in an effort to accommodate a bewildered father and twelve kids with their mother gone to her glory.

Everybody attended midnight mass at St. Mary's that Christmas, even Grandmother Scott and Aunt Rose, who seldom went to church, because Vinny would be singing a solo with the men's choir, *Sveta Noč* (Silent Night) in his mellow tenor voice. He had rewired our Christmas lights, and at every opportunity, we sat in the living room enjoying that beautiful tree with its tiers of light shimmering through a veil of angel hair until the needles dried out and fell off. Thus, we settled into the post-holiday routine, contending with a mild depression that cold weather brings with less sunlight and shortened days. Dad divined an idea that a family breadwinner would soon be in line for a job at Hubbard's, but Joe came home from the Army with an honorable discharge bonus and sublime ambitions.

First thing he did was purchase a phonograph to fill our house with classical music—*RCA, the Master's Voice*—only it was Joe's tenor voice singing along with 78 rpm operatic recordings that enchanted us kids. He told us stories of post-war Japan. Hiroshima and Nagasaki were gone. In the sky above Tokyo, he said that he had never seen so many bright stars. Everywhere in Japan, he saw succulents flourishing in imperial gardens and the *Budda* resting in hidden terraces. There he had enjoyed solitude and heard words that spoke to his heart: *Come sit by me for here exists a better heaven and a better earth.* He regarded eastern thought and would eventually pursue a deeper understanding of it. His experience there taught him to detest war, not the enemy. Music and the arts would be humanity's salvation as far as Joe was concerned.

He enrolled at the Pittsburgh Art Institute in town and carried his portfolio and art supplies back and forth on the streetcar. To pay his way, he worked an overnight job at a bakery in Aspinwall and in the morning brought home leftover baked goods still fresh with the aroma of the bakery oven. He built a drawing table between the two windows in the boy's bedroom. It looked more like an altar with his drawing pencils, pastel chalks, and paints and brushes neatly arranged on a ledge above the table. He used a palette and worked with pastels and oils, painting a range of perceptions from earthly landscapes to heavenly luminaries, inspired perhaps by what he read in his many books, such as the mediaeval battles of saints and angels against Lucifer's demons and mythological figures from Apollo to Zeus. How he managed to concentrate amidst the constant flow of traffic through the room was a mystery. Perhaps listening to the opera on the radio helped. Dad could be heard grumbling about Joe's choice of music and the useless waste of time doing artwork when he could be making money in a mill. *No chance, sorry Dad.*

The federal government announced a shortage of goods and released six million dollars' worth of war-hoarded merchandise to retail stores. Peacetime industry began to manufacture freezers, toasters, mixers, electric percolators, vacuum cleaners, radios, phonographs, and automatic washing machines and dryers. Refrigerators were in demand, and fortunately for us, our icebox was replaced with Aunt Olivia's vintage *Hot Point* with an ice cube freezer.

Vinny, in his studies at AV Tech, learned enough to go into a small electronics enterprise with his buddy Joe Rosco. They looked towards earning a few bucks on the side with good customer service, fixing everything electronic, including the new fad—TV. Television sets were costly, but Vinny wanted it for us right then as we were. He bought an eight by ten-inch screen, a cathode ray tube, and other guts, and built a black and white television set from scratch. Watching things going on in the world through that small screen mystified Dad. Pittsburgh did not yet have a TV station, but we sat up late one night to watch the famous *Louis vs. Conn* boxing match relayed by *stratovision* (transmitted by airplane) from Baltimore.

Vinny had invited our good neighbor, Polta Tomasich, a sports enthusiast, to join us. With every blow, he kept on saying, *Out of sight, out of Sight*, in his Yugoslavian accent. He worked at the Union Steel plant on Butler Street and was respected as a noteworthy philosopher on our hill. He used his old-world charm to greet us anytime one of the Scotts appeared before him. Days after the boxing event, Vinny encountered Polta sitting on his folding chair in front of his house.

He greeted Vinny with his familiar *How you was?* Vinny decided to challenge this and said, *Mr. Tomasich, you always ask me `how you was but you're supposed to ask how are you?* Polta chuckled and replied, *No, no, Vinny, I know how you are, I am looking at you. I want to know how you was.* For Vinny, everything was going swell. He glowed with with pride when he walked into our house and found our living room filled with kids sitting on the floor watching cartoons on his homemade tv.

Washington & Jefferson College in Washington County established a live broadcast of a word-game show. Dad usually had the correct definition on the tip of his tongue; he just couldn't always pull up the right answer on the spot. Richie sat through these episodes with Dad, trying to figure out what was going on. He was at that age when tiny people still lived inside the radio, let alone a television.

Huey had joined Skip at Central Catholic; both belonged to the Glee Club and performed in minstrel shows and operettas.

They would come home in time for supper and rush upstairs to groom and change clothes, then rush back to school for the evening's performance. They were presently billed for the nonsensical operetta *Naughty Marietta* and had to be on stage an hour ahead of showtime. Skip complained that Huey was taking too long getting ready. Huey emerged from the bathroom and meandered down the stairs looking as pleased with himself as he could be. Dad, awaiting at the foot of the stairs, asked in an irritated tone what the holdup was. Huey had taken his time because he wanted to look good in Dad's best tie. It never happened again.

Vinny earned his credentials at AV Tech and enrolled at the University of Pittsburgh in its engineering program under the GI Bill. He saw an ad in the paper that an agent of the Federal Communications Commission in Washington, D.C. was passing through town to administer tests for radio operators. He registered, took the test, and at the end of the day received a first-class radio operator's license, the hardest to achieve.

Radio Station WCAE hired him, and he was at last free to resign from mill work forever. He worked midafternoon to closing four days a week in a hut next to the radio transmission tower out in the middle of nowhere, beyond Forest Hills. There, he recorded data and monitored gauges that made it possible for the popular news and talk radio station to broadcast throughout metropolitan Pittsburgh.

Meanwhile, political bosses made job offers you could hardly refuse if you professed party loyalty. Vinny was offered a job as a city fireman, a respectable position in every way with good pay and benefits. It wasn't what Vinny wanted. Word got through to party bigwigs who got back to Vinny saying that he had insulted them. He responded by going to the voter registration office to change his affiliation from Democrat to Republican, and avoided mentioning this to Dad.

In his spare time, Vinny worked as a volunteer at the Slovenian Hall events on 57th Street. Good times included getting together for banquets, weddings, polka dances, K.S.K.J. (American Slovene Catholic Union) and S.N.P.J. (Slovenska Narodna Podporna Jednota). Movies you had no chance to see as first runs were featured there, maybe a few years behind.

During Lent that year, the Slovenski Dom featured Cecil B. de Mille's classic film *King of Kings*. The dark and distorted film was hard on the eyes but cost only a nickel to see. The velvet curtain would slowly rise and, behold, we were gazing at a mural of the Slovenia countryside commissioned by local artist, Joe Scott.

St. Mary's Drama Guild staged plays at the hall, the Scott boys made up most of the cast for the plays and Joe created the cardboard props. Vinny played a lead role in *Night Winds*, written and directed by the guild's chairman, Larry Canjar. Skip played *Antoine ze French Arteest* and our Larry played *Ignatz Stupovitz*, a little Jewish violin player. He didn't have a single line to say yet he stole the show. Frank Lokar, the church organist, accompanied the songs on an upright piano perched on a side stage. The hall was packed for every performance, and on the last night of the play the entire cast and crew received a thunderous applause.

Joe attended events all over town and hardly ever missed performances by the Pittsburgh Symphony Orchestra at the Syria Mosque under the direction of its renowned conductor, Fritz Reiner. He started a new job on the overnight shift at the Heinz food plant on the Northside, which paid better wages than the bakery shop job. In his spare time, he performed with the Civic Light Opera in the summer season at Pitt Stadium in singing and dancing roles. He had qualified as a professional entertainer dancing with the Tokyo ballet during his service in Japan with the U.S. Entertainment Forces.

Larry's good times—getting up at five a.m. to get ready for his morning paper route and trying not to make any noise with Dad home from night turn just falling asleep. Larry picked up his papers at Sunnyside School and delivered on a Stanton Heights route—an easy job in the summer when school was out. He was a candidate for scholarship at Central when school reopened, but had no desire to study Latin, a required course for graduation.

In September, he started Peabody High School, didn't like it there, and quit. However, his school counselor got him enrolled in the mechanical drafting program at Connelley Vocational. His homeroom teacher was concerned about what Larry had to contend with getting to school on time due to his paper route responsibilities and gladly approved the required admission slip. Grammar and English studies bored him, but he really enjoyed History and Current Events, and more so Politics.

Harry S. Truman was running for his first elected term as President. Even though Lawrenceville was a Democratic stronghold, some people didn't care for his style and personality. Members of St. Mary's asked Father Kebe for his opinion because they were afraid to vote for Thomas Dewey. The wise cleric explained that they had no choice but to vote their conscience. Truman was so unpopular that newspapers posted premature bold headlines the night of the election: *Dewey Defeats Truman*.

The nation awoke the next morning to learn that Truman had won. He was sworn into office on January 20, 1949 before the first national television audience. No one had more fun watching the presidential parade than the smiling man in a London Fog Signature Wool Overcoat and Stetson Hat sitting in the stands on that bitter cold and clear day. Dad cheered: *Give 'em hell, Harry*!

In the unforgiving climate of Pittsburgh, Joe completed his courses at the Art Institute and could not find a job in the field of commercial illustrating. He reflected on his dreams, considered his vocation, and entered the Jesuit Novitiate in Wernersville, Pennsylvania's Dutch country fifty miles east of Harrisburg. The whole family missed him, so Vinny went out and bought a 1938 Pontiac for three hundred dollars and took us to see Joe. It was a lot of money then but a good, solid car—no rust—well worth it for the two trips to get there. On the first two hundred and ninety mile drive down the brand new Pennsylvania turnpike, he took Dad, Sis, Huey, Larry, and Martha. On the second trip, he took his trained copilot Huey, and Dee, Anna, Eileen, Richie and me. Skip had just joined the Army.

Vinny had to work the day of the second trip and drove all that night to get to Wernersville. In Harrisburg he stopped to show us around. We were all feeling starved, so he took us to a roadside diner. An old man and woman served cold soup in dirty bowls. Vinny told them to take the food back and start over. They came back with hot soup in clean bowls and charged Vinny half price. When we arrived at the novitiate, Vinny slept in the car while Joe gave us an inspiring tour of those lavishly attended grounds. He took us to the dining hall, served us sandwiches, and played *Chopin* sonatas on a grand piano. It felt like we no sooner arrived and it was time to go home because we could not afford overnight accommodations anywhere. We were sad to leave but glad to see how at ease Joe seemed.

All the way back to Pittsburgh on that tiresome road trip, Huey had to nudge Vinny every so often to make sure he was awake. Huey said that staying awake for our family's safety almost killed him. The teachers at Central were killing him too. He had an after-school job and chores to do for Dad at home. At the eleventh hour, he sat at the dining room table in Skip's chair, running up the electric bill under the dim light of the chandelier, absorbing way too much academic information for his tired brain. He resisted Dad's early beckoning to rise and faced a rude awakening at the hands of the Christian Brothers for being late for school. Detention hardly addressed his concerns.

Dad wasted no time beckoning Richie; he went upstairs and tossed him out of bed. He was in second grade for the second time. Eileen and I walked him to school, but if a bully classmate approached, he would take off his glasses because he didn't want to be called *four eyes*. We tried to keep him on course to avoid delays or absent days, although we respected his assertiveness for manly independence.

Richie dallied on the way to school as nature tended to distract him. He would stop to pick stuff up off the ground like dry leaves, twigs, dead birds, and examine them. He would climb into a tree to pick a certain type of leaf, or a certain type of bug curled up underneath it. Eileen and I had to wait while he traveled into the brush for certain types of flat stones that he collected, adventures that guaranteed we would be late for morning Mass.

Eileen and I advanced to Sister Mary Fernando Fluehr's sixth grade class. She played the organ in church and taught music with the aid of a portable pump organ and a pitch pipe. One day the organ keys froze during the practice of a Slovenian hymn.

Sister started pumping the pedals wildly and still no sound came out; she made us finish the song *acapella.*

At home, we listened to a new song, the ringing of a telephone. Bell Telephone (*Ma Bell*) had been busy propagandizing in the neighborhood about the need for security in case of a burglary or murder; if you became a customer, you could dial a free number and get help. Under pressure, Dad let us get a phone and made a rule: *Okay to make a phone call to set a time to meet but no socializing over the phone.* The problem was that every time we needed to place a call, our party line was in use. Sometimes people would miss-dial and our phone would ring. Sis was in charge of taking calls and would politely explain that the person on the line had dialed the wrong number. The phone would ring again and Dad would get so mad that he'd holler into the phone, *This is shit for the birds.*

One day, himself picked up a call and swore at our party-liner, who happened to be Sis's girlfriend, Manna Chirico. Manna Mae swore back at Dad in her robust voice, knowing full well that swearing on the phone was against the law, so she quickly covered her tracks by threatening our Dad that she was going to sue him. The entirely ridiculous episode almost ruined a friendship until Larry stepped in. He called Manna Mae and apologized on Dad's behalf. In return, she invited Larry to join her bowling team at *Kobe's* Bowling Alley on Butler Street.

Vinny belonged to the Slovenski bowling team, presently engaged in a competition against the Morningstars. A new girl had joined that team, and Vinny inquired as to who she was—Dorothy Radick, who lived in the Ninth Ward. As rivals go, they made friends and started seeing each other on a regular basis. Dad got suspicious but didn't have the nerve to ask why Vinny, who had so little spare time to begin with, was spending less time at home. There did seem to be something different about big brother, like less intense and more cheerful. He took our three-year-old darling Martha everywhere with him, and she followed him everywhere when he was at home.

He'd carry a set of clean clothes to the basement, take a shower and get ready for his date. Martha would sit at the top of the cellar way stairs listening to his songs in Slovenian over the noise of the shower running. He would holler up to her, holding her spellbound with silly stories about two crazy characters named Sam and Pete who might one day visit her.

The holiday season was in progress and Dad gave me permission to paint a scene on our new front window; after all, I was a student at the Fitzpatrick free Saturday art classes at the Carnegie Institute in Oakland. Vinny made it clear that he was not in favor of using acrylic paint because it might never come off, but it was all that I could find in the attic trunk containing Joe's art supplies. Vinny grabbed his jacket, took his Pontiac for a ride, and came back with Dorothy; she wanted to see where he lived. I was at the window painting and came out to say *Hi.* Vinny looked at my messy art work and expressed concern, but his girlfriend told Vinny not to discourage me. He introduced her as *Dottie,* and she said, *Patty, your nativity scene is beautiful.* I never forgot this, but Vinny was right. I scraped paint off that window for a solid month.

That Christmas Eve, Vinny and Sis threw a BYOB party in our basement that lasted all night long. *Rudolph the Red-Nosed Reindeer* was the No. 1 hit tune, and KDKA radio played it all night and day. During the holidays, Vinny brought Dorothy to the house to meet the family and announced their engagement.

Dad sat bolt upright in his chair looking like a petrified tree stump until Vinny, in his smooth style, told him to relax. Dorothy, a bank teller, was a classy dresser with smartly styled auburn hair and gorgeous jewelry. Their pending marriage made for a tender closing of an incredible decade, and it seemed that we were heading for a new age of prosperity.

David L. Lawrence had won re-election by popular vote, thanks to Republican financier Richard K. Mellon, who put fifty million dollars' worth of development and construction contracts on the mayor's desk ready to be signed in preparation for Pittsburgh's Renaissance, beginning in the heart of the Golden Triangle with the development of Gateway Center—several modern office buildings, the Hilton Hotel, and a state park at the confluence, where converged our Three Rivers, the Allegheny, the Monongahela, and the Ohio—and with a commitment to clean up our rivers and the air.

Think of it, *the Point.* Our great-grandmother Brigid Feeney had called it an Irish shantytown and our great-grandfather Patrick O'Donnell had called it a veritable pig's wallow. Be assured, we Scotts living in a house on a hill that we claimed as our own would hold onto the privilege for as long as possible, even with the understanding that a day might come when we might have to let go—if and when the time came.

We prayed for laws more just, music more sweet, and hearts more gentle, and we looked forward to an era of peace—a peace like the settling of sweet morning dew on our city's vast and splendid hills. Sunlight broke through the overcast, the temperature reached the seventies, the January snow melted, heat waves rose from the pavements, and we tossed our winter coats aside.

1950

Dad took Richie to the Stanley Theatre downtown on his tenth birthday to see a live performance of *Rosie the Riveter*, a song and dance show about a fictional character who symbolized the millions of women who filled America's factories, munitions plants, and shipyards during World War II, a war that infected the culture to the extreme that war movies had long-standing reruns. Dad saw them all.

It had secretly bothered Dad that the draft board had rejected him because of too many kids, not that he wasn't relieved at the time with Mom needing so much more help. But as time passed by, and he saw his sons, one by one, join the service, he felt deprived of the opportunity to do something that would have boosted his sagging morale and deflated ego. With every pat on the back he gave Vinny, Joe, Skip, Huey, and Larry, when they left home, and with every hug he gave them when they returned, he had expressed his wish that he could have served, too. He loved his country.

Going to see war movies with Dad did Richie proud. One thing he noticed about Dad was that he never came up short when he treated us kids to a day out. He kept track of new films coming into town, but when his pin money came up short, he would say, *We'll have to wait for that one to come to the Dome.* On their way home from the show that day, they stopped at Neid's so Dad could wet his whistle. Richie sat beside him at the bar, making gurgling sounds sipping an orange pop from a straw until the bottle was drained. One more for the road for Dad, and they were on their way.

Dad had a way of walking with Richie, holding him close, not a bear hug, nothing effusive, just with Dad's pinkie finger wrapped around Richie's. They walked the block passed the *Protestant Home for the Aged and Incurables,* where Dad paused to reflect on earlier times with his father, Sam Scott the Milkman. From there to home it was slow going for Dad up the city steps

huffing and puffing. By the time they reached the top, he was wheezing heavily. Richie inquired, *Dad, how comes you make that weird noise when you breathe*? Dad replied, *Son, we live in the Smoky City.*

Dad had heard about emphysema, but his case would not be diagnosed for another decade, a disease that would eventually kill him. Air pollution laws were in effect and talk was that the price paid by industry to conform would send our mills south and into the third world. Our rivers, though cleaner, contained toxic discharges that contaminated the fish supply. The fish houses in the Strip District refused to carry local fish, but the provision house on Butler Street sold catfish for fifty-cents a pound, up a penny from forty-nine cents. Rounding prices off at a nickel or ten cents helped to ease the penny shortage. Finding pennies on the ground became an exciting pasttime for children. The local banks established *Penny Day* on which they did a brisk business exchanging coppers for quarters and two-half dollar coins for a paper dollar bill. The United States was doing what no other nation on earth could do, helping all of them over there and allowing prosperity to prevail over here.

My asthma took its seasonal hit of coughing and wheezing, and I was still scraping paint off the front window with a butter knife, all that I was allowed to work with. Richie felt so sorry for me that he went into Dad's shaving kit and borrowed two razor blades. We were forbidden to play with them but together made progress. Richie said he felt like a vandal slicing up a Michelangelo at the Vatican after I had turned our bay window into stained-glass art. Dad discovered the crime and took a conniption fit because Richie had once tried to scrape his face with Dad's razor knife. He didn't even have peach fuzz yet. Dad went to the hardware store and bought a paint scraper and paint remover to finish the job, making it known that the family artists were wearing him out and taking him broke.

No one we knew seemed to be as poor as the middle-aged black man in a blue cap and khakis who collected scrap on our hill. He drove a green pickup truck with bashed in fenders and crooked front wheels that seemed to turn faster than the back wheels. The exhaust pipe dragged on the ground and spewed black smoke. Above the din of his rattle trap, we could hear his mellow call from afar: *raaag man, raaag man, raaag man*. It signaled the neighborhood to bring our rags and metal scrap out to the curb or be at the curb to tell him where to find our junk. The day he hauled Mom's *Gain-a-Day* away, we all choked up. It was replaced with a modern *Speed Queen* washer and had been rusting away in the back yard. We desperately wanted to hold onto it and had to let it go; it was beyond repair. The rag man gave us a dollar for the washer and two dollars for the leaking copper cauldron, which was worth four dollars at the scrap yard. He also gave us kids a nickel apiece for helping him to pick up small scrap that lay scattered on the ground.

Our coins were burning holes in our pockets by the time the ice-cream truck rolled onto Duncan Street with its noisy bell clanging. A nickel bought a Popsicle to share or a Creamsicle not to share; a dime bought a Dixie cup or an ice cream sandwich, but fifteen cents bought a slice of chocolate ice cream cake roll—sweet treats to satisfy without ever leaving the hill.

Sis hardly ever had to leave the hill to buy what we needed. She home shopped the modern way with big food orders from Heinrichers and household cleaning products from the Fuller brush man. The Jewel Tea door-to-door salesman sold coffee, percolators, drip coffee pots, tea kettles, dinner plates and flat ware. Sis earned points towards these fancy items with every pound of coffee she bought. It took her a year to earn a free stoneware vacuum drip pot finished in a flowered base and gold trim. Dad enjoyed the coffee it brewed, way better than the aluminum percolator, he said.

Richie would hang around waiting for Sis to take time out for their afternoon tea—cracking jokes that only they were in on—a sacred ritual ever since our mother died. He was convinced that Sis had raised us, but she said we raised ourselves. One day, she took Richie to see *Grapes of Wrath* which was back at the Dome, their favorite place. Normally they walked, but Richie's clodhoppers were hurting his feet, so they waited for a streetcar. It never came, and they walked many blocks to the show, he limping. Sis said, *Next time we'll take a bus.* Henceforward, anytime a stressful situation challenged them, they would giggle at each other and yell aloud, *Take A Bus!* By the way, that movie made them feel rich!

Richie was always happy walking alongside Sis on their way somewhere, anywhere. She looked so glamourous, like in the movies, dressed in a dark dress and smoking a Lucky Strike. She treated him like a grown-up, sharing her opinion about members of the family who acted goofy, without mentioning Dad's name.

Dad swore at tv stars who played goofy characters in plotless sit coms, but he enjoyed the political dramas unfolding in televised investigations into alleged communist conspiracies to overthrow the government. A circus-like atmosphere created by Joseph McCarthy made Senate hearings so popular that local theaters installed big-screen TVs and offered free viewing. You could even watch it in downtown store windows. We cherished the fact that Vinny supplied our television entertainment even though he was too busy to watch it. He was getting married.

Dorothy Radick belonged to the Serbian Orthodox Church. Special arrangements had to be made for their marriage in the Roman Catholic Church. Father Kebe was a friend of the priest who had baptized her. Together, the clerics made for the lovebirds a beautiful ceremony. In anticipation of the big event, they set up housekeeping in the upstairs of Mrs. Radick's home in the Ninth Ward.

For the big day, Dad took Eileen and me shopping downtown for new clothes. Eileen picked out a green dress to match her eyes, and I picked out a blue dress to match mine. He told us to keep them on and told the clerk to put our old clothes in the store bag. He paid cash and walked us a few doors down the street to Strem's Studio to have a picture of us taken and framed. For ages, it shared space on our living room mantle with our military brothers; from time to time we looked at it and admired ourselves, and Dad reminded us that we were *his girls.* Of course, he drank too much at the wedding, but he made us feel as though we were the stars of that show.

Shortly afterwards our TV blew out. Dad told Eileen to get Vinny on the phone; she forgot he worked night shift at the radio transmission tower and apologized for waking him up. He stopped by to investigate and suggested it was time to buy a new television. Dad was miffed because he had expected Vinny's TV to hold up indefinitely. When it finally sunk into

Dad's great brain that the family genius had retired from the electronics business, he opened an account at Spears & Co., a furniture and appliance store in East Liberty. We went from an eight inch homemade to a store bought fourteen inch television. Vinny stopped by to take a look at it and said Dad got a pretty good deal.

Shortly, Dad received a letter from Joe saying he was resigning from the Jesuit Novitiate. He had treasured living in that serene environment absorbed in prayer and the study of philosophy, theology, and other lofty ideas. It got him to thinking there must be a great deal more to learn beyond the religious life in the practical world; his yearning to follow his heart brought him home.

Joe was a commercial artist and could find no work in his field. Dad mentioned this to his friend and confidant, Ted Neid, who commissioned Joe to paint a mural on the tavern wall. When the project was completed, us kids got dressed up and Dad took us to the opening—an illustrious full scale mural of a scene from Swan Lake. Much to our surprise, Eileen climbed up on a bar stool, spread her arms wide, and spoke up for all to hear, saying, *Our Joe painted this beautiful scene for everyone to enjoy, dancers in tutus doing ballet on their toes. Joe is a good dancer and a good artist. He sticks up for me when Dad's upset.* The opening was such a huge success for Neid's business that Dad shook Joe's hand and said, *Well, son, if dancing on one toe makes you happy, so be it*! He later let Eileen know that she didn't have to go that far.

He yelled at her every time she left a light on in the house. It made her cry, and he said, *Don't feel sorry for yourself, you'll lose the battle.* Joe told Dad he shouldn't talk to Eileen that way. She eventually figured out that Dad was right, but Joe was right, too. He and Dad disagreed regarding Joe's plans for his future. Dad harped on the idea that Hubbard's was a good option. Joe had to tell Dad straight up how he felt but said it in a nice way, *Look Dad, I don't want to spend the rest of my life in a mill. I want to work in the art world in New York City.* All he had to do now was figure out where to get funding for his sublime plan. All the work he could find was at odd jobs that paid poorly.

One day the Ringling Brothers Barnum & Bailey Circus came to town; Joe interviewed for a job and was hired. The circus left town with Joe. It seemed a natural thing for him to do, leaving home.

He felt sort of guilty that maybe he should have stuck around a little longer but thought no one would notice him being gone. He had always been drawn to the circus, ever since he was a lad going to the St. Mary's carnival fair. He had been leaving home ever since he climbed into the back of a grocery van when he was four years old and went on a thrilling ride through the bumpy streets of Lawrenceville. Now he traveled on a bumpy circus train for a season, and all that while we thought he was living the exciting life of a circus performer. It turned out that he had been hired to paint signs and build props for stage sets.

The stage was set for Vinny to graduate from the University of Pittsburgh with an engineering degree, and he was looking to a change of careers from his radio tower job. He found himself walking around downtown and stopped in front of the Westinghouse Corporation headquarters building in Gateway Center. He went in and talked to the receptionist. As fate would have it, one of the executives overheard the conversation, invited Vinny into his office and instantly made a connection between Vinny's experience and the company's work with nuclear reactor simulators. He placed a call to someone in charge of instrumentation and control who said that Vinny had exactly what they were looking for. Westinghouse hired him and assigned him to the Bettis Atomic Power Laboratory in West Mifflin. He resigned from WCAE, but in his spare time continued to use his

FCC license doing volunteer work for WQED as it struggled to beam up and become one of the finest public broadcasting stations in the country.

National television broadcasts of Senator Joseph McCarthy's investigations into a communist conspiracy to take over the country were operating at full tilt with fingers pointing at Hollywood. In light of its magnanimous contributions to boosting morale of American troops during the war, the accusations leveled at the stars seemed offensive, even for Dad. One night he tuned in on the hearings and recognized the man being questioned by the investigative panel. Matt Cvetic lived in Lawrenceville and belonged to St. Mary's on 57th Street. Dad had tipped a few glasses with him at Neid's. Mr. Cvetic revealed to Congress that he had been posing as a member of the Communist Party for the FBI for nine years. In the lengthy hearings, he exposed a number of Pittsburgh religious and civic organizations as communist fronts; arrests followed and people were prosecuted.

Due to the zealous nature of the FBI investigations, the home of a Slovenian family on 57th Street was searched and their chicken coop turned upside down. The terrified man of that household explained that his hobby was raising pigeons. The terrified woman of that household told Father Kebe that her *Anky* was telling the truth, but McCarthy suspected that the pigeons were being sent on clandestine missions to Yugoslavia carrying secret messages for the Kremlin, a preposterous accusation, knowing that pigeons rarely fly more than fifty miles over an ocean. Mrs. Anky further confessed the shame she felt because FBI thugs had gone through their personal belongings, and they had a nun in the family.

Vinny heard about it and let prominent citizens of our community know that the Slovenes were among war heroes who belonged to the American Veterans of Foreign Wars. He belonged to the local chapter of the American Slovene Vets and presently served as co-chairman. They held their meetings in the basement bar of the Slovenian Hall and held their patriotic parades from the Hall to St. Mary's Church on national holidays. How's that for being Irish!

Dad, still a dapper gent, was living on the edge of middle age in post wartime economy gabardines. His hair had thinned and his glasses were a few prescriptions thicker, but he had retained his cavalier charm and pedestrian manner. His friendly *hi how'ya doin'* as he strutted down Butler Street had won him a measure of trust around town.

Still, a mist lingered in his eyes. Something within him had changed, a change from a quick glance to a slow gaze, as if he was trying to see through a fog. When he brooded, his eyes looked so empty that it sometimes felt like he didn't even see us. His heavy smoking left him breathless though he still made no connection between that and one cigarette after the other. He struck a match and lit up at will and was rarely seen without a cigarette propped between the first two fingers of his right hand.

His *Martha girl* adored her father, unconditionally. She loved the aromatics of his *Old Spice* shave lotion and his handsome aura when he wore his gaberdine suit, white shirt and bow tie, his black wool overcoat and Stetson hat, his *Bogart* look, and took her someplace. She loved the earthy smell of his after-work clothes, his sweat so strong and sweet about him. He sometimes looked shabby and, a peculiar feeling of shame would engulf her because he was drunk and we were still poor, even though he went to work every day.

Skilled work was plentiful with positions hard to fill because Truman reinstated the draft, citing the international conflict in Korea and the need to expand the military. News of the conflict unfolded on television; Americans owned over a million sets. Proliferation of high-tech jobs impacted social change, and cultural change came swiftly. An explosion of sky scrapers on city skylines defined the sudden growth of corporate America with its relocation of technical professionals to all parts of the country.

The finishing touches of our remodeling were in progress. The front entrance hallway wall had been torn out to expand the living room. Dad was in there watching TV one night when part of the new ceiling collapsed on him. Sis was in the kitchen and heard the startling crash. She rushed onto the scene and, seeing Dad covered with plaster debris, said in a sarcastic tone, *Now you really look plastered Dad.* And he said, *This is really some shit for the birds.* Other than being stunned, no harm done to his great hard head, although he complained on high about the big mess and the big disruption to his routine until the ceiling was re-plastered and his lifestyle was restored.

Last but not the least project at 5614 was the attic, and a century of soot first had to be removed. You couldn't even sit on the front steps with all the soot soaring down to the ground. While this disruptive phase of the job was in progress, Sis made

arrangements to take Martha on a trip to Baltimore, Maryland, to visit her dear friend, Tess Heinricher, who had married and moved there. Sis took Martha downtown shopping for new clothes, a pink and a yellow dress, and black patent leather buckle shoes with bows. They packed a suitcase, made their way to the Pennsylvania Station and hopped aboard the B & O. Oh, what fun, what excitement for our baby sister, all dressed up in her new clothes and riding on that train with her beautiful *Sissy Mum*. Sis was twenty-four; Martha was four. Tess was thrilled to see Martha so well cared for and Sis looking wonderful. Tess and her husband had two kids and lived about a half mile from the Chesapeake Bay, where they went each day to swim and gather crabs for the evening cookout. They walked a long blacktop road in the blaring hot sun. It was Martha's first experience of vacationing. Sis had a great time with her friends, especially at night when it cooled down and the talking and laughter lasted into the night and the fireflies flickered like a million stars.

Our main ladies returned home happy and well-tanned to find a small room had been built at the head of the attic stairs with tongue and groove floor and new windows installed. We were to call it the *third floor*, not the attic, and it was to be Sis's private room. She was thrilled but, in the stifling heat, her lipstick melted. She started keeping it in the refrigerator, one of Auntie O's charitable donation.

Sis appreciated having a room of her own in the upper chambers of our busy household because it was a restful getaway. One day, Eileen took a walk up there to Sis's *apartment*, as she called it, to borrow a nickel to take me to Sullivan's candy store and found Sis in bed with the mattress on fire. She had fallen asleep smoking a cigarette, and Eileen saved her life.

Over four years since Mom died and Eileen and I felt pretty much on our own. It seemed we had free reign, could drift, and be gone for hours without being missed. Sis often had to leave pots and pans on the stove with the lids on and the gas jets turned off to go out looking for us when supper was ready. She knew where to look, first on the barricade corner where we played spy games, or in the Greenie below the barricade, a flat stretch of Homey Hill territory where kids on our hill created a ball field and kept it cleared. The most obvious place to look was the *WPA Wall*—the social center of our universe.

The older kids and their friends were known as *the gang on the wall.* This was a close-knit group of the unorganized innocent who grew up on the Wall and still gathered there to hang out, just goofing off, or making plans to go places and do things, like an afternoon picnic in North Park, an evening walk around the Highland Park reservoir, a night at the Dome. Some of the boys already had driver licenses and drove cars borrowed from their fathers. They took everybody who could squeeze in, no seat belts, for a ride to the Dairy Queen for a curly-topped ice cream cone, pay as you go. Usually, someone carried a portable radio to listen to the Pittsburgh Pirates baseball games. The gang on the wall also played a challenging rope game called *Higher and Higher.* Amazing how those fellows sustained no brain damage with all the hard falls they took and hitting their heads on the ground.

School started and Martha could hardly wait for Richie to come home. She could see the Wall from the middle bedroom window, and the minute she sighted him she'd start counting how many seconds before he reached the house: *five, ten, fifteen, twenty, twenty-five, thirty, thirty-five, forty, forty-five.* Uncanny how this magical child could count to a hundred and beyond, yet she always paused at forty-five, the year she was born.

Martha wanted to go to school with Richie. Sis told her she had to wait. She had attempted to start kindergarten at Sunnyside Public School. Dee walked her there on the first day and Martha walked right back home. Sis took her the second day and Martha refused to stay, explaining that other kids acted like they were better than she, like what Larry went through at that age. Perhaps, it was because these were the children of the *bible-believing Protestants* talked about at our house that Mom had so feared.

Eileen and I made our Confirmation and advanced from seventh to eighth grade. We were troubled to learn that Sister Mary Pietra Huckdstein, the kindest teacher we ever knew, had been transferred to Holy Name School on Troy Hill. Sister Mary Alexandrine Guntner was our new teacher and the new principal. She came from an all boys' school in Boston; we felt it at a trying age when our child-like spirits could have used a bit of feminine affirmation.

Fortunately, Anna attended to our maturing needs, which gave us a measure of self-confidence. Then Eileen came to school wearing lipstick; Sister Alexandrine was incensed. Eileen tried to explain that she borrowed Sis's lipstick because she wanted to look dressed up for school. Sister sent her to the lavatory to wipe it off.

Next, based on petty gossip that she flirted with men on the public works crew tearing down the wooden 57th Street steps and building concrete steps, Sister threatened to expel Eileen. She tried to explain that the crew were the flirts, not her; she wanted to be a nun. Sister instantly turned that request down on the excuse that there weren't any openings. In front of the whole class she made Eileen go out into the corridor and rap on the side door to the rectory and confess to Father Kebe that she flirted with boys. Miss Mary, the housekeeper, answered the door and said, *Father is sleeping*. Blessed are they who knock and the priest is sleeping.

I had a similar experience under that regime. The day after Labor Day was our first day in eighth grade. I wore a blue sweater set to school, a gift from Joe for my birthday the last day of August. Sister Alexandrine ordered me out into the unlit corridor and told me to never wear that outfit to school again because it was causing too much attention from the boys. I was mortified, completely unaware that boys even saw me. Eileen advised me not to take Sister too seriously because she favored boys. Eileen, when she felt up to it, still escorted me to dancing school. She loved ballet and couldn't take lessons due to her heart condition.

Vinny stopped by the house and heard Eileen out; she wanted to take piano lessons. He signed her up at St. Kieran's and arranged for the delivery of a second-hand piano. The relatives gave her a piano that needed tuning, and Vinny paid her seventy-five cents a lesson. Dad was working night turn and sleeping day turn. Eileen tried in earnest to practice quietly, but she kept hitting too many wrong notes and woke him up. He tore down the stairs in his underwear and tore into poor Eileen, saying that he had just about enough of her piano business. She explained that she needed a metronome; it was no use.

You would think it might have registered in Dad's consciousness what Patrick Quinn must have gone through in the old days when Dad tinkered on Mom's piano and sang his irritating tune. Instead, he told Eileen that her playing sounded like a funeral march, and she told him that cob webs in the piano was the cause, not her. This argument went round-and-round until Dad sent her on vacation to the relatives and took a crowbar and sledge hammer to the piano. Dad's unexpressed reasoning for his actions was that Eileen hardly ever practiced, the piano was not only collecting dust and bugs, but it was taking up too much space. Richie was sorriest of all to see it go; he had hidden his shoes in the piano so he could stay home from school.

During Indian summer, the season of changing leaves and the last warm spell, Richie took Martha on a hike up Quills Hill. She loved being with Richie. He gave her *Indian burns* by taking her arm in his hands, with one hand going clockwise, the other counterclockwise, and rubbing her arm back and forth until her skin burned enough to make her squeal. She didn't like that, so he tested his *knuckle sandwich*, making a fist with his knuckles placed firmly against the top of her head and twisting until she squealed. *Indian burns were actually less painful*, she said. On Quill's Hill, they explored the Indian caves looking for fossils and gathered a splendid assortment of dry leaves and branches to decorate our house. In no time, the holiday season approached and winter rushed in.

On Thanksgiving Day it started to snow. All we could see out our windows was snow—heavy, wet snow that stuck. Larry and his friends went sled riding that evening. He came home exhausted, went straight to bed, and got up at five in the morning to get ready for his paper route. He saw no need to turn on the lights because it was so bright inside. Outside, the landscape was buried beneath deep snow, and Duncan Street had vanished.

Larry had papers to deliver and didn't plan to end up behind the eight ball over a little snowstorm with money to be made. He bundled up, grabbed a shovel and went out to clear the sidewalk. The only sound he heard was himself shoveling snow, and it was snowing faster than he could shovel. He was panting by the time he found the curb and had to shovel his way back to the house to dry out his socks and shoes. Then it dawned on him that his newspapers hadn't been delivered to the back door. *Ah the heck with it*, he said to himself and went back to bed. It snowed thirty inches the day the city closed.

The National Guard was called in to maintain civil order. The mayor mustered every available piece of road equipment into service to clear the main roads and dump a million tons of snow into the river. Neighborhoods formed shovel brigades and cleared side streets and alleyways. Larry saw a challenge and recruited his buddies to clear our street. They set to work with a will sending great shovels full of snow flying, and they cleared a fire lane, piling snow in a compact wall along one side of the street, in some places four and five feet high. Once their community service work was accomplished, they built a snow fort and had a terrific snowball battle.

After the Big Snow of 1950 came the big freeze. People were ordered to walk in the streets for fear that the huge ice cycles falling off buildings would kill them. Traffic stood still, except for the countless sleds, tires, inner tubes, and pieces of cardboard on which the children of Pittsburgh rode joyfully down its slopes. The snow remained throughout the holidays, and before we knew it, a new year had rolled around.

The New Year 1951 became a year of strikes and lost wages. Layoffs followed strikes, and the organized union saved Dad's job. The men at the shop wisely decided not to strike, knowing that Hubbard's had started down a slippery slope, competing in a modern economy without modernizing. Wartime suppression of inventions had transformed into a war of new ideas like calculators and computers. New meant perfect, bigger meant better, and roomier cars were in demand. Car lots and tire shops started popping up all along Butler Street. Vast networks of new and improved highways were under construction, and shopping mall developments were driving neighborhood stores out of existence.

In Lawrenceville the effects would become devastating. A *Thorofare* supermarket went up overnight on the site of the old McCandless School across from the fire house on Butler Street. Butcher shops and grocery stores in the Tenth Ward went out of business. Old-timers said what they had been saying ever since post-World War One when Dad reached voting age and was introduced to local politics: *At city hall, our side of town does not exist.*

The volume of truck traffic that had once blocked main streets and clogged alleyways to unload merchandise started driving straight through our side of town. This and other hot issues mesmerized our do-nothing politicians. A complaint delivered by local leaders to city hall was that they were letting city neighborhoods rot to upgrade downtown. The report back to us was that if we wanted Lawrenceville to survive we would have to take care of it ourselves. The Arsenal Board of Trade was our city hall, the paramedic team that pumped oxygen into our economy and financed community programs.

Nothing compared to the heat of the sun beating down at high noon. It burned through smog and smoke and cauterized the landscape. Under the duress of primary elections, road crews converged on neighborhoods with a mandate from downtown to improve our city streets. Without a referendum of the people, a macadamized surface would destroy the beauty of the bumpy cobblestoned streets but would be less stressful on vehicles. A road crew arrived on the hill with brooms and shovels and cleared our streets of dirt and stones. A city asphalt truck followed, pouring the thick hot tar. A steam roller followed the asphalt truck, flattening the asphalt and removing air bubbles. The road crew put up a sign: *Road Closed. Wet Asphalt.* A day later they removed the sign. Kids on the hill brought out every wheeled vehicle in existence to test the new pavement—roller skates, scooters, wagons, and homemade carts called giggies. What a mess with everything sinking into that sticky black tar and impossible to avoid tracking it everywhere.

Larry wasn't happy about tracking the tar on his shoes from home to his after-school job way out in Bellevue, where he was employed in a machine shop school-work program. He was ambitious to earn money, got to work by two streetcars, and was gone all day. Eileen knew all about it; she packed his lunch, a healthy lunch of fruit, a baloney sandwich, celery stalks, and carrot sticks. He said he didn't want vegetables in his lunch and he wanted his orange peeled. She didn't feel like doing all that extra work but peeled his orange because she loved Larry.

Huey, working part time at Hubbard's, was two months from graduating Central Catholic when, out of nowhere, Dad decided to accompany him to school. Huey thought it must be a joke until Dad walked him to the principal's office to sign his withdrawal from school, asserting that Huey would have to work full-time to help support the family. This seemed absurd considering that six out of the twelve of us were already contributing to household expenses. We still ran up a bill at Heinrichers and paid it on payday, but Huey saw no reason for Dad's rash decision knowing that Huey's scholarship to Western Reserve was assured.

In a brief meeting, his homeroom teacher went over other options, and Dad said, *No, the only thing a diploma is good for is wiping your ass.* It was then that Huey realized that Dad had been drinking, apparently to get himself through the ordeal. In that stressful moment, Huey surrendered to Dad's will and, undaunted, secured a GED and enrolled at Duff's Business College taking night courses to aid placement in desk jobs during his pending military tour.

The whole family rallied around Huey in the face of Dad's action. Eileen told Huey not to judge Dad too harshly because he had a disease that needed treatment. Where had that been heard before? Eileen asked Sis to teach her how to make spaghetti and meatballs, so she could serve us a fantastic supper and cheer everybody up. Sis had not been exposed to Italian cuisine as a student of the culinary arts, so she asked one of our neighbors to teach her.

The six Italian families on our hill were native-born, but their parents were Italian immigrants who brought their recipes with them. Frank Chirico, a Union Steel worker, had saved our house from going up in flames when Sis had accidentally set the tea towels on fire. His wife, Josephine, worked dawn to dusk and then some taking care of her family. She maintained an amazing hillside garden which enhanced the nutritional value of everything she cooked. Moreover, she was single-handedly building a dirt road of about ten by one hundred feet from Duncan Street down to her house on the Keystone Street extension. For love of our family, she set pick and shovel aside to help Sis.

Josephine's daughter, Manna Mae, loved to eat, so she was told to stay out of the kitchen while Sis was in training and to clean up the kitchen after they were through. Mrs. Chirico made everything from scratch, even the pasta, but for expedience used the store-bought kind. After several sessions, Sis felt confident to make spaghetti and meatballs for our family, and Dad wouldn't eat it. Larry said it was the most delicious meal he had ever eaten.

Now, it was Eileen's turn, and Sis showed her how to make the spaghetti sauce in a pressure cooker. She was to lower the flame, and when the cooking time ended, let the pressure cooker cool down before removing the lid. At the appointed time, Eileen rushed to the stove but got there seconds too late. The lid blew off and the spaghetti sauce landed on the ceiling. Dad walked in asking for his supper and Eileen said, *It's up there, Dad, on the ceiling.* And he said, *Oh for crumps sake, what a circus*!

One season with the B & B circus was all that Joe could endure. He returned home and worked a few weeks at the Trilock Mill on Butler Street, a miserable experience, and then a few days at Kress Pattern Company next door, only to confirm his belief that harsh mill life and inadequate earnings would never support an artistic career. Again, he considered his fate and sorry fortune, promptly joined the Air Force, and was presently stationed at Selfridge Air Force Base south of Detroit, Michigan.

There, he met Daisy Nicolaides. She worked in an accounting firm and belonged to a group that bussed out to the base for the USO dances. Daisy said that the night she and Joe met happened to be square dance night. Joe said that when he chose who he wished to dance with, he picked the most beautiful lady on the dance floor. They had such a great time doing the square dance that they arranged to meet again on polka night. A sweet courtship unfolded, and it wasn't long before fate would place a big decision before them.

My dilemma was how to get over losing the joy of my Saturday ambitions. Ekl's studio no longer offered free lessons, and the free Fitzpatrick art classes ended after eighth grade. I had devoted four years of my life tolerating Dad's harping every Saturday about me being gone on house cleaning day so that I could take a bus and two streetcars from home to Oakland to downtown and the Northside and back home. In fear of being forced to give up these classes, I told no one of how, on the last leg of these journeys, I had to sit down half way up the 56th Street steps in dystrophic paralysis with my legs and feet tightened in cramps brought on by the physical demands of ballet and toe dancing. Joe, as he had stuck up for Eileen, would have done so for me when I was late for supper and faced a big kitchen cleanup; no wonder I missed him.

I felt hurt and disillusioned and Dad surely felt it too, but I noticed that he had stopped hounding me about housework, probably because Sis stepped in, trying to inspire me to learn a variety of domestic skills. I was making oatmeal one morning when Dad fetched his bucket of hand tools, a can of aluminum paint, and a brush and went into the yard. I was drawn towards the shiny silver paint that he was stirring and asked if I could help. He demonstrated how to dip the paint brush in the paint and wipe the excess against the paint can's rim and to skillfully apply the paint to our new wire fence. This I did, with such

precision that he told me to keep going. He had unwittingly rescued me from doing the dishes and all of the frustration that had been steaming inside me evaporated. I was glad for every chance to be outside all day. I loved using Dad's tools, his hammer and nails, the chisel, the pitchfork and shovel, although the pic-mattock and sledge hammer were too heavy for me to lift. It was impossible to stay mad at Dad for very long; he missed our mother.

The day after Labor Day, Eileen and I entered Peabody High School in the secretarial/business program. The school was a one-bus ride to East Liberty and an emotional shock after eight years at St. Mary's, which had one-hundred thirty students, four classrooms and a small library. Peabody had thirteen hundred students and forty classrooms. The school was bright, clean, and in orderly condition; the teaching staff was superb. The library occupied half the basement, the cafeteria the other half, and the food was nutritious. We ate the sandwich and apple we brought from home and drank the half-pint carton of milk provided by the public food fund.

After school, we were expected to go straight home to keep an eye on Richie and Martha. Sis waited for us to get there and then she dashed off to her new job on the 4:00 p.m. to midnight shift at Hubbard's, where Dad got her in on the hardware pole line as a shipping inspector. On her day off, Martha would find her *Sissy Mum* snoozing on the couch, so tired from so much work. She would tiptoe into the kitchen to find something to eat and go out back, catching the screen door so it wouldn't bang, and go find Richie. He'd take her for a ride on one of his giggies, those race carts he built with four or five and even six wheels. She loved looking for rocks with Richie. They'd go to the edge of the hill, and he'd teach her how to hurl flat stones a great distance. When the streetlights came on, he'd let her play kick the can with his pals and walk her home.

Martha started first grade and Richie started fifth grade for the second time. Sis walked them to and from school until Richie got the hang of that detail. Eileen and I looked out for them and got supper started. The torch had been passed, as in the beginning, when Vinny and Sis looked after Joe and Dee, then Joe and Dee looked after Skip and Anna, and then they looked after Huey and Larry, and now the torch belonged to me and my sister Eileen.

Sis expected Dad to blow up when she suggested that he pay us an allowance. He was not in favor of the idea because nobody at our house ever got paid for living there. Feeling the pressure, he offered to pay us twenty-five cents a week, which he paid us a few times and forgot about it, so Sis paid us and raised our allowance to fifty cents. At Hubbard's, she earned not much less than Dad did thanks to her previous factory experience. The mill was a dark and gloomy place, but it gave Sis an insight into how working there made Dad feel. She couldn't wait to get home, grab a bite, bathe, and recline in the privacy of her attic bedroom, never forgetting to set her alarm clock for six a.m. to take care of us kids. She really looked forward to weekends and getting all dressed up to join her friends at the Slovenian Hall polka dances.

Dee and Anna traveled by streetcar to West View Dance Land beyond the Northside. Anna had graduated from Peabody as a member of the National Honor Society and presently worked in an East Liberty law office; Dee now worked for an insurance company downtown. One evening as they were waiting for the next offer to dance a waltz or fox trot, a tall slender fellow in a blue business suit stepped forward and asked Anna if she'd like to dance. He introduced himself as Dave Smith. Anna took her time looking him over before saying she'd love to dance—one dance and they fell in love.

Dave was a native of Paden City, West Virginia, an Oklahoma State graduate working for an architecture firm. He lived at a downtown hotel and was preparing for his next assignment in Cleveland, Ohio, a promotion that put both of them in a quandary. How were they supposed to get to know each other if he moved so far away? She started thinking maybe break it off, but how? One day, Anna nervously announced that Dave was on his way to our house to meet the family. Words no sooner spoken and big as life he pulled up out front in a Cadillac with rusty fenders. She went out to greet him and brought him inside. Swift-thinking Anna already had a plan on how to introduce Dave to Dad, a plan that would kick in and take effect before Dad had a chance to react. As soon as she introduced them to each other, she swept us kids out to the curb and asked Dave to take the whole gang for a ride to Highland Park. Dave owned a movie camera and encouraged us to perform for the screen. We giggled our way through those candid flicks that were projected on a bed sheet tacked to the dining room wall. *Scott Home Theater*, Dad said. He and Dave got along.

When Dave's job transferred, he asked for Anna's hand so he could take her with him. She was torn between moving away and staying home, and felt she didn't know Dave well enough to marry him. She told Dad, and he agreed. She needed more time to make up her mind. She didn't want to rush into things, but going away with Dave unmarried felt wrong. Finally, she admitted that she could not live without him. She decided to move into the YWCA in Cleveland and support herself in an office job. Dad gave her his blessing and off she went on that blissful journey. Dave helped her move into the Y on Euclid Avenue and moved himself into a nearby apartment. However, he felt that this arrangement was not good enough for them and soon made arrangements to take Anna to New Martinsville, West Virginia, where they were married at First Christian Church—with Dave's family and God to bear witness. Blessed are they who can prove they were legally married, as Scott stories go!

1952

Dad was on the move, traveling by *Greyhound* between Pittsburgh and Cleveland with ideas for air travel flying around in his brain. He hadn't been in the air since he flew on an *aeroplane* to Gary, Indiana in 1930 at Postal Telegraph's expense. One thing he never regretted was turning down a position that would have gone against Mom's wishes. An unforeseen good outcome of losing his job at PT was that he got his sister hired as a tele-typist, a position that was secured when PT merged with Western Union. Aunt Rose made good money, which provided a means for her and our grandmother to move to Morningside in 1945. They had first moved to steep Baker Street, but a major landslide took the house. Their move to Bossart Street, a few blocks away from the affluent St. Raphael's Parish, *was the best thing that ever happened to them*, said our grandmother. No one knew who she was and, incognito, she returned to church. She welcomed us Scotts anytime we showed up for a visit, a five- or six-mile journey over hilly terrain. No one ever left without being served one of her homemade treats—strawberry ice cream, double-decker chocolate cake, orange pound cake, a bowl of fresh fruit. Best of all was her lemon meringue pie.

Eileen and I dropped by one day; she had just made a lemon pie and was sitting by the stove browning the meringue in the broiler. It was then that she told us the story of the day she was browning a lemon pie in the broiler of her stove on Holmes Street when Sam Scott barged in unannounced. She had lost her child support case against him, a court hearing that had created a huge rift among our dad and his brothers. She was so infuriated by Sam's imposition that she slammed the broiler drawer closed and the pie splattered all over the place.

Ever since, Dad had faithfully kept in touch with his mother and the family to the extent that it was possible. We were sometimes visited by Grandmother Scott, Uncle Sam, Aunt Rose, and on rare occasions, our cousin Sheila. She lived in a private boarding school and Eileen and I were the benefactors of her fancy hand-me-downs and brand-name shoes.

July 21, 1952 was Grandmother Mary O'Donnell Scott's sixty-seventh birthday. We were invited to the party, and it was to be a surprise. We walked the miles from our house to hers and the relatives were already there. Uncle Lawrence, who we barely knew, was expected at any moment with the birthday cake. We kids were to wait for him on the front porch, where we took turns riding on the swing and the glider—a wait of hours—and no Uncle Lawrence. Aunt Rose thought he forgot and decided to call him, but another man answered the phone. She asked to speak to *Lawrence Scott* and the man on the phone said, *I just killed him, come get him.*

A guarded family secret was about to be shockingly exposed. We learned that Uncle Lawrence had been sentenced to a five-year prison term on larceny and was paroled on good behavior after serving one year. Fool that he was, first thing he did was visit the Casino Burlesque Theater in the seedy district downtown. On his way out of the show, he was arrested and charged with a morals offense in violation of parole and sent back to prison to finish his time. He had recently been released and lived in an apartment in East Liberty that he shared with another man. Lawrence was the one son our grandmother most feared that she would one day discover listed in the newspaper crime list.

Aunt Rose hung up the phone, trembling uncontrollably. Unknown to her for the present was that the man who shared the apartment with Lawrence had served time with him at the State Penitentiary and was the man on the phone. She called the police and Dad asked Vinny and Dorothy to drive us kids home. In the days ahead, we learned why our uncle never made it to the party; he was bludgeoned to death with an ice pick.

Accounts in the *Pittsburgh Press* and the *Post-Gazette* dated July 22, 1952 reported two men arrested, questioned, and released. Both gave the same story: Lawrence went with them to a burlesque show. After the show, they went out with some women. Lawrence didn't go with them; he asked for the key to the apartment. They said Lawrence had family business to take care of, something about food for a party. One account implied a motive for the crime to be a homosexual love affair gone awry. It would take law enforcement ten years to indict one of the two men for the murder; he would be subsequently tried and convicted and put away for life. Shocking to think of it—Lawrence had gone to prison a lady's man, and now this.

Our grandmother broke down in despair; she wouldn't eat and couldn't sleep; her hair turned white overnight and she refused to see a doctor. Aunt Rose feared the worst.

Eileen started having nightmares and was afraid the murderer might come after her because she was with Aunt Rose when the murderer confessed over the phone. Eileen had to miss the funeral due to her fragile state of mind. Vinny and Dorothy took her to see Doctor Noden. He prescribed a liquid tranquilizer, *phenobarbital*, six months of hell, she said. She attended a retreat at St. Kieran's, and the counselor advised her to go home and turn on the radio, sing and dance, and take a nap every day, but she could not rest knowing our grandmother was going through hell. Eileen was sixteen years old.

On the second day of August 1952, Vinny stopped by our house bearing good news of the arrival of beautiful Rosanne Colleen Scott, the first grandchild for Dad's boasting. A month later, we received news of the birth of Dad's second grandchild, Teresa Smith of Cleveland, Ohio, the first of five children that Anna and Dave would inspire.

Larry, in his senior year at Conley Trade School, was inspired to join the Navy upon graduation, with a position as a machinist guaranteed once he finished boot camp. Sis asked him to teach her how to drive a car before he left home. He was not yet licensed but said he'd gladly teach her if she had something to drive. She had been saving up and bought a 1942 green Chevy sedan from a guy named Murphy for three hundred dollars. Larry got behind the wheel and discovered that the car wouldn't start. He told Sis that she got gypped. *Oh no,* she said, and sold the car back to the owner, recovered most of her money, and told Larry that she'd learn to drive when he got out of the Navy.

Sis had money to spend and got so excited when the Keystone Candy Shop and Soda Fountain opened for business on Butler Street that she treated all of us, one or two at a time, Larry first. She asked him to sample one of everything. *Oh no,* he said. *Not after what I went through with Auntie O.* Then it was Martha's turn, and Sis said, *Let's go to Keystones!* Oh boy, Martha's best treat of her childhood, so far. She ordered a cherry sundae. They sat in a booth and were waited on; they didn't need to talk. It was heaven just slurping up that cherry sundae and being with *Sissy Mum.*

Sis put coins in the tableside music box and let Martha choose three songs for a quarter. She chose *Peg O' My Heart, How Much is that Doggy in the Window, Woof Woof, and Cool Clear Water.* A veritable pop concert at a Butler Street soda shop. People really loved the songs of that era, lyrics that identified with feeling loved or hated, adored or ignored; melodies that described the depth and breadth of human passion that we all shared, whether living free or abandoned, wealthy or poor, incarcerated on death row, confined to a psychiatric institution, or bleeding on a battlefield—songs of woe, songs of hope, and songs of missing you—*oh my darling, I hunger for your touch!*

We were the happiest family on earth when Joe brought Daisy home to meet us, although we had our fingers crossed that all would go well at the formal introduction. Dad seemed a little nervous, but Eileen gave Daisy a big hug and terrific smile and told Dad to relax. I was in the dining room, stitching a green velvet trim fabric to the collar and sleeves of my old winter coat to make it look new. I had picked up this idea from my sewing class at Peabody. Daisy thought it was clever and offered a few suggestions. I immediately felt a bonding because she had taken an interest in what I was doing. Joe and Daisy had set their wedding date for the following spring, but with Joe's transfer to Guam imminent, they married on January 17, 1953 at St. Gabriel's Roman Catholic Church in Detroit.

Skip was home with an honorable discharge and Army money. First thing he did was buy a secondhand, powder blue Chrysler and wow what a boat! Fluid drive, whitewall tires, lots of chrome, and man was it ever long. It took fifteen hours to simonize, sucked up gas, and kept him broke. It sat parked at the curb most of the time but was a popular Duncan Street attraction. Skip had served as a paramedic in post-war Germany, where he picked up the language because, as Larry put it, the brothers at Central had pounded it into Skip's head so well that he sounded like an immigrant. He put both hands to the plow and re-vegetated our garden that summer.

After a few months of mill grit and grime on his old job at Hubbard's, Skip applied for and was hired as a medical aide at the recently opened Veteran's Administration Hospital in Fox Chapel. He eventually would quit that job because working nights made it difficult to keep up with the demanding school workload at Penn Tech that would eventually launch his IBM career.

We Scotts aspired to higher learning, not just through formal education, but in our personal quests for knowledge in the social and cultural dimensions and in the school of hard knocks. We were not the most ambitious of people, but we had an instinctive curiosity for exploring new ideas, creating new ways to do things, and keeping up with what was going on in the world. It seemed our nature was to always be moving on to better ourselves.

On April Fool's Day, Huey put the ladder against the side of the house and climbed up to repair the bedroom window. The mailman came by waving a big envelope and hollered up,

Hey Huey, come down here and get your Army induction notice. Dad heard about it and went berserk. Was it his nuerotic fear of losing a bread-winner? Or was it the abandoned car that had been deposited overnight on our vacant lot? He went straight to the basement, grabbed the ax, and with every swing he leveled at the abandoned car, he profaned the perpetrators of the evil deed. *Wait till I get my hands on the rotten nincompoops who put that pile of shit here. I'll teach them suns-a-bitches a lesson or two. Crise-sakes, this is our goddam property, geezus crise*! We kids did not yet know how to curse properly.

After six weeks of basic training, Huey returned home in full uniform. With a thirty-day leave to spare before heading for Seattle to serve the first phase of his tour of duty, he painted our house. That's Huey up there! Next up, Larry graduated and,

with Navy orders in hand, left for basic training in Boston on a promise to celebrate when he returned. In August, he arrived in full Navy uniform, bringing along with him some pretty spicy Navy language. Every other comment was: *What a pile of horseshit.* Word got around that he was throwing a party in our basement. A fair crowd showed up, many he did not know, and someone smuggled in a few cases of beer. Dad rarely hung out with the younger generation, but for Larry it was different. He and Dad had been through thick and thin together, ages ago.

Larry, in his youth, belonged to a sports club and dreamed of becoming the star player on the football team. Football season started and the team practiced after school. Dad told Larry he would have to clean the cellar before practice and wanted it done exactly as Dad had taught Richie when the cellar was first transformed into a basement. Dad didn't want any back talk either, but Larry was worried that he'd be late for the game if he spent too much time cleaning the cellar. One day he went to the attic and dropped his gear down into the back yard, then snuck out of the house and walked to Lawrence Park. He got there way early, and the team played two complete games that day. When Larry got home that night, he was tired and hungry. Dad said he could have his supper plate after he cleaned the cellar. Each stroke of that broom was a curse against Dad for putting him through such cruel punishment. Then one of Larry's big games came up at Arsenal Park. Dad went to watch it. Larry caught the ball and headed for the goal post. Dad ran down the sideline yelling for Larry to keep away from the big guys; he was smallest on the team, and Dad was his biggest fan. Sure, he partied with Larry and his friends for all it was worth—until he was smashed.

In that condition, he fixed his narrowed gaze on the abandoned car that was still sitting on our side lot. This time, he went ballistic, grabbed the sledge hammer, and totaled the car using every ounce of his one-hundred and thirty pounds of flesh. The party boys offered Dad a helping hand turning the car belly up and finishing the job. The following day, a few of the party boys returned in a pick-up truck looking for the rest of their beer. Larry said they could have it if they got rid of the heavy metal evidence to the crime. No problem. They set the car upright, ran a chain from its bumper to their truck and hauled it away, along with their leftover beer. Meanwhile, someone called the cops, and by the time they got there, the evidence had disappeared. With the coast clear, Skip sat down with Larry, put his arm around little brother and said, *I hope those kids don't plan to drink all that beer themselves.* He asked Larry how long he'd been smoking cigarettes. He couldn't remember and Skip suggested healthy alternatives. Larry smiled his cute smile and said, *Skip, you always were a good boy.*

Larry rejoined his shipmates and the *USS Cassin Young* sailed for Inchon, Korea—the thirty-eighth parallel. While negotiators manipulated peace plans between North and South Korea on the international chess board, the Pentagon ordered the Navy to maintain off-shore war units in the region.

Larry's ship stopped in every port along the way. He wrote home that the girls in other countries were gorgeous, but none as beautiful as the girls in Pittsburgh, none with such beautiful legs. He reached the Yellow Sea, off Inchon, and wrote home to say he had never been so cold in all his life, not even when we ran out of coal and our house was freezing.

A cold spell had Dad up earlier than usual building a fire in the furnace before he went to work. He expected Eileen and me home right after school and was annoyed that we had been chosen to join the thousand-voice All-City Chorus and had to practice after school. The concert was scheduled at Syria Mosque accompanied by the Pittsburgh Symphony Orchestra and conducted by William Steinberg. Dad said maintaining our house and home was more important. But then, he saw how upset we were over this and made good. He bought tickets and took the whole family to the concert.

Although Eileen and I had grown up like conjoined twins—same house, same bed, same classroom, same grade in school, we no longer had to travel together. We had separate interests and ran with separate friends. Boys who drove cars flirted with girls on our hill who hung out on the Wall. Five or six girls would pile into the back seat of a jalopy and go for a joyride down Butler Street, up Stanton Avenue, down Christopher Street, and back to Duncan Street. Before this escapade went forward, Sis and her girlfriend Manna Mae would jump in and take a ride around the road to make sure these boys knew how to drive and the vehicle was safe.

One night an Italian boy from Sharpsburg took Eileen to a drive-in movie, and she didn't tell Dad. It was well after midnight when she got home and Dad was waiting. She explained that the movie started late and there were two movies. Dad said she could hand that *cock and bull* line to someone else. While grounded she listened to the radio. Kate Smith came on singing: *You'll Never Walk Alone*, the Rogers and Hammerstein hit from the musical *Carousel.*

"*When you walk through a storm hold your head up high and don't be afraid of the dark. At the end of a storm is a golden sky and the sweet silver song of a lark. Walk on, walk on with hope in your heart though your dreams be tossed and blown. Walk on, walk on with hope in your heart and you'll never walk alone, you'll never walk alone."*

Once Eileen got hooked on that song, she sang it like a broken record for Dad's edification. She sang it in a drawn out parody, taking her good old time dusting furniture, especially if Dad was trying to read the paper and listen to the radio. She elevated her tone and kept it up until Dad relented and she was no longer grounded. Then he found out that Eileen and I were going for car rides with boys and made us stay in a whole week. I couldn't stand it and ran away as far as Sis's girlfriend Manna Mae's house at the bottom of her mother Josephine's road. She made me eat something—*pasta for fools*—is what I heard her say; I was hungry and ate, delicious!

Dad tracked me down and walked me home. He grounded me, I was miserable, and Sis paved my way to freedom. She told Dad that our stuffy house was bad for my asthma. He said that I could *sit on the front steps and breathe in the smog* after the supper dishes were done, which is what you get for running away. Richie sat with me and Sis on those steps after Dad went to bed. What amazed us was watching Sis light up, holding a cigarette with the delicacy of scenes in the movies. She would puff and drag and blow a stream of white smoke the way *Lauren Bacall* did to entice *Humphrey Bogart* and make that one cigarette last the whole night.

For the last thirty some years, Dad had nurtured a habit of two or three packs of Camel's a day. The price had jumped from fifteen to thirty cents a pack in the last five years. He smoked on the way to work, smoked at the gate before clocking in, chain-smoked on the job, on his break, on the way home and after supper. He smoked at the barricade corner and lit up before bedtime. A quick smoke while the morning brew dripped in our Jewel Tea coffee maker felt just right.

We knew something was up when he got all dressed up in suit, shirt, and tie one Saturday morning and came downstairs carrying his wing-tipped *Florsheim* shoes. He went to the living room and pulled from behind his chair his wooden shoe shine kit with a foot rest. He sat down to put on his shoes, grunting with the pain of strained muscles he never knew he had. He applied shoe polish and buffed his shoes to a high shine. He put away the shoe shine kit and announced that he was going down street. That could mean anything.

Turned out Dad went shopping at Donahoe's in town and got some real deals with discount food coupons clipped out of the newspapers. Here was Dad—a good father let's say fifty percent of the time with forty-five percent questionable, and five percent undecided because of the chocolate butter cream candies called *Bon Bons* he served after supper. That's when we got suspicious. Sweet treats indicated a high point of Dad's cycles, signaling that he was about to fall off the wagon. A binge could last a few days or a few weeks and would involve lost work and wages.

During these disconcerting periods, we hardly ever saw him; he was officially in hiding, sneaking late into the house and going straight to bed. No need to deprive his family of our peace and happiness, but for us it was a nightmare in the daytime and a daymare in the night time. He kept a running account at Neid's where he could board if need be. There, on one occasion, he climbed out of a bed not remembering where he was, found his way down two flights of stairs to the tavern in his *bee-vee-dees*, and the housekeeper screamed bloody murder. He lived to tell that story.

Most of the time he managed to make it home in one piece. We knew he suffered, but at least he didn't desert our family the way his so-called father Sam Scott had done. We held onto Mom's belief that Dad had a disease that needed treatment—a disease that progressed as time went by. His spell passed, and he gave me a quarter to go down to Isaly's Dairy in the Ninth Ward and bring home a quart of buttermilk and two *kosher* dill pickles, a sobering diet that snapped him back into reality. He must have thought about his health because the supplements he used were a cup of coffee for a headache, a bottle of beer for his nerves, and Carter's Little Liver Pills for a flush. Once cleaned up and changed, he felt better about himself and strolled over to Joe Monroe's basement barbershop for a haircut. Joe had been cutting Dad's hair since we moved to the hill and had been giving us kids free haircuts, too. The boys got G.I. cuts, but we girls got bowl cuts, meaning Mr. Monroe placed a bowl on our heads to get an even cut. As we became more aware of styles, he recommended his sister-in-law's beauty salon on Butler Street.

Dad resumed his normal routine and we resumed ours. It felt right to see him going to work in the morning and coming home for supper. For a time, we could relax and not worry about keeping our fingers crossed. Then he'd start needling us to get the house work done. He'd pace back and forth or go through the house turning off lights and complaining about the cost of electricity. He was fifty-two years old, and, with his edgy nerves getting edgier, his cycles were occurring in ever-shortening spans.

We had the idea that Dad paid less attention to us than he used to. We were wrong. Christmas rolled around and he came through in an abundance of good will and generosity. Sis couldn't wait for the holidays to be over, *too much work,* she said. She had to sleep on a couch in the dining room because her third-floor bedroom was unheated, freezing actually. She developed purple bags under her eyes from disrupted sleep with Dad pacing between the living room and kitchen like an inspector general until things were in order.

Dee had ideas about keeping our household organized and looked to Eileen and I to support the cause. Unknowingly, she blessed Eileen and I, so we thought. We loved dressing up in Dee's pretty clothes but always put them back before she came home from work, thinking she'd never know. She knew! One day she had about enough of our mischief and said, *You two, don't do that again or else*! We didn't really blame her. She came home from work exhausted between stress on the job, the streetcar ride home from town, and climbing the city steps to Duncan Street. She thought Eileen and I would have supper started by then. *Oh bless the Lord who forgives!*

Dee decided to set in motion a system that required everyone to participate so that things ran like a good clock, a clock that without family cooperation wasn't ticking. She asserted her feelings that we should make a better effort as a family working together, but it started to feel to her like a lost cause. Dad said, *Dee, stop rocking the boat; I'm the captain of this ship*. Dee knew what to do. She and her girlfriends went on a month's vacation to Wildwood Beach, New Jersey. Everybody was happy but me because Dad made me do the ironing. Dee came home a new person, transformed from dishwater to bleach blonde hair and wearing a classy sun dress, sun glasses, and a nice tan. Dad started calling her *glamourous* in a sarcastic tone, an insensitive remark to dish out to a hard worker. But, Dee gave me points for setting up my ironing board operation in the cool spot outside the kitchen door. *Why didn't I ever think of that?* she said.

As fate would have it, Hubbard's downsized again and Sis lost her job. In no time, she was back to work on the afternoon shift as a chef and waitress at the Union Steel Canteen, work she had wanted to do ever since high school. They mostly served soup and sandwiches, but Sis got creative and the mill workers said they enjoyed the cuisine. On payday, she brought her wages home in a four by six-inch manila envelope, gave Dad his portion, gave herself a portion, and left the coins for Martha, still contained in the pay envelope. Payday for Sis meant payday for Martha—candy money for *Black Jacks* at Sullivan's candy store.

At the Canteen, Sis met a truck driver who delivered big equipment for the mill. He would drop in for a cup of coffee and a bowl of soup. He seemed to be a gentleman and they eventually made friends and went out together a few times. He was not always available evenings and sometimes visited Sis at our house during the day, the tallest man we had ever seen. Dad didn't like her choice and made his feelings felt; we were afraid that he might get riled up and embarrass Sis. We kids surmised something was up, but what? We just had this feeling that her boyfriend was stealing our time.

Martha was eight years old and beginning to feel as though life was too free. Summer on our hill was wondrous for her, especially the nights. She would go into the narrow alley between our house and Besals and adorn herself with lanterns of lightning bugs. One hot but quiet evening, she took a potato from the corner cupboard in the kitchen and went to the Homey field, where she built a fire and cooked the potato until it turned black. She skinned it, drench it with salt, and ate it to her heart's content. Settling back on the scratchy army blanket that she brought with her, she gazed into the night sky, asking herself if

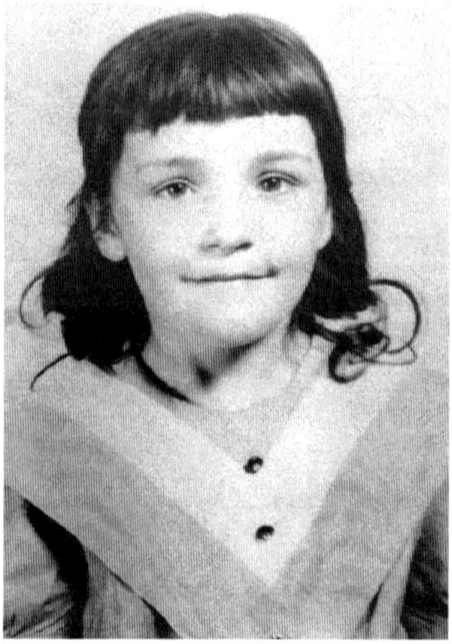

she really missed not having a mother. Being motherless made her feel different from her friends in unspoken ways. Other kids she knew did not cook potatoes in a fire in a field and sleep under the stars all by themselves. It seemed very late when she got home; she went straight to bed. Nobody missed her.

Martha followed a studious path, completing homework assignments at the dining room table right after supper without being told. She selected what to wear to school the next day before she went to bed at night, and she said night prayers before closing her eyes to keep spooky feelings away. If prayers didn't work, she turned on the light and read a book until she fell asleep. In the morning she came downstairs ready for her day with her hair combed in curls, her outfit in place, and her shoes buckled. Dad called her *doll baby* and always gave her a show of affection before heading out.

We had been in transition ever since Mom died. The subtle nuances were unlike what occurs in families where involved parents are present, yet similar to what every family goes through when, one by one, young birds discover their wings and fly away. Truth was, Dad couldn't take it—the flying away part. A tragic opera could be written to reflect Dad's mood:

The Flight of the Baby Birds from the Nest. He was concerned about Sis's lifestyle and was worried about Eileen; she turned seventeen and her heart doctor was uncertain that she'd live to see her twenty-first birthday.

Dad worried about me running around with a charmer from Sharpsburg. Dad didn't take all that easily to Italians for some reason. One day he announced to my drop-dead-tall-dark-and-handsome-just-stepped-out-of-a-Hollywood-movie-screen boyfriend: *You are not welcome in my house.* The worst parental reaction possible against two hopelessly romantic teenagers. If ever there was an Oscar drama queen born after that showdown, it was me.

I first met Tony one Sunday afternoon when I went over to the wall to hang out with my friends. It was the only day of the week that I enjoyed staying dressed up all day. Willy Saver, the only guy on the hill with a camera, was taking our pictures and took one of me. A jalopy pulled up and six boys got out. They had driven from across the river looking for girls to take for a ride. We girls said, *No, we're not allowed.* But we were friendly with them, and they started showing up when we hung out on the wall at night. Tony showed up with a friend named Jerry, who drove the car, and they took Eileen and me for a ride to

Highland Park. They wanted to park and Eileen said, *What the heck do you think we are? Take us home!* They did, but all too soon Eileen was going steady with Jerry, and I, suffering with a pathetic crush, was going steady with Tony. You could only do so much riding around in a car, to be honest. Anyhow, our dating went underground after Dad's ultimatum.

Meeting secretly was bound to create an atmosphere of promiscuity. I had no clue what I was in for, but I'm sure Dad did. Eileen had warned me that he was on a secret war path, but I showed no fear of Dad; I loved him. He had let me use his tools to build things and taught me how to play Solitaire with his cards. He had let me read his newspaper, so long as I folded it and put it on the end table by his reading lamp with his lead ashtray holding it down, the way he wanted it. He had taught me how to write letters to the editor with my opinion of the day.

Now it was orders from headquarters. *Patty, you can stay home and watch TV game shows with me!* In the fantasy love land where I existed, that was hardly possible. I couldn't wait to escape and go for a ride on my boyfriend's motorcycle with no fenders or exhaust pipe or anyplace to hold onto but him with my own mother's wild hair flying all over the place. She would have killed me!

One day, Dad stalled me on my way out the back door, saying I would have to do the dishes over because the pots weren't coming clean and I needed to use elbow grease. I stomped around searching for a can labeled *Elbow Grease*, boiling over with crocodile tears. He took a scratching pad and some cleanser and scrubbed the pots clean. *Now that's what you call elbow grease*, he said.

I wanted to do more gratifying work like my brothers did: sweeping the yard, hauling trash to the Homey dump, clearing the side lot, and beautifying the landscape. Dad offered an opinion that I was spending too much time in the mirror *trying to improve upon perfection.* Well, that comment went right over my head. One day I came downstairs with my hair curled and my face painted, and oh was he ever irked. *Patty,* he said, *there's a solution to all this beauty business. Why don't you go to Hollywood, the walk will do you good.* For one split second I thought, *Wow, maybe I could be a movie star.* Then the light bulb lit up.

Dad received a letter from USN Commander K.B. Brown that said what a fine job Larry was doing on board the *USS Cassin Young* in the Far East. We heard from Huey that his Army division was on its way to occupied Japan. A month later, he arrived in Yokohama on Christmas Eve and was able to attend Midnight Mass. He found it so touching to hear the beautiful sound of children singing Silent Night in Japanese. He was made editor of the *Depot Digest,* a weekly circulation in English and Japanese, and was also handling hometown news via *Stars and Stripes*—the Army paper, which kept him busy.

In Pittsburgh, police squads were kept busy on New Year's Day 1954, manning road blocks to halt striker violence. Teamster truck drivers called strikes against Kaufmann's, Horne's, Gimbel's, and other big stores in the area, disruptions that would last well into spring. Mayor David L. Lawrence won public confidence when he requested a federal investigation into possible illegal Teamster activities. Against the wishes of taxpayers, he convinced City Council to legislate a wage tax to fund ongoing rebuilding. Slums in the Northside and East Liberty were cleared for construction of shopping centers.

We thought Congress would have to intervene the day Dad gathered us for a *talk.* He was on a dry spell, but from the tone of his *listen up yins kids,* we thought we were going to be delivered to hell in a handbasket. Then he found the words choked up in his throat: *Something bad has happened to Sis.* He started shaking as tears rolled down his face; then he delivered the news: *Sis is going to have a baby.* He paused to catch his breath, looking up at the ceiling, and said, *We are going to love that baby and help Sis, starting today, and in every way we can, because of all things and of everything that Sis had to do for us ever since Mom died.* Heartbreaking to reflect on how much Sis had sacrificed for us and the thought of the suffering she now endured.

We had been noticing subtle changes in Sis. She stayed home more and walked around with a sad look on her face. She would look down into her cup of coffee, a cloud of smoke rising off a long ash at the end of her *Lucky*. She didn't joke around anymore, and there was a change in her appearance. Sis had informed Dad that the baby's father had betrayed her; he already had a wife and kids. Sis was treading in deep, dark waters and did not want us kids exposed to what she was going through. Her other trusted friend, Aggie Heinricher, had married and moved to Morningside. She and her husband took Sis in with her intention being to live there only until the baby was born.

School was out for the summer, and Eileen's open-heart surgery was scheduled at West Penn Hospital. Our friend and neighbor, Peggy Monroe, stopped by to visit Eileen the night before the surgery and found a team of surgeons hovering over Eileen. Peggy gasped and inadvertently blurted, *Eileen Scott, what if you die?* A sedative had to be administered to calm Eileen down. Nothing mattered but the procedure she was about to undergo. The surgeon opened her ribs, went through her lung, and sewed up her heart with a needle and thread. She had lost her voice in the surgery; however, it was deemed to have been successful, a miracle when you think that it was considered a new and risky procedure. Shortly, Dad received the surgery bill for $3,000. He calmly sat down and wrote the surgeon a letter, explaining his situation, and offered to send the doctor five dollars a month until the bill was paid, more if possible. The surgeon replied to Dad's letter and wrote off the bill.

Meanwhile, Dad was desperately trying to hold on and went to visit Sis. She wanted to know how Eileen was doing and how things were going at home. He told her things were not well. The little kids were sad, crying all the time because they missed Sis, and most especially, Martha's *Sissy Mum*. He begged Sis to move back home; she did and we rejoiced.

In that long Summer of 1954, Martha felt that she had Sis all to herself. They played cards. *Fight* and *500 Rummy*, morning to night at the dining room table. Sis was not one to have long conversations, but they listened to the radio and decided that *I'll be loving you always and will always understand* would be their song. The lyrics of so many of the popular songs that Sis sang around the house were essential to the unconditional love she gave us along the roads she traveled with us.

As for me, Mother Nature had quieted down, but by then I had lost my color and so much weight from morning sickness that Dad became alarmed and took me to see Doctor Noden who made the diagnosis. Dad said I didn't have to get married, I could just have the baby, but he was drunk when he said it and he was not at all convincing. All I ever wanted to do was become famous. I wanted to be a song and dance star on Broadway and a recording artist and an oil on canvas painter and a published author. I wanted to be free; a walk to Hollywood right then and there felt like a great idea.

That August turned out to be an interesting month in the life of us Scotts. The first weekend that month, Eileen stood as my bridesmaid with both of us wondering what it was all about. The veil between imagination and reality had lifted, that's what it was all about. I was sixteen years old and getting married.

Tony and I, on the advice of his relatives, went to see Father Kebe, thinking that he would turn down our ridiculous request to be married at St. Mary's. The good priest, still a friend of the family already in his eighties, saw right through our scheme to cover up our crime and reserved judgment, only to counsel us to attend Mass on Sunday, contribute to the Church, and raise our children likewise.

Eileen was first to visit me in my new home on Main Street in Sharpsburg, two rooms for fifteen dollars a month in a house leaning at a twenty-degree angle on the verge of collapse. She travelled from the hill on foot to Butler Street, caught a streetcar, and brought along all the ingredients to teach me how to make a good supper. I didn't own a pot to pee in so she borrowed one from the landlady. Tony came home from wherever and Eileen served supper. He told her that he didn't like chili and that made her mad. *Well, she said, what did you expect your highness, a seven-course dinner? I had to do all this cooking myself while Patty read a book.*

In the third week of August, Noreen was born. Dad cried tears of relief and joy holding his third grandchild in his arms for the first time. Then he braced himself to relive the days of a crying infant in the house, but she slept all night and cooed all day. He couldn't wait to get home from work and wash up and shave, just to sit in his chair by the window and hold *his baby girl* in his arms.

Sis thought he sometimes went overboard. He really loved Noreen and showed her off all over town. He made such a fuss that Sis had to remind him that he had more than one grandchild. She also reminded him again and again to treat all of them equally because there would be more—thirty-two more, to be precise.

Dad's fourth grandchild born in a February 1955 ice storm was named Patricia after me. Dad came to the hospital to visit, asked me where Tony was and expressed concern. Was there anything he could do for us? Right off, I proudly said, *No thanks, Dad, we'll manage.* I had no idea what needed managed, probably me. Then the hospital sent a bill for two hundred and some dollars and Tony's plan to buy a dream car vanished.

In Pittsburgh, the dream of a car in every family became a parking nightmare of two cars in every family. Competition for parking space in front of your own house turned streets into fortresses of chairs lined up along curbs and claims staked for parking rights in every block. A parking crisis never materialized on our hill where few still owned cars and most people walked up the road or used the city steps, which our Chirico neighbors swore was good for the heart. They were right!

Dad lately complained that living on the hill was too much of a strain. His job at the shop wore him out and he had a lot on his mind. Sobering rumors had surfaced that Hubbard's was going to close. Company leadership had changed following the death of CEO John W. Hubbard. Lawyers for the estate were managing the business. The most anyone could find out was that Hubbard's would phase out in stages. Dad began to shake with dread. He felt under seige with visions of luminaries and saints of ancient Ireland that he had never heard of. Out of nowhere he began to recite the prayer of St. Brendan:

Protect me oh Lord, my boat is so small and your sea is so big.

Fear undermined Dad's confidence and worked on his nerves, causing him to become agitated at the core of his being. He had not earned a living by deliberation, but as one steering a rocking boat towards an uncertain shore.

The workforce at the shop was distracted by negative talk, production slowed and accidents occurred. Those shrewd lawyers knew what to do. The phasing out and closing rumors were replaced with talk that Hubbard & Co. would reorganize. Dad was relieved and already had a job lined up for Huey when he returned from Japan.

Huey mustered out in April of 1955 via San Francisco to a big cheer on deck when his ship passed under the Golden Gate Bridge. He came home on a brief leave and then took a train to Ft. Meade, Maryland, where he completed the five months left of his Army duty. He said it was a good tour even though he was happy to be leaving, but he could feel times changing for the new recruits going in.

1955

Times—they were a changing, as the new-age music would prophesize. African Americans in the South launched campaigns against social injustice and the denial of the same rights that white people had had for a very long time. An era of social unrest swept across the country, giving rise to some of the greatest heroes of the time. Change came like a growth spurt, and the growing pains were everywhere.

Times were changing too fast for Dad. He liked everything to keep on going just the way it was. In truth, he had deep empathy for anyone struggling against The Oppressor, especially when they lifted families and communities up with them. And yet, he possessed a satirical view about unrest in the Deep South; there was enough unrest where he worked.

New rumors circulated that the hand tool division would be shut down in the first phase of Hubbard's restructuring. Dad was wiping down the pic-mattock line with an oil rag when the foreman asked him to stop by the office after he punched out for the day. Dad said *sure*, but then he started shaking so hard he could barely keep his hands steady enough to finish the clean-up. He went straight to the foreman's office and wasn't asked to sit down. He was handed a pink slip and told to go home, permanently. It was a low blow.

Sis was cooking supper when he arrived. He sat down at the table and laid that pink slip out in front of her. She asked him what it was, and he said it was the end of his career. *Career,* she said, *what career*? Then he told her his job was gone. She told him he'd find another job, a better job. He looked so sad. *Don't worry Dad. Don't take it so hard*, she said. Well, he didn't appreciate that comment. *What do you mean don't take it so hard? I'm all washed up. I'm going out and getting plastered*!

Men from the shop gathered at the union hall where they learned that the unprofitable tool division had closed but the profitable electrical division would remain in operation. Stockholders had elected a new president and chief executive officer to run the company. At first, Dad took the loss of his job really hard. But then he got to thinking something was wrong with the picture. He set to work with a will to get to the bottom of it. He started asking around from people in the know, accumulating information and fitting pieces of a puzzle together, intellectual curiosity that saved him from going crazy.

He paced back and forth from the living room to the kitchen, muttering: *Those blowhards that took over the shop might be laughing now; but don't worry, we'll get even*. Dad actually had an intelligent mind and the union leaders wanted to tap his brain. He had a knack for details and could recite the fine print in a contract. He advised the men who lost their jobs that they had a right to compensation and pension benefits. The union hired a lawyer, and the lawyer tapped Dad's brain.

It took time to settle the disputes in court, but they eventually won everything they were entitled to. Dad was a hero for a day. He made the front page of the *Lawrenceville Banner*. Sis went back to work and he took care of Noreen. During this challenging period, he remained sober and vigilant. He and Sis collaborated to keep the household going, pinching pennies and making do. In fact, everybody pitched in; even Vinny with a family of his own was still paying his half of the mortgage on our house.

To get to his job at the Bettis Laboratory, Vinny drove ten miles on a route that zigzagged from Lawrenceville to the *boondocks*, as he called West Mifflin. His work involved assisting with the training program for the crew of the first nuclear powered submarine and required frequent trips to the subbase at New London, Connecticut. Between long-distance commutes and demanding time on the job, he and Dorothy started looking for a more convenient place to live.

One day he stopped by the house to tell Dad he had located a house in Baldwin, a suburb south of the city. Ownership of our house would have to change hands, but a deal could be worked out to Dad's advantage. He could buy the house for one dollar, have the deed put in his name, and take over the fifty-dollar monthly mortgage payments. No one to this day understands why paying the whole fifty dollars seemed outrageous to Dad. We never thought of him as a cheapskate. He was collecting unemployment and Sis and Dee were pitching in; the mortgage could be managed. What a surprise!

In the machismo culture of the times, Dad considered his daughters more as domestics than as providers, and, completely ignoring the urgency of our predicament, went into a full-fledged rebellion, complaining loudly: *Why should I have to bankroll property that's gonna keep me busted broke*? This went on and on until his forehead erupted in hives. In the heat of a moment with an itch he couldn't scratch, he rambled about being *out of luck, up shit creek and needing a drink*. On his way out the door, he mumbled words to the effect: *Fifty dollars a month is a lot of hay and that's what kills it; this dump ain't worth a thin dime*. The primordial insult for all times!

Sis thought that Vinny should have made Dad pay the whole fifty dollars in the first place and it still would have been a good deal. Considering the loss of his job, Dad may have envied Vinny's rising success and mistaken his practical suggestions as condescending, making it difficult to negotiate. And, there was the strain between Sis and Dorothy; they had never quite shined up to each other, heaven knows why, but it created tension and an awkward communicating atmosphere. Maybe tomato soup and a grilled cheese sandwich would have saved the day.

As smart as Dad was, his behavior lacked intellectual certitude, or perhaps it was simply a lack of vision. He could just not get it through his head that paying an extra twenty-five dollars a month wouldn't kill us. He believed it was better to pay rent and keep money in his back pocket. We didn't understand why he kept saying that. He never had money in his back pocket. Money burned a hole in his pocket. He started harping that it was our house and no one had a right to sell it. Sis told Dad it was Vinny's house and he could sell it if he wanted to and burn it down if he wanted to; it didn't change Dad's mind. Sis wanted to believe in Dad but, for crumps sakes, he was tired of living on the hill, and Vinny didn't want to sell our house to anybody but Dad, period.

For Vinny to qualify for a mortgage on his new home under the GI Bill of Rights, the law said he could not hold two mortgages, making it necessary to sell 5614 Duncan Street. All Dad had to do was take it off Vinny's hands, and he said *NO*, a preposterous notion that resonated in his brain and became seasoned concrete. He conjured up the idea that there was no valid reason why Vinny should move from Lawrenceville, a jaded view that it was a great place to live in spite of its neglect by City Hall. The reality was that our neighborhoods were crumbling, our economic base was eroding, and the current recession was depleting our resources.

One person who had the means to at least encourage Dad to buy our house was Aunt Olivia; she had inherited her parents' estate—meaningful wealth. She also had financial and real estate knowledge, having worked in a downtown law firm for years. Instead, she called Vinny on the phone and remonstrated him for not covering Dad's ass. Vinny turned every stone over trying to help Dad come to terms with the situation. Without his cooperation, the problem could not be resolved. Perhaps, had Mom been there, she might have told Olivia to mind her own business and told Dad he didn't have to shoot himself in the foot. A *For Sale* sign went up, and Vinny stopped by to tell us that a real estate agent would be bringing prospective buyers to see the house.

He made apologies to us kids and asked if we could straighten up the place before people showed up. We were going to clean the whole house for Vinny, but Dad worked on our nerves and said to leave the dirty dishes in the sink. We were on Dad's side and we were on Vinny's side—torn in two for the love of our family and our home. Eileen told Dad she would pitch in for the mortgage as soon as she got her high school diploma; he acted like he didn't hear. It was like his mind was not right. He just kept saying, *No use cleaning the house; it's not our house anymore.*

Eileen had survived open-heart surgery, but this was too much. In fear of the unknown, she started sweeping dust balls out from under the beds and placing them on the furniture when prospective buyers were scheduled. She turned things over and spilled stuff all over the floors so nobody would want to buy our house and home. Had she received an explanation for what was happening, she might not have had those distressful anxiety attacks. Our family had never traveled this road. All the while, I was living across the river with my baby girl and wondering where my roaming spouse might be, completely unaware of the calamity going on at our house on the hill.

Dad started blasting the TV; Eileen thought he was going deaf, but he was drowning out the pain of his ill-begotten dreams. She wanted to watch the teen club, Paul Whiteman, but Dad couldn't stand the teenagers screaming on that show. He watched boxing matches on Saturday night and Eileen couldn't stand the violence. They got along watching Ed Sullivan and the comedy shows. Dad just wasn't himself, and the family had to put up with his bad mood. Eileen offered it up and prayed for Dad to buy our house, but he didn't want it. He just wanted his way, and once he got a plan fixed in his head, it carried him away. Eileen went to church and prayed that no one would want to buy our house.

The new St. Mary's on 57th Street opened in honor of Mary the Mother of God in May of 1955; its formal name, Saint Mary Assumption Church, was restored, a beautiful house of prayer erected to the glory of God and the Saints. Bishop John F. Dearden celebrated the dedication Mass along with a host of Slovenian priests from around the nation and the old country. The Reverend Matthew Francis Kebe had served St. Mary's for twenty some years and had never lost sight of his pastoral

May 1955

goals. Every church pew was filled and the crowd overflowed onto the sidewalk. Every person, from proud donor to humble worker, was listed in the souvenier booklet, along with the precise designation of funds to every project, from a three-thousand dollar gift to install the main altar of Italian marble to eight hundred dollars for the repainting of statues and memorial donations for the new church pews. God bless the Slovenians. They did themselves proud and within a year burned the half-million dollar mortgage.

In June, Richie graduated from St. Mary's. Thanks to his scholarship financier, Father Kebe, he would enter the hallowed halls of Central Catholic in the fall. He never knew of the trying time that Sister Mary Alexandrine, his scholarship sponsor, had given Eileen and me. Eileen said, *Don't worry about it Richie; it was because she favored boys.* Richie would always think of his seventh and eighth grade teacher with affection. Even though it took him ten years to get through eight grades, she had held high expectations for him, and he responded. To his good fortune, she steered him into academic studies rather than a vocational trade for which he assumed he was destined, and she got him thinking that he did not need mill work and a neighborhood bar to sustain his life.

He knew good people came out of that rough environment but he never felt like a snob about it. He looked up to Dad and appreciated how he made time to take Richie shopping and to the show and to kick around a few jokes, some real corkers, and chuckle at Richie's jokes like, *Hey Dad, I've been searching for years and I still can't find my glasses.* Pretty girls chased Richie everywhere and he stole kisses from all of them. On the *Wall*, he kissed his first love when he was seven, and she didn't even know he liked her. On the *Wall*, when he was eleven, he kissed Patsy O'Malley twelve times just before it got dark. There would be more girls to kiss, and he would even think of

giving up girls and becoming a priest! But the joy of that first kiss would resonate like the joy of sailing flat stones over the *Wall*, even as he faced the unknown, the ups and downs, the challenges and disappointments of life—like James Cagney's line in Yankee Doodle Dandy: *The road to happiness is paved with heartaches and stones.*

Joe left Pine Castle Air Force Base in Florida with an honorable discharge. He and Daisy dropped by for a day on their way to Detroit. She returned to her old job and he was hired as an illustrator for the yellow pages. With a feeling of prosperity in the air, they hired a contractor to build them a house in the suburbs, and they moved in with their firstborn, Douglas, on the way. Dad was back on a bus on the road to the Scotts of Michigan, beaming with pride and proclaiming, *It's about time we got a boy!*

Larry returned to the states from Korea and came home on two weeks leave, a fourteen hour drive from Boston. When he saw the *For Sale* sign on our house, he quietly on his own found out why, never uttering a word that might drive a wedge between the father he worshipped and the eldest brother he idolized. He always believed in two sides of every story, sort of like Mom's seeing Dad's drinking as a disease. Larry understood, and he helped the family start packing, him and Huey.

Huey was home with an honorable discharge; seeing the *For Sale* sign choked him up because he had painted our house. He had planned to move out on his own anyhow; his goal was to acquire a college education. He applied for funds through the GI Bill and started his freshman year in journalism at Duquesne University. All he had to do now was jump on the bandwagon and prepare for the big move. *After all, our family had grown out of the little house on a hill,* so said he.

In the midst of all this, Skip married the love of his life, Tony's sister Mary, a reliable partner. They met at my wedding and fell in love on the dance floor. They lived in East Liberty and, as busy as Skip was, he drove Dad around looking for a decent rental. Dad hadn't searched real estate ads in eighteen years, and the persistent housing shortage made single-family houses hard to find. Then he saw an ad for a spacious apartment on the North Aiken Avenue hilltop, an integrated neighborhood beyond Stanton Heights. Skip drove Dad over there to look at the place, a converted fire house. A butcher shop and a tavern occupied the ground floor of the building. Skip pulled in at the curb and, in his practical way, questioned Dad on how he planned to make it up and down that steep hill on foot. Dad's show of indifference to moving from one hill to another when he no longer liked hills was, to say the least, baffling. He stepped out of the car, encountered the landlady, Mrs. Katz, and introduced himself. She noticed his skeptical expression and talked him into seeing the place. Access to the flat involved a steep climb of many stairs. Once up there, he thought the place looked pretty good, but *where was the firehouse pole to slide back down on?* He'd think about it.

He searched more rental ads, found nothing adequate that he could afford, and pressure mounted to move before the new school year with Martha changing schools. He called a taxi and took Sis to look at *the ugly firehouse*, as she put it. He could tell that nothing there looked better to her than our house on a much better hill. He fumbled with words, sweated profusely, and pointed out upgrades that had been made—a ceramic tile bathroom and laundry, and a built-in kitchen. Access to the location would be inconvenient, but between them they decided that they would have to make do.

Days later, a Ryder Rental truck pulled up in front of our house. Everything was carried out and loaded on—two trips from our house to wherever took no time at all; the Scotts didn't own all that much stuff. Tony came through with a big hand on the heavy lifting; I looked after babies Noreen and Patti.

Who knew letting go would be so difficult? Every other time the Scotts had moved, it had been an adventure. Packing up, that was hard—going through what to keep and what to throw away. Everything we owned was a personal treasure. Who knew letting go would be so painful? Sure, there was the cathartic experience of pitching threadbare stuff and an accumulation of old clothes nobody else wanted to wear. Letting go in that case was easy. It was the letting go of a house on a hill that we had claimed as our own, the very heart of our universe. We did not see the train rolling down the track at full speed until it hit. Time came to say goodbye to our house and our hill and goodbye to the end of a great age. We all cried the day we said *goodbye*. We had held onto it for as long as possible with the understanding that a day might come when we would have to let go and might even have to embrace it.

Martha cried and said *I love you* and blew kisses to the only home she had known. She had enjoyed freedom to run unhindered through tall grass in open fields, sit down and catch her breath, suck on a stalk of grass, and listen to birds chirping in the trees. She would come home to find no one there and sit out on the front steps wondering, *Where did all the people go?* In the Homey she had listened to the secrets of the earth, communicated with nature. She had at times been gone from home for hours without being missed, the last of the Scotts to enjoy free reign. She had felt safe on our hill, until the day the moving truck pulled up in front of our house. She really cried the day she said *goodbye*. Martha was nine years old.

After the big move, she started having nightmares; Eileen's had never stopped. It was no way to live, she said: *Not even any trees to climb up or grass to slide down on or a wall to hang out on.* As far as she was concerned, we might have lost our house on the hill but we never lost our class. Dad said the situation was temporary and not to worry because we had moved to better ourselves.

It started to feel more like the experience of our ancestors, John and Ellen Scott, who had in the late 1800s departed their Motherland forever, taking with them all they possessed and the deepest yearnings of their hearts; they had gone away paupers and where they went turned out to be a worse hardship for them.

Uncomplaining, Sis made the trek from the firehouse apartment down to Penn Avenue in all kinds of weather and transferred at the fork of the road to the Butler Street line to get to her night shift job at the Union Steel Canteen. Ironic that it was this very transfer stop where Patrick and Margaret Quinn, with nothing between them but a well-traveled wooden trunk stamped *Made in* Belfast, had breathed in a feeling of hope and started a new life.

Like our venerable ancients, we Scotts would assert our fierce independence, master our own ships, brave our storms, assimilate into new-age cultures, pursue fruitful careers, raise our families, and with persistence, abundant talents and natural resources, we would succeed; Dad would always be extremely proud of us.

At fifty-three, he searched for work, an exercise in futility with no one hiring *old men*, as street gossip opined. Regret tormented his brain and guilt churned his gut. Had he made a terrible mistake? The unemployment office sent him on wild goose chases just to keep his account secure, but he was there for

Sis, taking care of his granddaughter and keeping the apartment clean while everybody else was at work or at school.

Martha started fifth grade and fretted on the lonely walk to her new school, wondering how she would ever survive life in Garfield. Bless the good nuns at St. Lawrence O'Toole who consoled her. She recovered her sense of purpose, bathed herself in the balm of acceptance, and sought out new friends. That took time but for her it meant *Friends for Life*. She had yet to learn it doesn't usually work that way, off the record, she said.

For the record, in the Office of the Deed Registrar of Allegheny County, in book Volume 3423, the sale of 5614 Duncan Street, Block 120-N, Lot 210 to William Sarhosis, *et ux* was recorded on October 13, 1955. We Scotts could hardly imagine anyone else living there but us, but for those in our family who had already left home, they saw our transition as no obstacle to progress. *Our Hill* as seen from the world at large was, after all, a provincial territory, a ghetto within a ghetto, a friendly but segregated parochial neighborhood.

Vinny checked in at the new family digs and offered his encouragement. He reflected on how hard the move was on our family and of the struggles of our early years, tough times, and how hard and how well we worked together. He said we had always shown appreciation for what he was able to do when he could do it, but it was a team effort. Nothing else could have worked. As far as he was concerned, there would never be any hard feelings or grudges held. Time would heal wounds, things would never be the same, but the memories would always be cherished with tender love.

Dad settled into a confounded routine of boredom, trying to relax in his chair by the window on the upper elevation of a remodeled firehouse, reading his newspaper, and making the best of a crisis he had orchestrated in the name of a grandiose idea of family greatness yet to be manifested, although there were significant signs that his *six of one and half dozen of the other*

were well on their way to letting Dad have it his way. The rub—our sometimes illogical father held onto ideas carried with him from childhood, ideas that collided with those of his modern-thinking children. Even then, anytime he became aware that his jaded thinking annoyed us, he cleverly changed the subject and drew us into engaging discussions on the state of the government, politics, and social and economic issues; and he let us express our point of view, even if he didn't agree with it.

As for our out-of-job-down-on-luck father, who carried a banner of honor and wore an armored shield, Dad was feeling like a wet noodle one day and went to see Doctor Noden at his Butler Street office. The good doctor worked him over with a medical fine-toothed comb and said ever so kindly but firmly, *Vince, you have to stop drinking and smoking now or you have a short time left to live. Do I have your word?*

Dad took a bus, then a streetcar, back home. He stopped at a lounge on Penn Avenue that had just opened. The neon sign in the window said: *Laverne's Tavern.* It appeared he was the only customer in the place. A woman of obvious elegance and stature standing behind the bar asked, *What will you have?* He moved from the bar to a table and asked, *Do you serve anything but booze? I'm just thirsty.* And she said, *How about a Coke? That'll do,* said he. She brought a large glass filled with ice and poured a Coke from the bottle into the glass. *Will that be all, sir?* said she. And he said, *Would you like to sit down for a minute?* The two became engaged in a friendly exchange of references when another customer walked in. She excused herself and went back to work. On his way out, he tipped his hat and said, *Hope to see you around.* And she said, *Me too.*

That very week, thanks to Dad's fine work with the men at the shop, their union and lawyers, his company separation payment and pension allotment kicked in, and he received his first check, enough to pay off his outstanding debts. He made a cautious descent on the firehouse stairs and down Aiken Avenue to a nearby bank, opened an account, and drew some cash. He strolled up the street in his cavalier way and turned in at *Laverne's Tavern.*

Herself was working the bar which overflowed with customers. The charmer in glittering armour stepped forward and asked for a Coke. She said, *We need an extra bartender if you're interested.* He walked around to the other side of the bar, put on an apron, and never smoked another cigarette or drank another drink again.

Therefore, we can honestly lift off Dad's shoulders the burden of alcoholism that he carried and its effect on him and all of us, and look at him with his load lightened and his face smiling. Here was a man full of generosity of spirit and affection for all of us.

Richie always had the feeling that Dad liked him best, though he could not speak for the others. But it could not be imagined, in that sometimes penniless domestic economy we all shared, anyone being denied whatever small change Dad could dig out of his pocket bottoms just so we could see the latest show at the old Dome movie house and with a bit of change left over to buy a scoop of candy corn or jellybeans to eat while we watched those fluttering black and white films. Richie did not recall ever being deprived by Dad in matters of great importance like that, not ever. He would remember with the dearest kind of affection going for a walk with Dad somewhere holding onto his pinkie finger and listening to his heavy breathing on those arduous climbs up the city steps to our house on our hill.

After all, it was *Our Hill*, you know!

Author's Note

First of all, I thank my brothers, Vincent (Vinny), Joseph (Joe), Francis (Skip), Eugene (Huey), Lawrence (Larry, deceased), Richard (Richie), and my sisters, Rosemary (Sis, deceased), Dolores (Dee), Anne (Anna), Eileen and Martha, for their literary contributions and enriching insights that brought our family memories to life. They supplied photographs, connected dots, and set the record straight. Counting me, Patricia Scott—tenth of the twelve, we are *Six of One, Half Dozen of the Other,* and this is our book!

It is revised from the original story, *The Scotts From The Hill in Pittsburgh, Pennsylvania*, which was a limited publication in 2001. Friends and family alike offered corrections and updates to it, all reflected in this new edition. The original was research and history oriented, whereas this edition tells the larger story of the family itself. The title is changed to *The Scotts From A Hill* because the original title created confusion between the hill we lived on and the Hill District of Pittsburgh, renowned as *The Hill.*

To approach writing this story, I grounded myself in local history at the Lawrenceville Branch of the Carnegie Library of Pittsburgh. At Carnegie's Main Library in Oakland, I obtained copies of documents and photographs thanks to formidable assistance of its staff. At the Office of the Recorder of Deeds of Allegheny County on Grant Street, I copied property records and plat maps showing where people lived and where they did business. At the nearby Court House, I searched birth, adoption, marriage, and death records. At the Commonwealth Bureau of Vital Statistics in New Castle, Pennsylvania, I obtained even more records.

Exploring the archives of the Catholic Diocese of Pittsburgh followed. The Family History Center of the Church of Jesus Christ of Latter Day Saints assisted in my searches of their web sites. Many records that established the storyline of our Irish immigrants were acquired through our second cousin, Nora Hopkins Grant FitzGerald, who traveled to Ireland many times to search ancestral archives.

I thank Aunt Rose Scott Kobert (deceased) for her diligent work on the history of the Scott side of the family. I thank Aunt Mary Quinn Marzolf (deceased) for resurrecting quaint tales of the Quinn side of the family, and others of our clans who spontaneously told what they knew.These wonderful people not only helped me put this book together, they helped me build a family genealogy going back to the mid-1800s.

I thank brother and artist, Joseph Scott, for creating the cover and illustrations for the book. I thank daughter, artist and teacher, Josephine Coniglio, for the digital polishing of the book cover. I thank brother and published author, Gene Scott, for his lively story-telling contributions. I thank niece and published author, Rosanne Colleen Scott, for her professional editing, literary advice, and encouragement during the writing of the original story, and I thank granddaughter Naomi North for her solid editing of the revised edition.

I thank good friend and published author, Jude Wudarczyk, of the Lawrenceville Historical Society, for an astute reading of the book and scholarly recommendations. I thank dear friend Doug Florey, Executive Director of Laughlin Children's Center in Sewickley, Pennsylvania, for opening the doors to my discovery of the history of the Sewickley Fresh Air Home for Children.

A saying goes: Consider it an achievement to get a family story past a good editor, and a miracle to get it past the family, especially while they are still alive, not to mention that ours proudly holds a place in America's Greatest Generation. It was a privilege and honor to write this story all about us!

About the Author

Patricia Scott is a homegrown Pittsburgher. There she was born, grew up, was educated, worked downtown, raised a family, and enjoyed the enrichment of the good city life. She now resides at the Passavant Retirement Community in Zelienople, Pa., way out in the country as the old folks say.